AMERICA'S NATURAL PLACES

Regional Volumes in *America's Natural Places*

East and Northeast, Donelle Nicole Dreese

Pacific and West, Methea Kathleen Sapp

Rocky Mountains and Great Plains, Kelly Enright

South and Southeast, Stacy Kowtko

The Midwest, Jason Ney and Terri Nichols

AMERICA'S NATURAL PLACES

EAST AND NORTHEAST

Donelle Nicole Dreese

Stacy Kowtko, General Editor

GREENWOOD PRESS
An Imprint of ABC-CLIO, LLC

A B C • C L I O

Santa Barbara, California • Denver, Colorado • Oxford, England

Library of Congress Cataloging-in-Publication Data

Dreese, Donelle N. (Donelle Nicole), 1968–
   America's natural places. East and Northeast / Donelle Nicole Dreese.
      p. cm. — (Regional volumes in America's natural places)
   Includes bibliographical references and index.
   ISBN 978-0-313-35088-7 (set hardcover : alk. paper) — ISBN 978-0-313-35089-4 (set ebook) —
ISBN 978-0-313-35312-3 (hardcover : alk. paper) — ISBN 978-0-313-35313-0 (ebook)
   1. Protected areas—East (U.S.)   2. Endangered ecosystems—East (U.S.)   I. Title.
   S932.E22D74   2010
   333.780974—dc22   2009032383

14   13   12   11   10   1   2   3   4   5

This book is also available on the World Wide Web as an eBook.
Visit www.abc-clio.com for details.

ABC-CLIO, LLC
130 Cremona Drive, P.O. Box 1911
Santa Barbara, California 93116-1911

This book is printed on acid-free paper (∞)
Manufactured in the United States of America

CONTENTS

Series Foreword   *xi*
Preface   *xv*
Introduction   *xix*

CONNECTICUT   1
Connecticut River   2

Devil's Den Preserve   4

Last Green Valley   6

Pawcatuck Borderlands   8

Robbins Swamp   10

DELAWARE   13
Blackbird-Millington Corridor   14

Burrows Run Preserve   15

Middleford North Preserve   17

Pemberton Forest   18

Prime Hook National Wildlife Refuge   19

Kentucky   23

Blanton Forest   24

Dinsmore Woods and State Nature Preserve   26

Eastview Barrens Preserve   27

Green River Bioreserve   29

Griffith Woods   30

Natural Bridge State Park Nature Preserve   32

Red River Gorge Geological Area   34

Maine   37

Acadia National Park   38

Caribou Bog Wetland Complex   40

Cobscook Bay   41

Debsconeag Lakes Wilderness Area   42

Kennebec Highlands   44

Kennebunk Plains and Wells Barrens   45

Mount Agamenticus   47

Saco Heath Preserve   48

Upper Saco River   49

Maryland   53

Battle Creek Cypress Swamp   54

Crabtree Cave   55

Finzel Swamp Preserve   57

Nassawango Creek Preserve   58

Potomac Gorge   60

Soldiers Delight Natural Environment Area   62

Massachusetts   65

Cape Cod National Seashore   66

David H. Smith Preserve and Fire Trail   68

Mount Greylock State Reservation   69

Reed Brook Preserve   71

Walden Pond State Reservation   73

New Hampshire   77

Fourth Connecticut Lake Preserve   78

Great Bay Reserve   80

Loverens Mill Cedar Swamp Preserve   81

Mount Monadnock   82

Mount Washington   84

Ossipee Lake Natural Area   86

Vickie Bunnell Preserve   88

New Jersey   91

Cape May Migratory Bird Refuge   92

Cape May National Wildlife Refuge   93

Cheesequake State Park   95

Delaware Water Gap   97

Muckshaw Ponds Preserve   98

Wharton State Forest   99

New York   103

Adirondack Park   104

Albany Pine Bush Preserve   106

Atlantic Double Dunes   108

Chaumont Barrens Preserve   109

Finger Lakes   111

Sam's Point Preserve   113

Southern Lake Champlain Valley   114

Pennsylvania   117

Aitkin Cave   118

Bear Run Nature Reserve   120

Bushkill Falls   121

Delaware Water Gap   122

Goat Hill Serpentine Barrens   124

Gull Point Natural Area   125

Tannersville Cranberry Bog Preserve   127

Tionesta Research and Scenic Natural Areas   128

World's End State Park   129

RHODE ISLAND   133

Ell/Long Pond Preserve   134

Lime Rock Preserve   136

Narragansett Bay Reserve   137

Rodman's Hollow   139

Wood River   140

VERMONT   143

Camel's Hump Natural Area and State Park   144

Equinox Highlands   146

Helen W. Buckner Preserve at Bald Mountain   147

Little Averill Lake Natural Area   149

Marsh-Billings-Rockefeller National Historic Park   150

White River Ledges Natural Area   152

Williams Woods Natural Area   154

VIRGINIA   157

Cumberland Marsh   158

Fortune's Cove Preserve   160

Goshen Pass Natural Area   161

Great Dismal Swamp National Wildlife Refuge and Natural Area   162

Mount Rogers   164

Poor Mountain Natural Area   165

Shenandoah National Park   167

Virginia Coast Reserve   168

WEST VIRGINIA   **171**

Bear Rocks Preserve   172

Cranberry Glades and Wilderness   174

Cranesville Swamp Preserve   175

Greenbrier Valley   176

New River Gorge   178

North Fork Mountain   180

Glossary   *183*
Bibliography   *187*
Index   *193*

SERIES FOREWORD

The United States possesses within its borders some of the most diverse and beautiful natural wonders and resources of any country on earth. Many of these valuable natural places exist under a constant threat of damage from environmental pollution, climatic change, and encroaching civilization, just to name a few of the more destructive forces. Some natural areas enjoy the care and protection of neighboring human societies, but some have fallen to the wayside of concern. This series of reference volumes represents a collection of distinct areas of preservation concern in the following five geographical divisions of the United States: the East and Northeast, the Pacific and West, the Rocky Mountains and Great Plains, the South and Southeast, and the Midwest. The goal is to present representative challenges faced across the country, providing information on historical and ongoing preservation efforts through the process of identifying specific sites that representatively define the United States as an environmental entity. Individual entries were chosen based on the following criteria: biodiversity, ecology, rare or endangered species habitats, or unique environmental character. Many of the entries are nature preserves, state or national parks, wildlife habitats, or scenic vistas. Each selection focuses on a particular area and describes the site's importance, resident flora and fauna, and threats to the area's survival, along with historical and current information on preservation efforts. For sites that are physically accessible, there is information on location, access methods, and visiting tips. Although each volume is organized by state, many natural places cross state borders, and so the larger focus is on environmental ecosystem representation rather than state definition. The goals are to inform readers about the wide variety of natural places across the country as well as portray these natural places as more than just an exercise in academic study. The reality of natural preservation in the United States has an immediate impact on everyone.

Each volume contains a short introduction to the geographical region, including specific information on the states' natural environments and regionally specific concerns of restoration and preservation. Content entries represent one or more of the following criteria: ecological uniqueness; biodiversity; rare or endangered species habitat; exceptional natural beauty; or aging, fragile, or disappearing natural environs. By reading the various entries in each volume, readers will gain understanding concerning environmental issues of consequence as demonstrated by the representative entry choices. The audiences especially suited to benefit from this series are high school and undergraduate students as well as hobbyists and nature enthusiasts. Readers with an interest in local, regional, and environmental health will find easily accessible, useable information throughout the series. The following paragraphs offer short excerpts from the introductions of the regional volumes in *America's Natural Places*.

The East and Northeast United States is a corridor, a doorway to America that has facilitated movement and migration into the continent. The subject of corridors is revisited frequently in the East and Northeast volume as it covers natural areas beginning as far west as Kentucky, as far south as Virginia, and voyages up the coast to Maine. Smaller corridors are described here as well, because many of the places featured in this book have their own respective passageways, some more wild than others. This volume is also about larger corridors—those that connect the past to the present and the present to the future. These natural areas are storytellers chronicling the narratives of cultural and ecological histories that not only have much to tell about the region's past, but also are microcosmic indicators of the earth's current global health. They are corridors into our future as they tell us where our planet is going—toward the loss of countless native species, archeological treasures, and ecosystems that are vital for a sustainable planet. These natural areas are themselves guided paths, passageways into a healthier future as they teach us what is happening within their fragile ecological significance before their lessons are lost forever.

The American Pacific and West is a place of legendary proportions; its natural resources have beckoned to entrepreneurs, prospectors, immigrants, adventurers, naturalists, writers, and photographers, thereby deeply embedding the region into U.S. history, culture, commerce, and art. J. S. Holliday wrote. "I think that the West is the most powerful reality in the history of this country. It's always had a power, a presence, an attraction that differentiated it from the rest of the United States. Whether the West was a place to be conquered, or the West as it is today, a place to be protected and nurtured. It is the regenerative force of America." Over the course of its history, the ecosystems of the Pacific and West have been subject to a variety of forces, both restorative and destructive. Individual entries in the Pacific and West volume seek to not only detail the effects of these forces but to describe the flora, fauna, and topography that make each entry unique. As a cumulative effect, the volume offers an inclusive depiction of the region as a whole while echoing the famous call to "Go West."

"The western landscape is of the wildest variety," Wallace Stegner wrote of his homeland. "There is nothing in the East," he continued, "like the granite horns of Grand Teton or Teewinot, nothing like the volcanic neck of Devil's Tower, nothing like the travertine terraces of Mammoth Hot Springs." Consisting of deserts, grasslands, alpine mountains, plateaus, canyons, cliffs, and geyser basins, the Rocky Mountains and Great Plains is a region of great biodiversity and natural beauty. From the 100th meridian over the peaks of the Rocky Mountains, this landscape has been the source of frontier legends, central to the nation's geography as well as its identity. Home to the world's first national park and some of the most extractive industries in the nation, this landscape displays the best and worst of human interactions with the natural world. Fossils in Colorado are evidence of ancient inland seas. Tall-grass prairies reveal pre-Anglo American ecology. This volume teaches students to read natural landscapes as products of interacting dynamics between culture and nature. People of many backgrounds, ethnicities, and cultures have contributed to the current state of the environment, giving readers a strong, provocative look at the dynamics of this ever-changing landscape.

"The American South is a geographical entity, a historical fact, a place in the imagination, and the homeland for an array of Americans who consider themselves southerners. The region is often shrouded in romance and myth, but its realities are as intriguing, as intricate as its legends." So states Bill Ferris. This volume explores the variable, dynamic South and Southeast through the details of its ecoregions and distinct areas of preservation. Individual entries provide the elements necessary for examining and understanding the threats, challenges, and promises inherent to this region. State partitions serve as geographical divisions for regional treatment, but the overall goal of this work is to present representative examples of the varying ecosystems across the area rather than focusing on the environmental character of individual states. When combined, the sections present a total picture of the South and Southeast through careful selections that portray not only the coastal wetlands and piedmont areas characteristic of the region but also the plateaus, mountains, highlands, plains, and woodlands that define the inland South and Southeast. The goal is to produce a comprehensive picture of the South and Southeast natural environs as they combine to present a unique character and quality that shapes Southern reality today.

The Midwest stands historically as the crossroads of America, the gateway to the West. The region is incredibly diverse, long shaped by geological forces such as the advance and retreat of glaciers. It is a transitional region, where the eastern temperate forests meet the Great Plains of the West and where the southern extent of the northern forests transitions from the mixed-wood plains to the Ozark forests and southeastern plains of the South. Human presence and interaction, however, have greatly reduced and currently threaten this diversity. The Midwest's rich soils and forests, along with its abundant lakes and streams, make this region's natural resources some of the county's most desirable for farming, logging, and development. As a result, little of the once-vast prairies, forests, and wetlands remains. Nonetheless, many efforts, both public and private, are underway to restore and protect the diversity of the Midwest. By taking a holistic approach, individual entries in this volume exemplify the varied ecosystems of the region with the volume as a whole covering all the major Midwest ecoregions. As readers explore the various entries, a comprehensive understanding of the natural systems of the Midwest will emerge, grounded in the region's natural and cultural history and shaped by its current and future challenges.

PREFACE

A corridor is a passageway, a doorway, a guided path that facilitates movement and migration. The subject of corridors is revisited frequently in this book as it covers natural areas beginning as far west as Kentucky, as far south as Virginia, and voyages up the northeast corridor to Maine. There are much smaller corridors described here as well, because many of the places featured in this book have their own respective passageways, some more wild than others because popular places for tourism are profiled as well as preserves that are closed to public access. But *America's Natural Places: East and Northeast* is also about larger corridors—those that connect the past to the present and the present to the future. These natural areas are storytellers chronicling the narratives of cultural and ecological histories that not only have much to tell about the region's past, but also are microcosmic indicators of the earth's current global health. They are corridors into our future as they tell us where our planet is going—toward the loss of countless native species, archeological treasures, and ecosystems that are vital for a sustainable planet. These natural areas are themselves guided paths, passageways into a healthier future as they teach us what is happening within their fragile landscapes and seascapes and what can be done to preserve their historical, cultural, and ecological significance before their lessons are lost to us forever.

Working from the perspective that all places are ecologically important makes identifying specific areas to include in this book particularly challenging. The selection criteria included choosing discrete areas that: harbor endangered species, represent extraordinary biodiversity or sensitive ecosystems, demonstrate critical importance to the broader region, bear historical or cultural significance, present key examples of human impact on the natural areas, clarify the link between humans and regional ecosystems, and present landscapes with exceptional scenic value.

There are two basic audiences for this book. One is a general audience including readers of interest who are environmental enthusiasts, hikers, nature photographers, travelers, and those who simply want to learn more about the natural areas in their region and beyond. For academic purposes, the intended audience is undergraduate nonscience majors at two-year and four-year colleges and universities and advanced high school students. The book will be used primarily by students to write papers, prepare for research projects, and otherwise become better informed about the nature of the environment in the United States. The book is not a textbook to train environmental scientists but a work of nature writing that identifies and describes sites of priority preservation due to their ecological fragility or historical, cultural, and environmental significance.

The purpose of the book is ultimately to provide a detailed description and discussion of natural environments in the eastern and northeastern United States. This book supports current local, national, and global movements toward sustainability and enhances efforts currently underway that promote environmental awareness and regional stewardship. In a time of ecological crisis, it is critical that resources such as this book are available to students and the community in order to change the perception that how we treat the earth has no impact on our lives and well-being.

EAST AND NORTHEAST

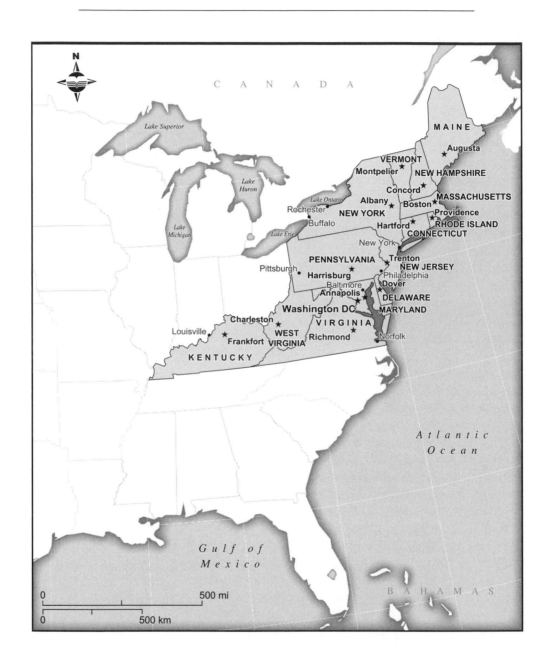

CANADA

Lake Superior

Lake Huron

Lake Michigan

Lake Ontario

Rochester

Buffalo

Lake Erie

MAINE

Augusta ★

VERMONT

Montpelier ★

NEW HAMPSHIRE

Concord ★

Albany ★

Boston ★

MASSACHUSETTS

Providence ★

RHODE ISLAND

Hartford ★

CONNECTICUT

NEW YORK

New York

PENNSYLVANIA

Pittsburgh ●

Harrisburg ★

Trenton ★

NEW JERSEY

Philadelphia

Dover ★

Baltimore

Annapolis ★

DELAWARE

Washington DC

MARYLAND

Charleston ★

Louisville ●

Frankfort ★

WEST VIRGINIA

VIRGINIA

Richmond ★

Norfolk ●

KENTUCKY

Atlantic Ocean

Gulf of Mexico

BAHAMAS

0   500 mi

0   500 km

INTRODUCTION

"But the first salt wind from the east, the first sight of a lighthouse set boldly on its outer rock, the flash of a gull, the waiting procession of seaward-bound firs on an island, made me feel solid and definite again, instead of a poor, incoherent being," composed regionalist writer Sarah Orne Jewett about the coast of Maine in *The Country of Pointed Firs*. The East and Northeast United States is an anchor of sorts, a rock extending into the sea, heavy with natural resources and the colonial roots of a nation. It is a metaphor for beginnings. For some, the East and Northeast was the beginning of a new way of life—a New World. For others, it is where the loss of a way of life has its origins—the beginnings of a cultural genocide that would make its way across the country and never end, but rather keep circulating back east, manifesting itself in different ways. This volume is a walk through natural areas and ecoregions that are rich in environmental diversity, exceptional beauty, imperiled landscapes, and archeological and historical goldmines. Because of the heavy burden of development on states in the East and Northeast, many of the areas explored are high-priority areas of preservation as the threat of commercial and industrial enterprise is ever increasing. But still, this part of the country is a repository of dark forests, savannas, remote beaches, barrens, berry bogs, cliffs, mountains, lush valleys, cavern systems, and wetlands, all teeming with legend and folklore. Many of these preserves, parks, and forests highlight areas of such critical importance that, if they were to succumb to economic or agricultural development, globally rare species, ecosystems, regional pure water qualities, as well as historical and cultural information would be lost forever.

The Northeast's landscapes and seascapes barely resemble those rocky shores, wild wetlands, and cool, dark forests encountered by European colonists upon their arrival centuries ago. What seemed a land of infinite abundance has become a region in recovery after forests and woodlands were indiscriminately cleared for timber and agriculture. In the process of this colonization of the land, wildlife habitats were destroyed, and hunting and fur trading resulted in the extirpation and displacement of countless species.

It would be misleading to suggest that only European settlement is responsible for altering the northeast territory. American Indians cleared land for planting and to persuade wildlife out of their roosts to be hunted. "Just as ecosystems have been changed by the historical activities of human beings, so too have they had their own less-recorded history: forests have been transformed by disease, drought, and fire, species have become extinct, and landscapes have been drastically altered by climate change," claims William Cronon. And yet, while it is true that all human societies have an impact on the environment, the vast indigenous populations that inhabited the East and Northeast impacted the land very differently compared to the Europeans. According to Cronon, "the choice is not between two landscapes, one with or one without a human influence; it is between two human ways of living, two ways of belonging to an ecosystem." Both ways clearly realized that the land was necessary for survival, but the European worldview converted the land and its natural resources into a monetary value for the benefit of the economic systems in Europe and for the burgeoning economy in the United States.

Despite the extensive loss of forestlands from logging, many states in the East and Northeast United States have more forest cover now than they did in 1900. This restoration is a result of citizens and organizations recognizing that their homelands were rapidly diminishing and that something needed to be done to protect the beauty, health, and biodiversity of their communities and surrounding areas. The acquisition of land is at the forefront of many conservation efforts taking place in the Northeast. Lands that join other protected areas are of particular interest for acquisition, because they can help create large contiguous greenways that provide more extensive regions for wildlife to roam. They also create buffer zones for the already protected areas. Land acquisition is critically important to the East and Northeast United States because of its highly developed coastal areas and cities that are continuing to spread into undeveloped regions that are at risk of being permanently lost.

Connecticut, for example, is a state that is trying to safeguard what remains of its undeveloped lands. One such conservation effort that attempts to connect already protected lands is called the Pawcatuck Borderlands Project. This borderlands region is a large forest system that crosses the Rhode Island and Connecticut border, stretching from Boston to Washington, DC. As with many large-scale conservation projects taking place in the Northeast, balancing natural resource protection with strategies that enhance economic vitality of the region is essential, and an important aspect of the Pawcatuck Borderlands Project. Another example is the Last Green Valley in northeast Connecticut. This region is sometimes referred to as the Quinebaug Highlands or the Quinebaug and Shetucket Rivers Valley National Heritage Corridor. It is often called the Last Green Valley because it is one of the last undeveloped green areas along the highly populated northeast urban corridor spanning from Washington, DC, to Boston. The region is situated east of the New London and Hartford, Connecticut, areas and west of Providence, Rhode Island, and Boston. While the Last Green Valley has its share of development, it is an oasis of natural resources along the highly urbanized eastern seaboard. Many organizations are involved in the protection of this area, including the Green Valley Institute, the Nature Conservancy, and other agencies that work with farmers and landowners to promote sustainable land use in the Last Green Valley.

Like the Last Green Valley, many of the places explored in *America's Natural Places: East and Northeast* are among the last of their kind. They are some of the most compelling natural areas and ecosystems in the Northeast United States that include savannas of Kentucky bluegrass, the Blue Ridge Mountains, parks with Pennsylvania's waterfalls, the lakes and loons of New Hampshire's north country, Vermont's Green Mountains, New Jersey's Pine Barrens, remote Maine wilderness, rocky coastal beaches, boreal bogs, prairie grasslands, meadows of wildflowers, vast cave systems, and the Adirondack Mountains. But this book is not just about places. It is also about home, watersheds, health, and activism. It is a journey through Appalachian corridors and through ecological passageways that are archeological, haunting, vibrant, polluted, and devastated. Central to any study of the ecology of the East and Northeast United States is the extraordinary Appalachian Mountain range that stretches from Georgia to Canada. The profound and enduring impact of the Appalachians on the eastern landscape, weather, and the people who live on its hills and in its hollows cannot be overstated.

Although the chapters of *America's Natural Places: East and Northeast* have been organized by state, readers should approach the natural areas in relation to their region, for ecosystems are not bound to geopolitical borders and are often gradually in flux as climate change and other forces influence their range. Ultimately, this book is an urgent call for a renewed commitment to conservation and personal stewardship as inappropriate development, invasive species, and pollution continue to promote habitat loss and the degradation of natural resources. It is, at the same time, a celebration of some of the inspiring conservation projects that have saved, protected, and restored many of the East and Northeast's most beautiful and imperiled ecosystems.

Connecticut River, 2
Devil's Den Preserve, 4
Last Green Valley, 6
Pawcatuck Borderlands, 8
Robbins Swamp, 10

CONNECTICUT

Three regions play a prominent role in Connecticut's natural heritage: the Long Island Sound coastal region, the Connecticut River valley, and the Litchfield region in the northwest. The Connecticut River valley is where the Connecticut River bisects the state and meanders through urban areas, small rural towns, open spaces, and forests. This valley is known for its scenic beauty, recreational opportunities, and natural areas that contribute to the state's biodiversity. The Litchfield region is where the classic images and landscapes of New England are at their finest. The green hills, Housatonic River, historic colonial villages, and churches nestled in the valleys capture the rural character of the Northeast. The Long Island Sound region is home to eight million people who rely on the health of its watershed and enjoy the appeal and recreation of its seaside atmosphere. It is the body of water where the Connecticut River and all of its tributaries drain, making it the downstream recipient of pollution that enters New England's waterways as far north as northern New Hampshire. It was designated a national estuary in 1987, and it is a critical location for the nesting and feeding of birds and coastal wildlife as well as a home to rare plant species for the state. Because of its tourism and fishing industries, Long Island Sound is essential to the state's economy.

There are other regions of Connecticut that are significant. One example is the Last Green Valley region in northeast Connecticut. This region is sometimes referred to as the Quinebaug Highlands or the Quinebaug and Shetucket Rivers Valley National Heritage Corridor. It is often called the Last Green Valley because it is one of the last undeveloped green areas along the highly populated northeast urban corridor spanning from Washington, D.C., to Boston. Another example is the Pawcatuck Borderlands. This region is a large forest system that crosses the Rhode Island and Connecticut border, stretching from Boston to Washington, D.C. The Pawcatuck Borderlands includes important wetland areas as well as several important rivers and hardwood forests. It also contains substantial yet unique pitch pine forest natural communities, but the borderlands region is most known for its giant rhododendron forest and Atlantic white cedar.

The primary environmental concerns for Connecticut are mercury levels in water, climate change, the state's aquifers, and brownfields, which are land areas, often postindustrial, that are not being used due to the possible presence of dangerous contaminants. The state's Urban Site Remedial Action Program was created to clean up abandoned, potentially hazardous sites for public safety and to prepare these sites for possible reuse and development.

Connecticut is also actively researching the impact of climate change on the state's environmental health. The state's Climate Change Action Plan investigates the existing and potential negative impacts of climate change to Connecticut's ecology and economy. It also seeks to discover new ways to reduce greenhouse gas emissions and provide education to citizens and business about energy conservation and reducing carbon emissions.

The state of Connecticut recognizes the importance of water quality and the risks of mercury-laden products that, through disposal, advance the presence of mercury in the environment. Mercury is dangerous to the health of humans and wildlife and can cause reproductive and neurological disorders. The state's Environmental Protection Agency discourages the use of products containing mercury and encourages citizens to take the products they do use with mercury to a proper hazardous waste facility site. Finally, Connecticut's aquifers are essential for providing healthy drinking water for its citizens. The Aquifer Protection Area Program enforces land use regulations in aquifer areas and promotes educational activities that inform citizens of the necessity of protecting groundwater for the health and safety of everyone.

CONNECTICUT RIVER

In 1972, the passing of the Federal Clean Water Act put to an end more than a century of the Connecticut River being used as a garbage and sewage dump. In the last few decades, improvements in the water quality and overall health of the Connecticut River, which is the largest river system in New England, have been remarkable. With its headwaters near the Canadian border, this ecologically rich and historic river meanders through New Hampshire, Vermont, Massachusetts, and Connecticut before emptying into the Long Island Sound and out to sea.

Its watershed covers more than 11,000 square miles, and the river travels about 410 miles from its headwaters to the Long Island Sound. Its name was derived from the Native American word *quenticut*, which means "the long tidal river."

Flowing into the Connecticut River are the waters from 38 tributaries. Two important tributaries in Connecticut are the Eight Mile River and Salmon River. The Eight Mile River watershed is predominantly comprised of lush, dense forests, which help to keep this river pure and provide habitat for river otters, bobcats, and songbirds. The river also hosts a diversity of fish and aquatic life, including freshwater mussels, which

Sunset over the Connecticut River. (Dreamstime)

require healthy environments to survive. After a 12-year process, in 2008, the Eight Mile River in Connecticut was officially designated a wild and scenic river. This designation protects the river from any activity that might compromise its ecological and cultural integrity. The Salmon River is another river that is valued for its high water quality and excellent habitat for diversity of fish and rare species, especially in its lower portion. It has been identified as a site for the restoration of wild salmon, provides drainage for 96,000 acres in central Connecticut influencing 10 small towns, and supports a wintering roosting site for bald eagles.

Of special concern is the lower Connecticut River, which is home to tidal marsh communities that have been internationally recognized for their extraordinary ecological value. This wetland complex hosts numerous rare and endangered species, native brackish grasses, seaside sparrows, marsh wrens, egrets, and green-winged teals. The tidelands have been threatened by *phragmites australis,* or the common reed, which is an incredibly hardy plant that spreads easily and crowds out other important plants. At the mouth of the Connecticut River in Old Lyme is the Griswold Point Preserve, a 25-acre scenic beach preserve where piping plovers and least terns nest. The piping plover birds and their eggs rely on their camouflaged appearance for protection, but an increase in predators, loss of habitat, and human disturbance have significantly compromised this beautiful beach bird. This lovely preserve of blowing beach grasses offers views of the Long Island Sound but is closed during piping plover nesting periods in the summer.

The critical importance of this river system is well understood, and much is being done to continue to improve upon its health and vitality. The Connecticut River Project hosts workshops that involve state and federal agencies, nonprofit organizations, scientists, and academics from the four states through which the river passes to discuss planning strategies for optimum conservation. At these meetings, focus areas for protection are established and threats are identified. Key strategies are discussed for minimizing invasive species, restoring the river's floodplain areas, protecting and restoring the lands and forests that surround the river, and restoring connectivity and the natural flow of the river and its tributaries. Roads, dams, bridges, and other forms of development alter the natural flow patterns of the river and greatly impact the biodiversity and habitats along the river. The Connecticut River impacts the lives of many people as it traverses through urban areas, small rural towns, open spaces, and forests, and keeping it clean and vital is an environmental priority for New England— not only for the people who live there but for all of the life forms that are sustained by this majestic river.

Further Reading

Connecticut River Watershed Council. http://www.ctriver.org.

Henshaw, Carol. *Natural Wonders of Connecticut & Rhode Island: Exploring Wild and Scenic Places*. New York: McGraw-Hill, 2000.

Stekl, William F., and Evan Hill. *The Connecticut River*. Middletown, CT: Wesleyan University Press, 1972.

DEVIL'S DEN PRESERVE

Located in Weston and Redding, Connecticut, Devil's Den Preserve is a fascinating mosaic of wetlands, woodlands, swamps, streams, wildflowers, outcroppings, a gorge, rocky cliffs, scenic ravines, and a remarkable number of plant and animal species. Totaling 1,756 acres, this highly visited preserve lies in Connecticut's bustling southwest corner and is the largest parcel of protected land in Fairfield County. Coyote, red fox, bobcat, ruffed grouse, and many other birds and animals live at Devil's Den along with a vibrant array of flowers, including Indian pipe, pink lady's slipper, and cardinal flower.

Perhaps the most important features of Devil's Den Preserve are its size and ecological context. Devil's Den is part of the larger Saugatuck Forestlands that embrace roughly 60,000 acres of healthy woodland. Many species need large tracts of intact forestland to thrive. When such a large unfragmented forest rests in a densely populated area, it becomes even more important. Devil's Den Preserve will help to keep southwest Connecticut from becoming entirely developed. Six ecological zones in the preserve characterize its forest composition: the lower slopes, midslopes, upper slopes, crests, riparian areas, and wetlands. The high-moisture wetlands feature red maples, black tupelo, elm, and ash trees. The diverse lower slopes are dominated by ash, hickory, beech, birch, sugar maples, and tulip trees. The mid- and upper slopes are comprised of mostly oak, hickory, and chestnut trees. The crest areas are dry and rocky with much less diversity.

There is substantial archeological evidence at Devil's Den that the region was used for hunting by Native Americans, who also used the overhanging rock formations for shelter. An old sawmill from the 1700s and Godfrey Pond can be seen at the preserve. The Godfrey family ran the sawmill for almost 100 years, providing evidence of the area's history in lumbering. Charcoal production also occurred in the area that is now Devil's Den until the early 20th century, when other emerging forms of fuel made it unnecessary. Much credit for the preservation of this area goes to Katherine Ordway, who donated the money to the Nature Conservancy to purchase the property.

Because of the ecological sensitivity of the preserve, visitors are encouraged to engage in recreational activities that have less impact on the land, such as hiking and bird-watching. With more than 20 miles of hiking trails available, there is ample opportunity for visitors to experience the beauty of this scenic landscape. In addition to the Godfrey sawmill and pond, other places of interest within the preserve are the Saugatuck Wildlife Refuge, Ambler Gorge, and the Great Ledge, from which the Saugatuck Reservoir can be seen. The larger Saugatuck Forestlands hold other natural areas including Trout Brook Valley, Centennial Watershed State Forest, and Huntington State Park.

Devil's Den Preserve. (Courtesy of Nancy Bray Cardozo)

Activities aimed at protecting Devil's Den involve removing invasive species, trail maintenance, and monitoring water quality of the wetlands in the preserve and surrounding areas. Established in 2006, the Saugatuck River Watershed Partnership brought together representatives from the 11 towns in the watershed area who all agreed that conservation of the region is a priority. Workshops highlight that the main threats to the watershed are land management, invasive species, incompatible development, dams, and reservoir management. A few of the key conservation strategies of the partnership include protecting and restoring water quality by identifying sources of water degradation and developing water enhancement programs. The partnership addresses invasive species by regularly removing threatening plants through the help of volunteers. Restoring original water flow patterns is an important consideration for the protection of fish species. The partnership actively gathers information that is shared with the 11 municipalities in order for more sustainable decisions to be made in the future regarding land and water use within the watershed. Educational workshops and programs are also conducted to develop a stronger sense of stewardship in the watershed communities.

Further Reading

Chapman, William K., Valerie Conley Chapman, Alan E. Bessette, and Arleen R. Bessette. *Wildflowers of Massachusetts, Connecticut, and Rhode Island in Color.* Syracuse, NY: Syracuse University Press, 2008.

Hammerson, Geoffrey A. *Connecticut Wildlife: Biodiversity, Natural History, and Conservation.* Lebanon, NH: University Press of New England, 2004.

Nature Conservancy. "Devil's Den Preserve." http://www.nature.org/wherewework/ northamerica/states/connecticut/preserves/art17963.html.

Wharton, Eric. *The Forests of Connecticut.* Newtown Square, PA: USDA Forest Service Publications Distribution, 2004.

LAST GREEN VALLEY

There are some natural areas in the Northeast United States where the ecological importance is hard to channel into a specific preserve, park, or sanctuary because the entire region has such extraordinary significance. The Last Green Valley in northeast Connecticut is a region that is sometimes referred to as the Quinebaug Highlands or the Quinebaug and Shetucket Rivers Valley National Heritage Corridor. It is often called the Last Green Valley, because it is one of the last undeveloped green areas along the highly populated northeast urban corridor spanning from Washington, D.C., to Boston. A satellite view of the region at night reveals a sharp contrast between the valley's dark, undeveloped appearance amid the long line of urban and suburban glow that indicates high levels of human activity. The region is situated east of the New London and Hartford,

Connecticut, areas and west of Providence, Rhode Island, and Boston. Although the Last Green Valley has its share of development, it is an oasis of natural resources along the highly urbanized eastern seaboard.

The Last Green Valley region has within its boundaries seven state parks, an abundance of wildlife, over 80 ponds and lakes, many miles of hiking trails, 16 state wildlife management areas, and the Quinebaug and Shetucket rivers systems. The region is primarily forest and farmland and is a critical resource for southern New England not only because it does an exceptional job of helping to keep the air and water clean through natural purification processes, but also because it preserves the region's rural character. Recognized for its exceptional value to New England, the region was designated a national heritage corridor in 1994. It offers a vast area for wildlife to roam, such as black bear and bobcats, and includes some rare species such as the frosted elfin butterfly and the ringed boghaunter dragonfly. Spanning more than 200 square miles, the Last Green Valley is an ideal place for many recreational activities. Visitors can explore boating, canoeing, and fishing opportunities on the many lakes and river systems while hikers, birdwatchers, and bicyclists can enjoy the many trails, state forests, and nature preserves in the area. The Nature Conservancy has several nature preserves in the region, including Dennis Farm, Ayers Gap, and Rock Spring. These preserves protect areas of special interest because they harbor rare plants species or critical animal habitats. Other exceptional places to visit include Bigelow Hollow State Park, Laurel Sanctuary, and Goodwin State Forest.

Southern New England is at risk of losing this critical area primarily because of incompatible development. It is a beautiful rural landscape cloaked in hemlock, hickory, oak, and white birch that is also close to the Atlantic coast and urban centers, making it desirable for all kinds of development. Many organizations are involved in the protection of this area, including the Green Valley Institute, the Nature Conservancy, and other agencies that work with farmers and landowners to promote sustainable land use in the Last Green Valley. The Green Valley Institute provides workshops and activities to educate the local community about ways to protect the natural resources of the region. The Source to Sea Expedition is a paddling event that begins at the headwaters of the Quinebaug and the Shetucket rivers and meanders down to where these rivers eventually empty into the Long Island Sound. Goals of this event are to raise awareness about the importance of healthy watersheds, show the links between land use and water quality, and emphasize how pollution from upstream negatively impacts the waters of the Long Island Sound. The annual Tastes of the Valley event celebrates the food grown by local farmers, and the Walktober event invites residents to walk a trail and relish in the breathtaking beauty of Connecticut in October.

Further Reading

Chapman, William K., Valerie Conley Chapman, Alan E. Bessette, and Arleen R. Bessette. *Wildflowers of Massachusetts, Connecticut, and Rhode Island in Color.* Syracuse, NY: Syracuse University Press, 2008.

Green Valley Institute. http://www.greenvalleyinstitute.org/.

Hammerson, Geoffery A. *Connecticut Wildlife: Biodiversity, Natural History, and Conservation.* Lebanon, NH: University Press of New England, 2004.

Last Green Valley. www.thelastgreenvalley.org.

PAWCATUCK BORDERLANDS

The Pawcatuck Borderlands is a large forest system that crosses the Rhode Island and Connecticut border stretching from Boston to Washington, DC. This incredible East Coast conservation effort continues to grow through land acquisitions and land management initiatives that recognize the ever-increasing threats that are compromising the health of New England's coastal areas. The Pawcatuck Borderlands includes important wetland areas, such as Ell/Long Pond Preserve in Rhode Island as well as several important rivers and hardwood forests. It also contains substantial yet unique pitch pine forest natural communities that are common for coastal areas but have been decreasing due to high demands for commercial and residential development. But the borderlands region is most known for its giant rhododendron forest and Atlantic white cedar. Classified as a cypress tree, the Atlantic white cedar in the Pawcatuck Borderlands is a wetland tree that is home to the Hessel's hairstreak, a globally endangered butterfly, and an equally rare dragonfly called the banded boghaunter.

Just south of Ell/Long Pond Preserve is Canonchet Brook Preserve, a 600-acre natural area in Rhode Island that contains a blend of old-growth and new-growth forest, where oaks, tulip poplars, white pines, hickory, maple, witch hazel, blueberry bushes, and mountain laurel can be seen among the slopes and rocky terrain. The Ell/Long Pond Preserve is a special place in and of itself, and its place nestled within the Pawcatuck Borderlands will ensure its protection as a federally recognized natural landmark.

Also located in this area is Poquetanuck Cove Preserve near Ledyard, Connecticut. Purchased in 1953 by Desire Parker, this preserve protects an important archeological site that provides evidence that it was once an area where Native Americans harvested oysters. To permanently protect this serene marshland area, Parker donated the property to the Nature Conservancy in 1988. Walking along the one-and-a-half-mile trail reveals an array of habitats, including an oak-beech forest, a hemlock ravine, the cove itself, and a pitch pine forest. Osprey and waterfowl can be observed in the marsh.

In North Stonington, Connecticut, in 2004, the Ashwillit Brook Preserve was created in the Pawcatuck Borderlands through the collaborative conservation efforts of the Nature Conservancy and the North Stonington Citizens' Land Alliance. This 123-acre parcel of land is ecologically significant because of its black water bogs rich in colored, organic, acidic material that provides a quality habitat for Atlantic white cedar. Situated near the Pauchaug State Forest, Ashwillit Brook Preserve will augment the protected areas within the borderlands to conserve larger tracts of important land.

View of a creek in the Pawcatuck Borderlands. (Courtesy of Rick Newton)

The challenge for the communities in the Pawcatuck Borderlands is to explore and discover ways to manage growth and support economic and community vitality while maintaining the ecological integrity of this beautiful area. The Borderlands Project was created in 2001 with the goal of addressing those challenges. A more recent effort began in 2007 with the Village Innovation Pilot that focused on two communities within the Borderlands—Killingly, Connecticut, and Exeter, Rhode Island. The goal of this initiative is to conserve environmental resources by directing growth into planned village centers. Town hall meetings have been held regularly in both towns to explore the most realistic and effective strategies to promote growth while conserving critical lands. Considered one of Connecticut's "last great places" by the Nature Conservancy, the Pawcatuck Borderlands covers 200 square miles connecting rural lands and hardwood forests with the quiet corner of northeast Connecticut. Through land acquisition and the collaborative efforts of state, local, and federal agencies, the Pawcatuck Borderlands communities are exploring innovative ways to prosper economically while preserving their natural heritage.

Further Reading
Borderlands Project. http://www.borderlandsproject.org.

Henshaw, Carol. *Natural Wonders of Connecticut & Rhode Island: Exploring Wild and Scenic Places.* New York: McGraw-Hill, 2000.

Kricher, John, and Gordon Morrison. *A Field Guide to Eastern Forests, North America.* Boston: Houghton Mifflin, 1998.

The Nature Conservancy. "Pawcatuck Borderlands." http://www.nature.org/wherewework/ northamerica/states/rhodeisland/preserves/art9945.html.

ROBBINS SWAMP

The northwest corner of Connecticut is like no other part of the state. Known as the Northwest Highlands, this area is blanketed in dense forest that has been able to resist the seemingly insatiable demands of the logging industry for the last century. There are mountains in this region, wetlands, and more than 100 rare and endangered species. The largest inland wetland in Connecticut is in the Northwest Highlands, and it is called Robbins Swamp. Typically perceived as wastelands, wetlands such as Robbins Swamp are receiving more recognition as ecological environments critical for their contributions to regional health. While many wetlands have vanished into residential and commercial development because of the negative perception, Robbins Swamp is a thriving ecosystem because of the increased understanding of the valuable natural resources of these underappreciated areas.

Formed over limestone bedrock, Robbins Swamp is a calcareous swamp that is highly alkaline. Many of the wetland areas in New England are highly acidic, making this swamp quite unique. The soils contain high levels of calcium carbonate, creating a fertile environment for unusual species. The endangered timber rattlesnake and northern metalmark butterfly can be found in this region of Connecticut. Trees in the swamp include red maple, black ash, and American elm. The rare spreading globeflower and a swamp orchid called yellow lady's slipper can be found in this wetland along with showy lady's slipper, grass-of-Parnassus, and fringed gentian. Other rare species include shrubby cinquefoil, swamp birch, and tamarack. The state endangered bog turtle lives at Robbins Swamp.

The major ecological threats to the swamp are invasive species, fertilizer and septic runoff, chemical and heavy metal pollution, and disruption of natural water movement and drainage patterns. Some rare and endangered species (such as the bog turtle) require open areas for their habitats, but if the swamp receives too many nutrients, red maple trees may close the open spaces and threaten those habitats.

The Northwest Highlands of Connecticut are ecologically strong in part due to their proximity to the spectacular Berkshire Taconic Landscape, which reaches across western Massachusetts, Connecticut, and New York. Its span encompasses the Berkshire and Taconic mountains and connects them to the Appalachian range. Covering more than 155,000 acres, there is no other place quite like it in southern New England. It is a lush wilderness, but not too intimidating for the occasional nature observer. Comprised of rich wetlands, northern hardwood forests, the Appalachian Trail, lakes, river systems, more than 150 rare and endangered species, and extraordinary views, the Berkshire Taconic Landscape is a conservation success story. Many organizations and landowners are involved in the preservation of this diverse area that is vibrating with health and vitality.

Also of interest in the Northwest Highlands are Canaan Mountain, Hollenbeck Preserve, and Cathedral Pines Nature Preserve. Canaan Mountain is a range that extends for eight miles with scenic peaks and rock outcrops hovering above dense woodland. Its highest peak reaches over 1,900 feet. Cathedral Pines Preserve contains a stand of old-growth white pine and hemlock trees. Located within the Hollenbeck River watershed, Hollenbeck Preserve is home to a number of rare plant and animal species and grassland birds of concern in Connecticut. The Hollenbeck River bubbles through Robbins Swamp, making its water quality important to this special wetland. Thousands of acres are protected within the Northwest Highlands of Connecticut, and, as conservation efforts from various organizations continue, the region and its natural communities will continue to thrive. Through land acquisition, promoting sustainable development, invasive species control, and water quality monitoring, Robbins Swamp has a good chance of maintaining its status as one of the most important natural areas in Connecticut.

Further Reading

Chapman, William K., Valerie Conley Chapman, Alan E. Bessette, and Arleen R. Bessette. *Wildflowers of Massachusetts, Connecticut, and Rhode Island in Color.* Syracuse, NY: Syracuse University Press, 2008.

Hammerson, Geoffery A. *Connecticut Wildlife: Biodiversity, Natural History, and Conservation.* Lebanon, NH: University Press of New England, 2004.

Henshaw, Carol. *Natural Wonders of Connecticut & Rhode Island: Exploring Wild and Scenic Places.* New York: McGraw-Hill, 2000.

Nature Conservancy. "Northwest Highlands." http://www.nature.org/wherewework/northamerica/states/connecticut/preserves/art21228.html.

Blackbird-Millington Corridor, 14
Burrows Run Preserve, 15
Middleford North Preserve, 17
Pemberton Forest, 18
Prime Hook National Wildlife Refuge, 19

DELAWARE

Delaware is an eastern seaboard, coastal plain state and the second smallest in the country. It is bordered by Pennsylvania, New Jersey, Maryland, the Atlantic Ocean, and the Delaware Bay. Less than a century ago, Delaware was covered in native forest and piedmont ecosystems common for eastern U.S. coastal regions. Now, only 20 percent of Delaware's forests remain, and most of its shoreline has been developed. Still, Delaware has maintained a healthy population of wildlife and native plant species and provides habitats for rare and endangered species. Although its wetland ecosystems have been greatly compromised by the pollution from commercial, industrial, and residential development, it still contains beaches, dunes, fields, and upland forests that are filled with wildlife. It shares the Delmarva Peninsula with Maryland and Virginia and shares many of the same coastal conservation concerns as these other states.

Because Delaware is largely defined by its coastal ecology, water quality and the health of its wetlands are conservation priorities for the state. Many of the state's rivers and estuarine water sources are contaminated by bacteria as well as residential and urban pollution. The Delaware Wetlands Conservation Strategy is a collaborative effort that monitors wetlands in the state and helps to restore these areas for the enhancement of wildlife habitats and ecological benefits associated with wetlands, including the filtration and purification of water sources, the reduction of flooding, and the promotion of wetland education and biodiversity in the state. This strategy is also committed to education and outreach to encourage local and state stewardship for these wetlands that are essential to the state's environmental health. Also of importance to Delaware are its rivers. The Nanticoke Watershed Alliance, an organization that serves to promote sustainability within the watershed, provides cultural and educational resources for people who live within the Nanticoke River watershed.

Delaware participates in other conservation programs that are designed to maintain and restore the ecological integrity of the state. The foundation for Delaware's natural heritage is its wildlife. The Delaware Wildlife Action Plan was created in response to an undeniable decline in the state's wildlife populations in recent decades. Habitat loss is one of the primary factors contributing to this decline. The primary goal of this plan is to "keep common things common" while also protecting those species that are rare.

Also important to the state is the Blackbird-Millington Corridor Conservation Plan in 2004 that brought together citizens of the Delmarva Peninsula, environmental experts, the Delaware Department of Natural Resources and Environmental Control, and the Nature Conservancy in Delaware to develop a five-year plan to protect a 52,000-acre tract of land that reaches from the Delaware Bay to the Chester River in Maryland. The conservation plan for the corridor includes activities that foster habitat and species protection and promote education and research opportunities in the corridor. The forest areas are critical for Delaware because of the significant role they play in the air and water quality of the region.

BLACKBIRD-MILLINGTON CORRIDOR

There are places in America that inspire such strong feelings of stewardship that a community of people will come together and work to protect them despite the challenges. In 2004, it was this kind of unprecedented group effort that proposed the Blackbird-Millington Corridor Conservation Plan that brought together more than 150 residents of the Delmarva Peninsula, over 60 experts from 30 organizations, the Delaware Department of Natural Resources and Environmental Control, and the Nature Conservancy in Delaware to develop a five-year plan to protect the 52,000-acre tract of land that reaches from the Delaware Bay to the Chester River in Maryland. The goal entailed protecting the area from the ever-increasing intensity of development on the eastern seaboard.

The Blackbird-Millington Corridor includes the Chesapeake Bay Lowlands and the North Atlantic Coast ecoregions. It is valued as a high priority area for its undeveloped state and private forests, its wetlands that provide home to roughly 125 rare species of plants and animals, and its biodiversity. The area gets its name from two public land holdings that are part of the corridor: Delaware's Blackbird State Forest and Millington Wildlife Management Area. Historically, it was an area traveled by the Lenape and Nanticoke Indians before a portion of the corridor was used for agriculture. Peach farming was once essential to the local income, and it has been said that Harriet Tubman, in her attempt to free slaves, found refuge at Clearfield Farm in Blackbird Hundred under the protection of abolitionist John Corbit.

The conservation plan for the Blackbird-Millington Corridor includes 37 actions that address habitat restoration, land protection, compatible economic uses, and education and research opportunities. Of primary concern is protection of the forest areas because of the significant role they play in the air and water quality of the region. The forests also provide recreation areas for the local residents as well as sanctuary for enjoyment of the corridor's wooded natural beauty. With the vast majority of Delaware's original forest lands gone, preservation of those that still remain is of critical importance.

Still it would be a mistake to overlook the corridor's streams—Blackbird Creek and Cypress Branch—and the tidal wetlands, ponds, and bird habitats that support the migratory avian populations that pass through the corridor. Blackbird Creek is managed by the Delaware National Estuarine Research Reserve as a site representative of the mix of freshwater and brackish ecosystems common on the Atlantic Coast. Brackish bodies of water in estuaries have a higher amount of salinity, or salt content, than fresh water, but less than the sea. Estuaries, partly enclosed coastal bodies of water, connect to the sea through a system of rivers and streams and are known for their rich biodiversity. An estuary is often referred to as a bay or a sound. The Chesapeake Bay is one of the largest and most complex estuaries in the United States and lies to the west of the corridor.

The Blackbird-Millington Corridor has resisted devastating pollution and development for this long due to the conscientious stewardship of private farmowners who have cared for the quiet beauty and life-affirming natural resources of this area. Without their dedication to preserving their local landscapes, much of what this green corridor has to offer would have been lost to development. And now the community-based conservation plan is an example of how a better future can be created for these important areas through the unified efforts of organizations, concerned residents, and government agencies that come together to preserve the natural heritage of the place they call home.

Further Reading

Blackbird-Millington Corridor Conservation Plan. http://www.dnrec.state.de.us/nhp/information/blackbird.asp.

Stutz, Bruce. *Natural Lives, Modern Times: People and Places of the Delaware River.* Philadelphia: University of Pennsylvania Press, 1998.

BURROWS RUN PRESERVE

In northern Delaware, there is a place known for its butterflies, birds, and wildflower blossoms. That place is the 352-acre Burrows Run Preserve managed by Delaware's Nature Society. This area, located near Old Kennett Road and the Delaware-Pennsylvania state line, is primarily used as a wildlife conservation area and as a site for environmental education. Although the preserve is not open to the public, natural history programs and tours allow for visitation.

Burrows Run is a site frequently used for ecological research. Records indicate that the preserve has 115 wildflower species and 179 species of birds, and 13 rare plants have been found here, including the American ginseng. American sycamore and white ash trees flourish in the preserve, and close to 100 species of wildflowers such as the trout lily, false hellebore, and common blue violet dazzle the preserve. Since establishing a vital habitat for butterflies, the increase in butterfly populations at Burrows Run has allowed the preserve to work with a local school district—Red Clay School District—to educate students of the role of butterflies in the ecosystem.

Another important activity taking place in the preserve is the ongoing study of the water quality of the Burrows Run stream that runs through the preserve. Studies conducted by the Nature Society suggest that the stream remains relatively clean and unpolluted based on the substantial macroinvertebrate populations in that they require a healthy aquatic environment to survive. Nineteen fish species live in the Burrows Run, including the green sunfish, which has not been seen anywhere else in Delaware. The stream, bubbling in shallow areas and slow moving through its deep pools, provides excellent habitat for species that thrive in well-oxygenated areas as well as space for those who hide in deeper areas or along undercut banks. The stream is an excellent water source for the preserve's wood frogs, salamanders, eastern painted turtles, and garter snakes. To protect the stream, the Delaware Nature Society is committed to the preserve's educational value and working with the nearby community. In creating a local stewardship program, the society educates streamside landowners of the connection between stream health, water quality, wildlife, and vegetation to help protect Burrows Run's watershed ecosystem. Many landowners have donated property to the Nature Society or have agreed not to develop lands within the watershed, helping to protect the stream corridor lands.

The Burrows Run nature preserve began when Crawford and Margaretta Greenewalt donated 110 acres of land to the Nature Society in 1990. They had owned and farmed the land since the early 1930s. Other donations to the Nature Society have contributed to what is today a vibrant preserve that will be permanently protected. Coverdale Farm, which lies within the preserve, is home to the largest champion black tupelo tree in Delaware. Like the preserve itself, the farm is not open to the public, but there are a host of educational programs in place at Coverdale. Participants can learn about raising and managing livestock; organic farming; the importance of clean soil, water, and air for human health and survival; wildlife; and the surrounding areas that include old-growth forest and the Burrows Run stream. The farm complex dates back to the 19th century with a barn that dates back as far as the 1700s. Visitors can learn a great deal about farm life among the acres of corn, soybean, and hay and a lot about the natural environment at Burrows Run Preserve. It is a place that not only offers scenic beauty with its wildflowers and butterflies, but also a place that has been fully utilized for its research and educational value.

Further Reading

Delaware Nature Society. http://www.delawarenaturesociety.org/.

Tatnall, Robert. *Flora of Delaware and the Eastern Shore: An Annotated List of the Ferns and Flowering Plants of the Peninsula of Delaware, Maryland and Virginia.* Wilmington: Society of Natural History of Delaware, 1946.

MIDDLEFORD NORTH PRESERVE

Within the Nanticoke River watershed in Sussex County, Delaware, lies the wild swamps and forests of Middleford North Preserve. Here the Nanticoke River bubbles and dances through Middleforth as the only portion of the river that has not been channeled or dredged. Perhaps this is one of the reasons that the Nanticoke is one of the cleanest rivers that empties into the Delaware Bay. Roughly 440 acres near Seaford, Middleforth North is home to the Hessel's hairstreak butterfly, a globally endangered creature that can only find food during its caterpillar stage in the Atlantic white cedar groves at the preserve. Other trees at Middleford include the loblolly pine, red maple, blackgum, and sweetgum. Because of its wetlands, forests, groves, and floodplain, Middleford North has rich biological diversity and has become home to numerous rare species.

Like many of the East Coast preserves, parks, and refuges, Middleford North is also a haven for migratory birds. The preserve provides home and habitat for more than 80 species, including the American redstart, Louisiana waterthrush, and black and white warbler. A rare sighting of the blackburnian warbler has occurred at this preserve. Seen during its flight south during migration, the blackburnian population lives predominately in Canada. Although its population is considered stable, rapid deforestation in the United States and Canada indicate that the warbler's mature and old-growth forests habitats are diminishing.

Perhaps of utmost importance at Middleford North is its location within the Nanticoke River watershed. A watershed is an area that gathers water and drains it into a common point. Basically, everyone lives in a watershed, because the precipitation in any given area drains to a certain body of water depending upon the hills, ridges, and valleys of the land. The Nanticoke River was named by early American explorer Captain John Smith, who coined the river after the Indians who lived nearby. The Nanticoke River watershed is 725,000 acres and includes a mix of freshwater tidal wetlands and brackish wetlands. The river and its watershed are under threat due to incompatible farming practices, sewage, and the clear-cutting of trees, which removes an important means of filtration for the water as it seeps down into the soil. The high degree of development in the watershed region also promotes polluted runoff after rain and storms as the water travels over concrete and eventually drains into the Chesapeake Bay. The Nature Conservancy, along with a host of state and local agencies, works to protect the watershed. Along with continuing to acquire more acres of land in the watershed for preservation, the conservancy conducts workshops with landowners in the area to educate residents in sustainable stewardship of their properties. Also of importance is the Nanticoke Watershed Alliance, an organization that promotes sustainability within the watershed, provides cultural and educational resources for people who live in the watershed, and offers volunteer opportunities for those who want to help.

Middleford North Preserve is a step toward improving the quality of the Nanticoke River, the watershed, and creating a healthy environment for all beings that are sustained by it. The river is a vital spawning ground for river herring, striped bass, and redbreast sunfish, and plants such as Long's bittercress, seaside alder, and Parker's piperwort are endangered species that find a suitable habitat at Middleford North. As with many of the extremely fragile natural areas in Delaware, Middleford North is not open to the public. The preserve, which includes two and a half miles of the scenic Nanticoke riverfront, is a natural area where the future of Delaware's ecological balance is taking a foothold.

Further Reading

Hess, Gene K., Richard L. West, Lorraine M. Fleming, and Maruce V. Barnhill III, eds. *Birds of Delaware*. Pittsburgh, PA: University of Pittsburgh Press, 2000.

Nanticoke Watershed Alliance. http://www.nanticokeriver.org.

Nature Conservancy. "Middleford North Preserve." http://www.nature.org/wherewework/northamerica/states/delaware/preserves/art10709.html.

PEMBERTON FOREST

It is hard to imagine a world without forests, but that is a possible future for the state of Delaware due to rapid development and the timber industry. Less than a century ago, Delaware was carpeted by native forest land and a piedmont ecosystem common for coastal regions. Now, only 20 percent of Delaware's forests remain. Fortunately, Pemberton Forest, located in Sussex County, is a high-priority preservation area for the Nature Conservancy. This forest, which totals more than 1,300 acres, is a combination of the original Pemberton tract of 456 acres and the Ponders tract of 908 acres, which was acquired in 2004 for $9.8 million. Together, these two tracts that make up the preserve help protect streams, wetlands, habitat for rare plant and animal species, and are the best examples of bogs and Atlantic cedar swamps that Delaware has to offer. Also, Pemberton is the only location where the curly-grass fern can be found in Delaware.

To protect Pemberton Forest Preserve, the Nature Conservancy has taken on what it considers the largest forest restoration project ever for the state of Delaware. The Ponders tract, once owned by a timber company, used to be a loblolly pine plantation. By gently thinning a substantial population of the loblolly pine through techniques that imitate natural forest disturbances, the conservancy is revitalizing the native coastal hardwood forest and shrubs. Oak, tulip, hickory, sassafras, red maple, and Virginia pine trees are being restored, while nonnative species are being carefully monitored. In fall 2005, the Nature Conservancy began taking a close look at the invasive species at the preserve, some of which are quite aggressive and a threat to the native budding trees and shoots. Some of the invasive species include Japanese honeysuckle, phragmites, and spotted knapweed. Next to the Ponders tract, the highly aggressive Japanese knotweed was found. This in-depth survey helped the conservancy control the invasive plants in preparation for the tree planting that took place the following year. On Earth Day 2006, through the conservancy's Add-a-Tree program, 170 trees were planted by volunteers and conservancy staff. This large-scale tree planting was later followed by the construction of habitat islands, corridors of green that attract birds and wildlife. Habitat islands are commonly seen in rural areas that are dominated by agricultural production. The islands provide pathways from one natural area to another to optimize habitat space for plants and animals.

A few waterways will be impacted by this restoration project. The Ponders tract is home to a shallow creek called Ingram Branch that flows into the Broadkill River. The Broadkill then empties into the Delaware Bay. Restoration of Pemberton Forest preserve protects the water quality of these local waterways that eventually impact the health of larger bodies of water, including the Atlantic Ocean. Improving the quality of world oceans begins with restoring creeks and rivers.

Currently, the preserve is not open to the public because of the fragility of the area, but ideally, the conservancy would like to discover ways to allow for the forest to be enjoyed by local residents and visitors while still keeping the forest's ecological qualities intact. Fundraising is underway to raise money for a parking lot, hiking trails, benches, and an observation deck for visitors. The forest restoration efforts taking place at Pemberton are unprecedented for the state of Delaware, but without these initiatives, the forest tracts would continue to decline. This is a time when large-scale projects to save what little remains of natural areas is a necessity requiring substantial time and money from dedicated individuals who realize that they are contributing not just to the health of a forest tract in Delaware but to a sustainable planet for all.

Further Reading

Rappole, John H. *Wildlife of the Mid-Atlantic: A Complete Reference Manual.* Philadelphia: University of Pennsylvania Press, 2007.

Silberhorn, Gene M. *Common Plants of the Mid-Atlantic Coast: A Field Guide.* Baltimore: Johns Hopkins University Press, 1999.

Tatnall, Robert. *Flora of Delaware and the Eastern Shore: An Annotated List of the Ferns and Flowering Plants of the Peninsula of Delaware, Maryland and Virginia.* Wilmington: Society of Natural History of Delaware, 1946.

PRIME HOOK NATIONAL WILDLIFE REFUGE

In the United Sates, more than 530 national wildlife refuges exist due to the work of the U.S. Fish and Wildlife Service, and Prime Hook is one of them. Located off Turkle Pond Road in Milton, Delaware, Prime Hook National Wildlife Refuge was once an area populated by farms and houses. In 1963, the refuge was established primarily to support wintering waterfowl and the migratory bird passages along the Atlantic Flyway. Prime Hook encompasses 10,000 acres along the eastern seaboard for the protection of migratory birds, which includes 4,200 acres of freshwater feeding grounds. The refuge also houses many species of salamanders, turtles, insects, and frogs, and the endangered Delmarva fox squirrel is protected at Prime Hook. The refuge carefully monitors this rare squirrel population as well as protects the mature hardwood forest areas where the squirrel can thrive. Forest conservation is a priority at the refuge, which features a diverse array of maple, oak, pine, hickory, and poplar. Additionally, the upland shrub habitat areas of the refuge are small but provide necessary breeding opportunities for the coastal plain swamp sparrow, a bird that is very unusual for Delaware. The invasive common reed, or *phragmites australis*, is a threat to other native species of plants and is carefully controlled by the refuge. Also, phragmites is not good for nesting or feeding, providing few survival necessities for wildlife.

Prime Hook, meaning Plum Point in Dutch, was named after the region's abundance of purple beach plums by Dutch settlers in the 17th century. This coastal shrub with white flowers thrives in a sand dune habitat and contains a small purple fruit that was used in jams and pies. The refuge also supports nursing fish and crabs in its tidal salt marsh communities, and its carefully managed water levels help to promote the growth of grains such as wild rice and millet.

The most popular recreational activities at Prime Hook are fishing, hiking, canoeing, bird-watching, and nature photography. The refuge provides many educational opportunities by working with local public schools and providing guided tours and field trips for classes. The refuge offers a self-guided seven-mile canoe trail along Prime Hook Creek that weaves through wooded wetlands and leads into a freshwater impoundment,

Prime Hook National Wildlife Refuge. (Flickr—JD Bennett)

a shallow pond area. Along the trail, canoeists might see red maple, sweetbay magnolia, green ash, sweet gum, American holly, and sandbar willows. Shrubs such as marsh mallow, seaside alder, winterberry, and bayberry can be seen. Beavers, herons, snow geese, egrets, and many other birds can be seen year-round. The refuge also maintains six foot trails where visitors may observe nature and encounter wildlife despite the fact that there are four state highways running through the refuge.

What is admirable about Prime Hook is its commitment to educating visitors about the ecological importance and beauty of wetlands. It is essential that the value of marshes be recognized in the United States. These marshy areas are often considered useless and unattractive, thus explaining the loss of the vast majority of wetland areas to development and exploitation in the last century. In addition to keeping water cleaner, marshes absorb water during flooding and gradually release water during dry periods, thus helping to maintain a balanced water supply at all times. The canoe trail and other activities at Prime Hook are aimed toward sharing the incredible biodiversity of Delaware's wetlands, which is why it is critically important that they are preserved. Opportunities to support Prime Hook are available through volunteer opportunities and also through purchasing duck stamps that were issued after the passing of the Migratory Bird Hunting and Conservation Stamp Act in 1934. Millions of dollars have been raised to help purchase and maintain wetland areas and coastal wildlife refuges.

Further Reading
Prime Hook National Wildlife Refuge. http://www.fws.gov/northeast/primehook/.
Rappole, John H. *Wildlife of the Mid-Atlantic: A Complete Reference Manual*. Philadelphia: University of Pennsylvania Press, 2007.

Blanton Forest, 24

Dinsmore Woods and State Nature Preserve, 26

Eastview Barrens Preserve, 27

Green River Bioreserve, 29

Griffith Woods, 30

Natural Bridge State Park Nature Preserve, 32

Red River Gorge Geological Area, 34

KENTUCKY

Kentucky is comprised of six geographic regions: the Jackson Purchase in the far west corner, the Western Coal Fields, the Pennroyal region that contains the Big Barrens of Kentucky, the Bluegrass region in the north-central part of the state, the hills called the Knobs that surround the Bluegrass region, and the Eastern Mountains and Coal Fields. These six regions have formed the rich natural and cultural history that Kentucky is known for today. Places such as the Red River Gorge, Natural Bridge, Mammoth Cave, the gently rolling horse farms of central Kentucky, and the Appalachian Mountains and forests to the east have defined the unique character and diversity of the state. The Appalachian culture to the east with its music, labor struggles, coal mining legacy, and economic hardship exists as a sharp counterpoint to the picturesque horse farms and opulence of the Kentucky Derby that brings wealth and roses to the state each year.

Kentucky has programs that are actively engaged in protecting the state's wetlands, wildlife, grasslands, and agricultural lands. But urban and agricultural runoff, acid mine drainage, and the state's coal industry have created enormous conservation challenges for Kentucky. Surface mining and mountaintop removal have devastated wildlife habitats, natural communities, and water sources and have compromised the health of all people, plant, and animal species in the mining regions. The ancient mountain ranges of Kentucky have been turned into rubble wastelands as a result of mountaintop removal. Additionally, the water quality in the state's rivers and lakes is a major problem in Kentucky. Pollution from farms, septic systems, and sewage sources has impaired many of Kentucky's waterways by adding high quantities of bacteria into the water.

At one time in U.S. history, Kentucky was the west. It was a frontier where English, French, and Spanish explorers came into contact with Native American tribes in the midst of a wild landscape roaring with buffalo and the beating wings of wild turkeys. This contact proved to be disastrous for the indigenous cultures and for the buffalo. While many of the original inhabitants of Kentucky either died of European diseases or were forced into territories beyond their homelands, the buffalo were hunted to near extinction. Still, there is something remaining of those buffalo—their footpaths. These primitive routes that were carved by the region's roaming wildlife laid the groundwork for many of Kentucky's modern highways.

It took a long time for English settlement to gain a foothold in Kentucky because of the Appalachian Mountain Range to the east that formed a barrier between Kentucky and the states to the east, but settlers found their way to the region down the Ohio River or through the Cumberland Gap. There are some places in the state that still beckon these earlier times, particularly in the eastern mountain region. In an essay titled "An Entrance to the Woods," Wendell Berry wrote of the Red River Gorge: "There are haunted places, or at least it is easy to feel haunted in them, alone at nightfall. As the air darkens and the cool of the night rises, one feels the immanence of the wraiths of the ancient tribesmen who used to inhabit the rock houses of the cliffs." Berry, who is well known for being a Kentucky farmer, author, and conservationist, has written many works that express his commitment to agrarian values that also speak out against environmental destruction. His writings have helped to bring environmental awareness to the state of Kentucky while also encouraging a philosophy of stewardship and neighborliness, not simply as a form of activism but as a way of life.

BLANTON FOREST

In 1928, Grover and Oxie Blanton purchased a vast stretch of forest on the southern slopes of Pine Mountain in Harlan County, Kentucky, with the decision that the property should never be logged. The Blantons passed the land on to their daughters, who followed their parents' wishes to protect the land. As a result, Blanton Forest is Kentucky's largest, most diverse old-growth forest. With trees that dating back to the 1600s, researchers have marveled at the fact that this area has been able to escape commercial development for so long. In 1995 and 2001, two portions of the forest were designated a state nature preserve, therefore permanently protecting this extraordinary natural resource and environmental treasure.

Blanton Forest is a rare example of a mixed mesophytic forest, a forest region comprised of mixed species that have adapted to a moderately moist water supply. With a stunning mosaic of old-growth oak, hemlock, beech, and poplar, Blanton Forest has trees that measure three or four feet in diameter. Rhododendrons, mountain bogs, and more than 400 plant species, including sphagnum moss and cinnamon ferns, can be found in Blanton Forest, some of which have thrived in the forest for hundreds of years. The federally endangered blackside dace still survives in Watt's Creek, which bubbles deep within the forest's dark interior. In 1995, 1,075 acres of the forest were dedicated as a nature preserve, but the preserve has grown to now encompass 3,098 acres. Still, more than 3,600 acres of forest are in need of protection, some of which include buffer lands necessary to protect the ancient forest.

The efforts to preserve this globally rare ancient forest are unprecedented in the state of Kentucky. The Kentucky Natural Lands Trust (KNLT), along with support from other state agencies, is leading the campaign to protect Blanton Forest. The goals of the KNLT are to protect the forest's biodiversity, provide low-impact educational and recreational activities, promote research within Blanton as a living laboratory that acts as an indicator of the overall health and well being of the planet, and explore opportunities for an environmentally sound ecotourism industry. Additionally, the creation of a stewardship endowment has enabled the KNLT to hire a steward to provide full-time management of Blanton Forest. More recently, the Kentucky State Nature Preserves Commission has led an effort to hunt for an insect called the hemlock wooly adelgid. This destructive and invasive insect has been devastating hemlock forests in the eastern United States.

But it is not just the ecological diversity that makes Blanton Forest important. This natural area bears beneath its canopy the rich cultural heritage of central Appalachia. It is located approximately five miles west of the city of Harlan, sometimes referred to as "bloody Harlan" because of its history of violence related to coal miners struggling with corrupt coal companies for better wages and safer working conditions. It is a link to the past when white settlers and pioneers traveled through its ridges and hollows, and a window into the region's Native American history. Spears and arrowheads can still be found within the lush vegetation that some say resembles a tropical rainforest.

Knobby Rock in Blanton Forest. (Courtesy of Heather Spaulding)

Visitors usually hike one of the scenic trails in the forest accessed from Kentucky Route 840. One trail loop leads to Knobby Rock, offering magnificent views above the forest canopy, while another winds near Watts Creek. Hikers can view an abundance of wildlife, plant species, and trees that reach higher than 100 feet above the forest floor. There is a four-mile trail system in the forest, but the vast majority of Blanton Forest is still revered as one of the few remaining places where forest ecosystems have endured unaltered by human encroachment.

Further Reading

Jones, Ronald L. *Plant Life of Kentucky: An Illustrated Guide to the Vascular Flora.* Lexington: University Press of Kentucky, 2005.
Kentucky Natural Lands Trust. "Blanton Forest." http://www.knlt.org/blanton.htm.
Kentucky State Nature Preserves Commission. "Blanton Forest State Nature Preserve." http://www.naturepreserves.ky.gov/stewardship/blanton.htm.

DINSMORE WOODS AND STATE NATURE PRESERVE

In 1842, James and Martha Dinsmore built their home amid acres of old-growth forest in Western Boone County, Kentucky. Located in the northern section of the Bluegrass region, this area has remained relatively undisturbed and provides Kentucky's only example of Pleistocene glaciations. These early glacier deposits created moist, fertile, and acidic soil unique to this region. The nature preserve surrounding the Dinsmore homestead consists of 107 acres of mature forest that includes oak, sugar maple, and white ash. The area is known for its spectacular display of wildflowers, including dwarf larkspur, wood poppy, and trout lily. Of top priority for the Dinsmore Woods and State Nature Preserve is to protect the federally endangered running buffalo clover and encourage it to spread while trying to maintain invasive garlic mustard growth. One of the main reasons for the clover's decline is that the plant is dependent upon large herbivore animals, such as bison, to periodically disturb the soil, create habitat, and carry the seeds to other locations. Once believed to be extinct, running buffalo clover populations have only been found in a few states in the country.

The 107 acres are owned by the Nature Conservancy, donated to the organization by Martha Breasted in 1985. Currently, the site is managed by both the Nature Conservancy and the Kentucky State Nature Preserves Commission (KSNPC). In 1990, both agencies dedicated the property, which provides it with the highest level of legal protection in Kentucky. Part of the KSNPC's mission is to manage and maintain natural areas that contain rare native species and natural communities important to the region's biodiversity. The KSNPC is also committed to educating Kentuckians and visitors of the importance of nature preserves and conservation. The 30 acres surrounding the house and grounds are protected by the Dinsmore Homestead Foundation. The preserve is located near the intersection of Middle Creek Road and Kentucky Route 18.

Dinsmore Woods attracts students, scholars, historians, conservationists, and hikers for its beauty and its historic and natural resources. Artists often visit Dinsmore to paint or sketch the picturesque landscape. The hiking trails offer ridge-top views, forest floors blanketed in lush green vegetation, groves of spring wildflowers, trees with intricate vine systems, winding streams, and a diversity of songbirds and wildlife. With the nearby horse farms in the Boone County area, it is not unlikely to see horseback riders entering the designated horse trail. While Dinsmore sees many visitors—more than 6,000 a year—the trails are marked by fragile habitat signs that encourage footpath traveling only, helping to preserve the landscape.

The Nature Conservancy's interest in Dinsmore involves its historical significance. The Dinsmore Homestead features the farmhouse, graveyard, carriage house, and entry to the nature preserve and other hiking trails. Originally from New Hampshire, James Dinsmore acquired his wealth through sugar cane, cotton, and slavery while living in Mississippi and Louisiana. Finally, he moved to Boone County, Kentucky, to be a farmer where he grew grapes, raised sheep, and grew willows for basket making. He brought with him his wife, Martha, and 11 slaves. The couple had three children together—Isabella, Julia, and Susan. Of particular interest to historians are the old farmhouse and the graveyard, which marks the resting place of family members and the slaves that worked at Dinsmore. The family graves are marked with roughly three-foot-high carved gravestones, while the slave graves are marked by unnamed small field stones. Of the three daughters, Julia spent the most time on the property, 54 years maintaining its upkeep. A writer and a poet, she kept a detailed journal of life at Dinsmore, adding to the extensive collection of historical documents available on microfilm for research. The homestead offers many opportunities to learn about Kentucky rural life in the 19th and early 20th centuries.

Further Reading

Barnes, Thomas G., Deborah White, and Marc Evans. *Rare Wildflowers of Kentucky*. Lexington: University Press of Kentucky, 2008.

Boone Conservancy. http://www.thebooneconservancy.org/.

Dinsmore Homestead. http://www.dinsmorefarm.org.

Jones, Ronald L. *Plant Life of Kentucky: An Illustrated Guide to the Vascular Flora*. Lexington: University Press of Kentucky, 2005.

EASTVIEW BARRENS PRESERVE

Dedicated in 1997 as Kentucky's 37th state nature preserve, Eastview Barrens is roughly 120 acres of prairie grassland and the largest remaining example of the "Big Barrens" that used to cover Kentucky's western midlands. Since most of the barrens that used to expand across Kentucky have been converted to farmland, other examples of barrens vegetation are small and isolated. The large tract of land that is now Eastview

Barrens Preserve remained undeveloped because of its sandy soil quality that is ill suited for agriculture and because of periodic burning due to sparks flying from a nearby railroad. Because barrens are historically fire-maintained systems, the sparks from the neighboring railroad played an important role in preserving this area. The fires kept the area open, reducing the number of shade-producing species, allowing for the native grasses to thrive. The Kentucky State Nature Preserves Commission and the Nature Conservancy, who jointly own Eastview Barrens, regularly maintain the area by conducting ecological burns that help to preserve the prairielike ecosystem. Much research is being done to study the impact of fire on rare plant species at Eastview.

Located in Harden County near Elizabethtown, Kentucky, the significance of Eastview as a natural area of high-priority preservation is the array of globally endangered plant species that thrive at Eastview, some of which include frostweed, spikemoss, barrens silky aster, prairie gentian, and long-haired hawkweed. Other native plants in the preserve may not be globally rare, but they are protected at Eastview because of their decline in Kentucky. Rare species of insects are also found at Eastview because they are dependent on the kind of plants that a prairie ecosystem supports. Because of the ecological fragility of this landscape, Eastview Barrens is only accessible through guided tours conducted by the Nature Conservancy and the Kentucky State Nature Preserves Commission.

Beginning in fall 2001, the Nature Conservancy started a project to conserve the barrens region of Kentucky because of its biodiversity and historic importance. The region spans six counties in central and western Kentucky, with Eastview having the largest tract of grassland. The fires that maintained this vast area in Kentucky occurred naturally and were started by Native American who lived in the region. Large herbivores such as elk and bison also helped to maintain this prairie landscape.

Another protected area in the region is Baumberger Barrens Preserve in Grayson County. Donated as a gift to the Nature Conservancy from Mary Alice Baumberger in 1992, this preserve provides an example of a unique dry limestone community amid a scenic blend of woodland and grassland.

The primary threats to the barrens are invasive species, development, agriculture, fire suppression, and improper forestry practices. In 2002, Kentucky's Purchase of Agriculture Conservation Easement program inspired many landowners in the region to apply for protection of their lands. Since then, the Nature Conservancy assists landowners every fall and spring with regular burns of well over 500 acres in the region. Additionally, the Kentucky Department of Fish and Wildlife Resources loans a no-till drill to landowners to plant more native grasses and forbs (broad-leaved flowering plants) on their lands. They are also encouraging trees and shrub buffers around the grasslands whenever possible and are helping to promote best management practices (BMPs) during timber harvesting. BMPs are designed to make the least amount of disturbance to an area during forestry activities in order to maintain a proper balance between water and land quality by controlling the movement of sediment, nutrients, and pollution. While Eastview State Nature Preserve is the largest protected barrens in the area, the preserve is supported by a much larger ecosystem that covers roughly one million acres in Kentucky. The preservation of Eastview Barrens is dependent upon the preservation of this entire ecosystem that is under threat and critical to Kentucky's history and ecological health.

Further Reading

Anderson, Roger, C., James S. Fralish, and Jerry M. Baskin, eds. *Savannas, Barrens, and Rock Outcrop Plant Communities of North America.* New York: Cambridge University Press, 1999.

Barnes, Thomas G. *Kentucky's Last Great Places.* Lexington: University Press of Kentucky, 2002.

Nature Conservancy. "Eastview Barrens State Nature Preserve." http://www.nature.org/wherewework/northamerica/states/kentucky/preserves/art10906.html.

GREEN RIVER BIORESERVE

Located in south-central Kentucky, the Green River meanders through the interior plateau of Kentucky and through Mammoth Cave National Park before spilling into the Ohio River system. Lined with vibrant wildflowers and dense trees that canopy its edges, the Green River is home to the spreading false foxglove, southern maidenhair fern, and Eggert's sunflower. Twenty-six miles of the Green River has been designated a Kentucky Wild River.

Celebrated in John Prine's song "Paradise," the Green River is Kentucky's most abundant source of aquatic biodiversity and considered the fourth richest river system in the United States. A total of 151 species of freshwater fish and 71 species of mussels have been identified in the Green River, some of which can be found nowhere else on the planet. While the Green River is home to this diverse array of rare aquatic life, 35 species have been recognized as endangered. The primary threats to the Green River are development, damming, and toxic chemical runoff from agricultural farms.

Fortunately, much is being done to protect this river, nicknamed the crown jewel of Kentucky. As part of the Sustainable Rivers Project, the Nature Conservancy and the Army Corps of Engineers are working together to restore natural flowing patterns in the river by altering the Green River Dam so that it supports the river's wildlife. By delaying the release of the dam's reservoir until the end of spawning periods, the conservancy and corps will promote fish and mussel species populations and improve the overall ecological health of the river. The Nature Conservancy's Green River Project works to protect the river's water quality and supports the bioreserve as a critical habitat for the species that call the Green River home. Additionally, the Nature Conservancy has created a program—PACE, Purchase of Agricultural Conservation Easements—to protect the Green River corridor from incompatible rural development by selling property to buyers who are willing to devote the land to conservation practices and agree to not develop the property. The Fish and Wildlife Service also works with the Nature Conservancy in a variety of restoration efforts, including reducing river sediment from local development, managing erosion, promoting sustainable agricultural practices to reduce toxic runoff, cleaning illegal dumping, hosting meetings, and creating community-involved activities that help to maintain the river's ecological balance. The biological richness of this 1,350-square-mile watershed makes this area an environmental priority for the Nature Conservancy.

The Green River region is an ecological wonder. The karst topography—a landscape created by groundwater dissolving sedimentary rock—and its creation of caves, tunnels, and sinkholes make this area undeniably unique. But the river's importance to the region is also undeniable. The Green River watershed comprises roughly 8,288 miles of streams and rivers in Kentucky, and the Upper Green River Basin is the water source for well over 100,000 people.

The most famous ecological feature of the Green River region is Mammoth Cave, which is the largest cave system in the world, with more than 350 miles of known subterranean passageways, and Kentucky's biggest tourist attraction. The Green River played an important role in the formation of the unparalleled enormity of Mammoth Cave's network of caverns through erosion and the river cutting deep into the limestone layers. Deeper channels are still in the process of being formed today. Another place to visit along the Green River watershed is Hundred Springs, a scenic location where water gushes from the ground and 100-foot waterfalls cascade into the Green River. There is also Hundred Acre Pond, where a sinkhole that has no drainage outlet created a rich wetland area.

Further Reading

Barnes, Thomas G. *Kentucky's Last Great Places*. Lexington: University Press of Kentucky, 2002.

Native Fish Conservancy. "Fishes of the Green River Bioreserve, Kentucky." http://www.nativefish.org/programs/greenriver.php.

Nature Conservancy. "Green River Bioreserve." http://www.nature.org/wherewework/northamerica/states/kentucky/preserves/art10997.html.

Wallace, David Rains. *Mammoth Cave: Mammoth Cave National Park, Kentucky*. Washington, DC: National Park Service, 2003.

GRIFFITH WOODS

Nestled in central Kentucky's Harrison County lies a 750-acre tract of land that is thought to be the largest remaining bluegrass savanna woodland in Kentucky. Griffith Woods, maintained by the Nature Conservancy, the University of Kentucky, and the Kentucky State Nature Preserves Commission, is an example of an ecosystem that used to spread widely over the central Kentucky region. Bluegrass savannas typically featured fields of clover and grasses, cane, and salt licks intermingled with rich woodland and open meadows. With extensive development and agricultural activities, these rare savanna woodlands continue to rapidly decline, making Griffith Woods a natural area critically important to a state whose nickname is the Bluegrass State. Once named Silver Lake Farm, Griffith Woods exists in its current state partly because of William Griffith, who, in the 19th century, forbade logging on the property, preserving a magnificent display of oak, hickory, and ash woodland. In addition to the bluegrass savanna, in Griffith

Woods lives the world's largest chinquapin oak as well as other trees that are estimated to be over 300 years old.

Griffith Woods is the natural area of primary concern for the Bluegrass Restoration Project, a research and restoration program initiated in 2002 to address ecological conservation in Kentucky's central counties. Located on U.S. Highway 62 near Cynthiana, Griffith Woods is not only significant to Kentucky's environmental history, but it comprises a collection of unique communities that can be found nowhere else in the world. Part old pastureland and agricultural fields from raising livestock, alfalfa, corn, and tobacco and part savanna and forest, Griffith Woods is a diverse ecological wonder. In addition to the regeneration of species such as cane and blue ash, historical preservation, and research of the soil composition of Griffith, the Bluegrass Restoration Project is monitoring changes in the forest structure with a technology called LiDAR (light detection and ranging), which collects topographical data from air flights over an area in order to closely monitor changes in the landscape. Using this technology helps researchers to better understand the ecosystem under study and how it responds to restoration efforts.

Additionally, a nonprofit group called Friends of Griffith Woods also plays a significant role in the restoration of this area. Committed to raising funds that support Griffith Woods, this group promotes educational research of Griffith as a historical, ecological, and archeological site of interest to students, researchers, and community members. Since Griffith Woods is not open for public access, Friends of Griffith Woods also funds and hosts activities that offer guided tours, workshops, and seminars that explore the native vegetation. One of the primary goals of the Friends of Griffith Woods and the other agencies managing this landscape is to restore Griffith to a condition close to what it looked like prior to European settlement. They are working toward this goal by operating a nursery to restore indigenous plant species and scheduling volunteer events to remove invasive species from the imperiled running buffalo clover beds. Botanical experts of the bluegrass region are studying Griffith Woods to determine and understand the biodiversity of the area prior to European transformation of the landscape.

At the center of the farm is an old building built in 1827 that is being restored and turned into an educational center and trailhead for Griffith Woods. Once called Silver Lake Place by a family that occupied the building for six generations, this federal-style historical structure also used to be an inn and tavern that served travelers who voyaged along the Lexington-Cincinnati Turnpike. Damaged by time and weather, Griffith Tavern serves as a rare architectural monument to Kentucky's colonial past.

Further Reading

Friends of Griffith Woods. http://www.friendsofgriffithwoods.org/.

Griffith Woods. http://moondancerfarm.com/griffithwoods.html.

Jones, Ronald L. *Plant Life of Kentucky: An Illustrated Guide to the Vascular Flora*. Lexington: University Press of Kentucky, 2005.

Wharton, Mary E., and Roger W. Barbour. *Bluegrass Land & Life: Land Character, Plants, and Animals of the Inner Bluegrass Region of Kentucky: Past, Present, and Future*. Lexington: University Press of Kentucky, 1991.

NATURAL BRIDGE STATE PARK NATURE PRESERVE

Situated in the Daniel Boone National Forest in Powell County, Kentucky, the sandstone Natural Bridge is considered a natural wonder. Standing 65 feet high, 78 feet in length, and 20 feet wide, geologists estimate that this arch, which was carved by the Red River, is at least a million years old and has been forming for the past 65 million years. Composed of Pottsville conglomeratic sandstone, Natural Bridge was formed from rocks falling from a sandstone ridge. Weather and progressing root systems also helped to create the arch formation.

While considerable commercial development has taken place in the surrounding areas, in 1981, the Kentucky Nature Preserves Commission designated 994 acres within the state park as a nature preserve to protect the stunning beauty of this natural structure and also to protect a rare species habitat. The Hood Branch watershed receives full protection within the boundaries of the preserve, enhancing the state's rich aquatic community. The Virginia big-eared bat, listed as a federally endangered species, lives within the realms of the nature preserve along with macroinvertebrate communities that are considered the most diverse in the Kentucky River System. Human disturbance is considered the most probable cause for the decline in the Virginia big-eared bat population. If the cave habitat is disturbed during hibernation, bats may lose their stored fat reserves and not survive until spring, when the insects are available. If a pregnant female is disturbed during hibernation, the whole colony may abandon the location.

The Natural Bridge State Park, within which the preserve is located, is roughly 2,300 total acres. Dating back to 1896, the park was founded by the Lexington and Eastern Kentucky Railroad Company. The park offers a wide range of hiking trails from the short and easy three-quarter-mile Original Trail to the Sand Gap Trail, which is seven and a half miles of moderate to difficult terrain. Disturbing the wildlife or plants and hiking off trail are illegal in order to preserve this special Kentucky natural area. Every weekend in the summer season, visitors can experience traditional Appalachian square dancing at the park as well as a host of other outdoor activities.

The park offers a wide variety of educational opportunities. As a member of the Leave No Trace Center for Outdoor Ethics, the park provides guided backpacking and hiking excursions designed to educate participants about not only the spectacular natural beauty of the area but also how to experience natural places responsibly by making as little of an impact on the land as possible. While learning how to respect wildlife and dispose of wastes properly, participants see rugged cliff lines, lesser-known arches, and rock houses unique to the park. Natural Bridge State Park also offers volunteer opportunities, including an invasive species workshop, where volunteers assist the naturalist staff in removing highly invasive plants that threaten the environmental health of the area. Annual events open to the public include Herpetology Weekend each May, Natural Arches Weekend each February, and the Kentucky Native Plant Society's Wildflower Weekend each April. Located in Slade, Kentucky, the park is accessible from Kentucky Route 11 and is well marked to encourage visitors.

Natural Bridge State Park Nature Preserve. (Courtesy of Mark Donovan)

It is important to mention that Natural Bridge is adjacent to the Red River Gorge Geological Area. There are more than 80 arches in the area, which comprises the largest concentration of rock shelters and arches east of the Rocky Mountains, some of which were homes to ancient Native Americans and explorers. Considered a rare opportunity to explore cultural resources, the gorge is an outstanding site for archeological studies into the lives of the Shawnee and other tribes native to the region. Most of the arches can be viewed by the extensive network of hiking trails, even though large portions of the gorge have been set aside as preservation areas by the National Wilderness Preservation System. The Red River, responsible for carving Natural Bridge, is designated a Kentucky wild river and has been recently named the only national wild and scenic river in Kentucky.

Further Reading

Kentucky State Parks. "Natural Bridge." http://parks.ky.gov/findparks/resortparks/nb/.

Mohlenbrock, Robert H. *This Land: A Guide to Eastern National Forests.* Berkeley: University of California Press, 2006.

Ruchhoft, R. H. *Kentucky's Land of the Arches.* Cincinnati, OH: Pucelle Press, 1986.

RED RIVER GORGE GEOLOGICAL AREA

Part of the Cumberland District of the Daniel Boone National Forest, the Red River Gorge Geological Area is prized for its watersheds, unique rock formations, sandstone cliffs, archeological sites, natural stone arches, and habitat diversity. The area, consisting of 29,000 acres, was designated in 1974; in 1976, the Red River Gorge was listed as a national natural landmark by the National Park Service. A nine-mile portion of the Red River, which tumbles through the gorge's unusual topography, was the first river in Kentucky to be named a national wild and scenic river in 1985. Additionally, this jagged yet wooded landscape of cliff-line ridges and deep green valleys provides a rich habitat for trees, including tulip poplar, yellow buckeye, bigleaf magnolia, sweet birch, oak, and pine, and an abundance of wildlife.

The Red River Gorge formed as a result of millions of years of weathering and erosion of the ancient Appalachian Mountains. In no other place east of the Rocky Mountains in there such a collection of rock formations. With more than 100 known natural stone arches and cliff lines, the gorge is a marvel of geological strata and a destination spot for climbers. Sandstone cliffs that jut out from the hillsides offer breathtaking views overlooking the forested landscape, but they are also quite dangerous. Each year, some visitors find themselves caught in the tight crevasses between rock faces, and a few lose their lives from accidental falls down the rocky cliffs.

It is estimated that the first humans to inhabit the area arrived 13,000 years ago, when northern regions were covered with ice. The Paleo-Indians followed large land animals such as mastodons to the area to take advantage of the rich natural resources. There is evidence that people inhabited the many rock shelters of the gorge. The rock shelters provide a wealth of information about the gorge's ancient human and ecological past. The nitrate-rich soils preserve artifacts and plant remains, providing insight into ancient agricultural practices and plant domestication. Later, the Shawnee and frontiersman found refuge in the gorge's rocky wilderness, and, in the 1900s, the gorge brought economic prosperity to the region through the mining of iron ore and tree harvesting. But, in 2003, the gorge was named a national archeological district and placed on the National Register of Historic Places. There is still much to be explored and discovered in the gorge's concentration of rock formations.

Currently, the primary threat to the Red River Gorge Geological Area is from recreational use, especially camping, climbing, and rappelling. To address the impact on the gorge from human visitation, the U.S. Forest Service has created a program called Limits of Acceptable Change, which invites the public to work with the Forest Service to discover ways to protect the natural resources of the area while also permitting opportunities for enjoyment and solitude within the gorge's lush wilderness. The Forest Service warns that mistreatment of areas on and around the rock shelters could destroy ancient remains and cause a repository of important archaeological information to be lost forever.

Other unique aspects of the Red River Gorge Geological Area are the Nada Tunnel and Clifty Wilderness. Considered the gateway into the Red River Gorge, the Nada

Red River Valley, close to sunset. (Courtesy of Kate Haverland)

Tunnel is a narrow 900-foot, one-lane tunnel that only measures roughly 13 by 13 feet along Kentucky Route 77. At one time used for a logging railroad in the 1900s, the tunnel is listed on the National Register of Historic Places. Also, roughly half of the geological area is called Clifty Wilderness. The Kentucky Wilderness Act of 1985 prompted the designation of half the gorge as a wilderness area to protect its primitive natural environment and to prohibit human habitation.

Further Reading

Berry, Wendell. *The Unforeseen Wilderness: Kentucky's Red River Gorge*. Berkeley, CA: Shoemaker and Hoard, 2006.

Mohlenbrock, Robert H. *This Land: A Guide to Eastern National Forests*. Berkeley: University of California Press, 2006.

Snell, John, and Hal Rogers. *Red River Gorge: The Elegant Landscape*. Morley, MO: Acclaim Press, 2006.

U.S. Forest Service. "Red River Gorge Geological Area." http://www.fs.fed.us/r8/boone/districts/cumberland/redriver_gorge.shtml.

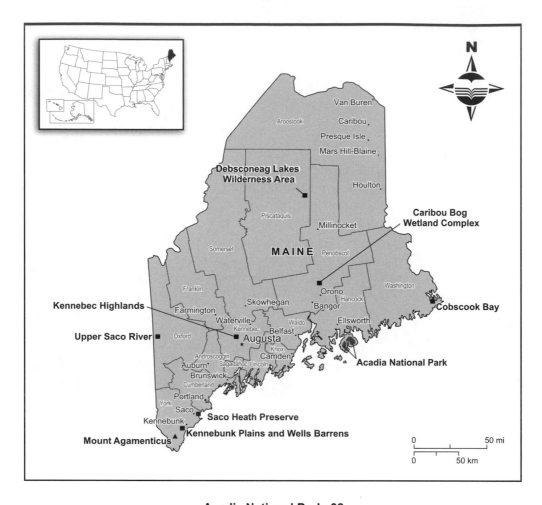

Acadia National Park, 38

Caribou Bog Wetland Complex, 40

Cobscook Bay, 41

Debsconeag Lakes Wilderness Area, 42

Kennebec Highlands, 44

Kennebunk Plains and Wells Barrens, 45

Mount Agamenticus, 47

Saco Heath Preserve, 48

Upper Saco River, 49

MAINE

In 1864, Henry David Thoreau immortalized the Maine wilderness of the 19th century when he wrote *The Maine Woods*, which chronicles his experiences traversing some of Maine's most extraordinary places. In the essay "Ktaadn," Thoreau describes Maine as "primeval, untamed," and "not lawn, nor pasture, not mead, nor woodland, nor lea, nor arable, nor wasteland. It was the fresh and natural surface of planet Earth." Maine is perhaps most ecologically defined by its northern woods, Mount Katahdin, Acadia National Park, its long, rocky coastline, its blueberry barrens and heath bogs, its moose population, puffins, and loons that wade in the lakes at dusk. It is also the state where a stretch of the Appalachian Trail corridor reaches its northernmost point in Baxter State Park. Maine contains three ecoregions. The western half of the state is the Northeast Highlands. This thinly populated region is dominated by northern hardwood forests and spruce-fir forests. The eastern half of the state is called the Laurentian Plains and Hills ecoregion. This area is defined by its abundance of glacial lakes and spruce-fir forests. The smallest ecoregion in Maine is the Northeastern Coastal Zone, which is located at the southern tip of the state. This region is the most densely population area of the state and is mostly comprised of pine, oak, and hickory forests.

While the vast majority of Maine is still forested, it has changed a great deal since Thoreau's time. Few people live in the northern, remote regions of Maine, but it is "far from wild," according to Christopher Klyza, who states that Maine's northern forests "are largely owned by multinational forest products corporations and in family management holdings, which have 25,000 miles of logging roads in the region." One of the conservation challenges for Maine rests in discovering ways to protect its natural resources while maintaining a thriving economy, which is primarily supported by timber, commercial fishing, wildlife recreation, and tourism industries.

Maine also has a growing Native American population. The Houlton Band of Maliseet Tribe, Pasamaquoddy Tribe, Penobscot Indian Nation, and the Aroostook Band of Micmacs live in Maine and have a history of conflicts with the state over land ownership and hunting and fishing rights. The relationship between the tribal peoples and the state of Maine has been contentious at best. Maine was the last state in the United States to permit tribal members to vote in national elections, but this voting right was only given to two recognized tribes: the Penobscot and the Pasamaquoddy. The Micmac and Maliseet tribes were not recognized until 1973.

In addition to the many agencies and programs that target air, land, and water conservation needs, Maine also places a high priority on protecting its wildlife, particularly as residential and commercial development continue to grow. A program called Beginning with Habitat takes a land approach to conservation by providing important information regarding plant and wildlife communities to local municipalities to promote land use practices that support growth while also protecting natural resources and habitats. Ecological fragmentation due to sprawl and inappropriate development threatens a natural area's plant biodiversity and makes it more vulnerable to the invasion of aggressive nonnative species.

Another important program designed to provide sound ecological information to decision makers is the Maine Natural Areas Program, which researches and compiles important data on Maine's rare species and natural communities that occur within the state's wetlands, bays, forests, mountains, lakes, and rivers in order to make conservation suggestions for the preservation of Maine's native ecosystems and natural heritage. Other major entities deeply involved in Maine's conservation activities are the Maine Department of Environmental Protection, the Maine Audubon Society, Maine chapters of the Nature Conservancy, the Maine Department of Conservation, and the Maine Department of Inland Fisheries and Wildlife.

ACADIA NATIONAL PARK

Established in 1916, Acadia National Park receives millions of visitors each year and for good reasons. Located on Maine's Mount Desert Island, Acadia was the first national park established east of the Mississippi. Acadia is a national treasure of granite cliffs, evergreen forests, sandy and rocky beaches, streams, wetlands, mountains, pristine lakes, and abundant wildlife. More than 40,000 acres in size, much of Acadia has been preserved with little human impact, while the eastern portion of park is used primarily for recreation activities. One of the main attractions at Acadia is Cadillac Mountain. At 1,530 feet, Cadillac Mountain is the highest elevation in the park; it provides panoramic views of the park and is notably the highest peak on the Atlantic coast north of Brazil.

Acadia is a landscape formed from glaciers as large ice sheets carved valleys, shaped mountains, and moved boulders. Early history of the area indicates that the original inhabitants of Mount Desert Island were the Wabanaki people, who hunted, fished, and foraged for food on the island after traveling across the water by birch-bark canoe. European explorers such as Samuel Champlain, who named Mount Desert Island, and Antoine Laumet de la Mothe, sieur de Cadillac, who named Cadillac Mountain, were early explorers of the island, and, by the mid-19th century, the number of settlers and summer visitors grew quickly as Acadia was prized for its resources and for its dramatic wilderness.

Indeed, there is no shortage of exceptional flora and fauna in this national park. The forests of Acadia are towering with red spruce, white spruce, sugar maple, and other trees. Known as the Pine Tree State, a diverse selection of pine trees can be found in Acadia, such as white pine, pitch pine, jack pine, and red pine. Animals found at the park are white-tailed deer, red fox, eastern coyote, beaver, and snowshoe hare. The shoreline is decked with masses of seaweed such as kelp and Irish moss; in their hairlike tangles can be found crabs, sea urchins, sea anemones, starfish, and jellyfish. Acadia is also a bird-watcher's paradise. Common loons, warblers, bald eagles, and peregrine falcons can be seen in the park as well other extraordinary birds such as buffleheads, red-breasted mergansers, common eiders, white-winged scoters, surf scoters, and black scoters. Off the coast of Acadia on the smaller surrounding islands, puffins playfully swim on the shores.

With more than 120 miles of historic hiking trails, over 500 campsites, miles and miles of carriage roads with breathtaking views, Acadia offers a wide range of outdoor activities for photographers, nature observers, and the adventurous. Ultimately, all of this recreation has its price. Offering such exceptional beauty and an abundance of wildlife on the land and by the sea, it comes as no surprise that the biggest threat to Acadia is visitor use. Being one of the most visited national parks in the United States, Acadia is subjected to heavy human foot traffic. Cadillac Mountain, because of its fragile subalpine vegetation, is an area under threat as the sensitive plants risk being trampled. Wetland areas along the Ship Harbor Nature Trail are showing damage from the high amount of human traffic, and Mount Desert Island's sea caves have suffered substantial loss of marine life from human visitation. Fortunately, park officials and naturalists are consistently monitoring the human impact on Acadia and developing strategies to minimize foot traffic by redirecting visitors to other locations in the park and limiting access to certain fragile areas. Also, an organization called Friends of Acadia has created numerous programs to preserve Acadia, one of which is a campaign called the Tranquility Project whose purpose is to restore the pristine wilderness of Acadia by acquiring funds to continue educational park programs and to reduce automobile traffic through the park by expanding the low-emissions bus system. As the number of visitors to Acadia increases each year, so will the need increase to preserve the ecological vitality of this truly unique natural area.

Further Reading
Butcher, Russell. *Field Guide to Acadia National Park, Maine*. Lanham, MD: Taylor Trade, 2005.
Friends of Acadia. http://www.friendsofacadia.org.
Kaiser, James. *Acadia: The Complete Guide: Mt. Desert Island and Acadia National Park*. Shelburne, VT: Destination Press, 2005.

Caribou Bog Wetland Complex

One of the most extensive and diverse wetland systems in Maine appears in Penobscot County and spans close to 6,000 acres. The Caribou Bog Wetland Complex includes Mud Pond, Caribou Pond, Pushaw Stream, Pushaw Lake, and Penjajawoc Marsh. This lush wetland system is known for its biodiversity and for being home to important natural communities, rare plants, birds, mussels, and dragonflies. There are a number of threats to this area, not the least of which is development. Being close to Bangor, a number of sites in the complex are prime targets for commercial developers.

Of the ecologically significant natural communities present in the complex, the most exemplary is the domed bog ecosystem, a raised level bog that receives most of its nutrients from precipitation. Geogenous bogs—peatlands that receive most of their nutrients from underground water and surface water—are also present in the complex. Geogenous bogs are the least acidic, which allows for the growth of more alkaline-preferring wetland plants to thrive. The swamp birch and the sparse-flowered sedge are both rare plants found in the Caribous Bog Wetlands that grow in the alkaline-dominant peatlands. Pushaw Lake contains lacustrine shallow-bottom communities; the shallow depth of the water allows for sunlight to hit the muddy and sandy bottom, which supports the growth of rare plants such as water stargrass and American shore-grass. Other plants include narrow-leaved arrowhead and pipewort.

In the southern region of the Caribou Bog Wetlands Complex is Penjajawoc Marsh. This rich marshland is a location for many birds, some of which are rare, such as the least tern, American coot, bald eagle, sedge wren, black tern, and black-crowned night heron. Penjajawoc is classified as an emergent marsh, which means that half of the vegetation in the marsh is in the form of cattails and other emergent grasses and sedges. Evidence of an old railroad right-of-way is still present in the marsh, and the area is visible from the Bangor Mall. Its location near the mall has created ongoing dispute over the question of commercial development.

Caribou Bog Wetland Complex is also known for harboring state endangered freshwater mussels and dragonflies. Two species of mussels—yellow lampmussels and tidewater muckets—thrive in Pushaw Lake and in other areas of the complex. These mussels have been found only in the Penobscot, Kennebec, and St. George watersheds in the state of Maine, indicating that their range is quite narrow and making the wetland complex an area of critical importance for protection. Caribou Bog also is a prime habitat for three of the five state endangered species of dragonflies. Muskeg darner, delicate emerald, and war-paint emerald are dragonflies of special concern for the state of Maine that breed in the sphagnum hollows of the acidic Caribou Bog peatlands. More research of these bog dragonflies is needed to determine more precise information about their population and range.

Portions of the Caribou Bog Wetland Complex are owned by the University of Maine and the city of Bangor. The biggest threats to the wetlands are commercial and residential development, water quality, and invasive species. Freshwater mussels are very sensitive to toxins and changes in water quality, requiring careful management of the water across the wetlands region. Introduction of zebra mussels could potentially eviscerate current populations of the state's rare yellow lampmussels and tidewater muckets. Purple loosestrife is a nonnative invasive plant species that is a threat to the open wetlands and needs to be monitored. Additionally, state shoreland zoning specifications must be strictly followed to allow an adequate buffer area for the wetlands. Perhaps one of the most important conservation steps is education. Community outreach programs to educate local residents and landowners of the extraordinary qualities of the Caribou Bog Wetland Complex promote stewardship and community support to protect this valuable natural area.

Further Reading

Johnson, Charles W. *Bogs of the Northeast.* Hanover, NH: University Press of New England, 1985.

Tiner, Ralph W. *A Field Guide to Coastal Wetland Plants of the Northeast United States.* Amherst: University of Massachusetts Press, 1987.

COBSCOOK BAY

In Washington County in southeastern Maine, a 40-square-mile estuary by the name of Cobscook Bay has been able to escape the heavy development that has seriously compromised most coastal ecosystems in the eastern United States. Known for its large tides that can reach 24 feet, its breathtaking beauty, its nutrient-laden waters, and diverse ecosystem, Cobscook Bay is a relatively clean body of water that needs to stay that way.

Nine communities in the vicinity of the bay are supported by the Cobscook, and an exceptional list of wildlife depends on the health of this beautiful estuary. There are a number of characteristics that make Cobscook, with its convoluted shoreline, such a remarkable place. The bay is generally very shallow, allowing for sunlight to shine on its bottom. In the summer months, right whales, finback, and minke can be seen. It has a higher saltwater content than other estuaries in Maine due to its incredible tidal flow. These high tides wash nutrient-rich waters from the Gulf of Maine into the estuary, creating an ecosystem supportive of great biodiversity. The bay waters teem with phytoplankton, sea urchins, marine worms, sea scallops, and soft-shelled crab. Many of the local residents make their living from fishing the bay, and the Cobscook supports a multimillion-dollar aquaculture industry. The Cobscook Bay area is also populated with waterfowl and other coastal birds that find sources of food in the mudflats. Black ducks and Canada geese are particularly abundant in the bay area. Cobscook is also classified as an essential habitat for bald eagles. Protecting the bay as a nesting site for bald eagles will continue to improve bald eagle populations and support the tidal and freshwater waterfowl, shorebirds, and wading bird habitats.

Another perhaps underappreciated aspect of Cobscook Bay's vibrant ecosystem is the rockweed. This vegetation is the seaweed that clings to the shoreline when the tide leaves. Knotted wrack and bladder wrack are the two most common types of seaweed, but all of the types that wash ashore are full of intertidal marine life essential for the survival of many species that live in the bay. As the tide comes in, the fish follow the lush, floating seaweed manes and eat the small snails and fleas. The birds then chase after the fish for their daily meal. Rockweed that has broken apart from rocks floats in the tidal waters and not only provides food for marine life but also can be used as a hiding spot from hungry swooning birds. Decaying rockweed on the shore is a haven for insects and other bacteria that help accelerate the decomposition of the seaweed as continues to nourish life along the shoreline.

Although the well-being of the bay is relatively intact, there are threats to the Cobscook that seem to become more pronounced each year. The appearance of invasive species is on the rise, and water quality is always a significant concern. The invasive green crab population has grown exponentially in the last decade, creating a threat to young clams. The possibility of overfishing the bay due to the ever-increasing demand for shellfish could disrupt the fragile cyclical tidal patterns that keep the bay so rich. The Cobscook Bay Research Center provides education about the bay and promotes progressive research to discover ways to preserve both the bay and the economic vitality of the area. Striking this delicate balance to keep the Cobscook sustainable and productive is key as many organizations are working together to help the bay, as well as the people who depend on it, thrive.

Further Reading

Cobscook Bay Resource Center.:http://www.cobscook.org.

Nature Conservancy. "Ecosystem Modeling in Cobscook Bay, Maine: A Boreal, Macrotidal Estuary." *Northeastern Naturalist* 11, no. 2, (2004): 1–12.

Tiner, Ralph W. *A Field Guide to Coastal Wetland Plants of the Northeast United States*. Amherst: University of Massachusetts Press, 1987.

DEBSCONEAG LAKES WILDERNESS AREA

When northbound hikers who have braved the long Appalachian Trail starting in Georgia finally arrive at the Debsconeag Lakes Wilderness Area and Mount Katahdin in Maine, they know they are close to finishing the trail, but they also know that some challenging hiking is yet to come. In fact, Maine is considered to have the most difficult and rugged hiking terrain on the Appalachian Trail. The trail is rocky, slippery, layered in tree roots, and in many places covered in lush vegetation. The Debsconeag Lakes Wilderness Areas holds 15 miles of the famed Hundred Mile Wilderness portion of the Appalachian Trail. For these hikers heading north, Baxter State Park just north of Debsconeag is the destination, but not without crossing through this wilderness area that has the highest concentration of lakes in the state of Maine.

When the native people of this region traveled through the waterways in their birch-bark canoes, they frequently had to stop to carry the canoes through the rough and rapid areas. Debsconeag means "carrying place" for this reason. With some trees that are believed to be 300 years old, areas of Debsconeag have been able to resist the ravages of logging and offer remarkable examples of undisturbed forest. Debsconeag provides habitat to 215 plant species; possesses mesmerizing lakes that are bubbling with brook trout and rare freshwater mussels; and is cloaked with yellow birch, American beech, red spruce, sugar maple, hemlock, and white pine. Black bears, bobcats, moose, pine martins, bald eagles, and boreal chickadees are some of the wildlife that can be seen in this wilderness area. Classified as an ecological reserve for research and conservation of Maine's ecosystems, Debsconeag is also an imperative site that connects close to 500,000 acres of bordering conservation land.

Debsconeag Lakes Wilderness Area, near Millinocket, Maine, is part of a larger Katahdin Forest Project initiated by the Nature Conservancy in 2002. The project includes 46,000 acres of Debsconeag and tells the story of an unprecedented conservation effort and financial deal. The Nature Conservancy financed a struggling paper company and, in return, received the 46,000 acres at Debsconeag and gained a conservation easement of 195,000 additional acres near Mount Katahdin that buffers Baxter State Park. In 2006, the Nature Conservancy donated the easement property to the State of Maine along with substantial funds in the form of a stewardship endowment. The goal of this remarkable deal is to conserve the natural resources in the Katahdin and Debsconeag Lakes area while also protecting the region's paper mill and timber industries. A conservation organization providing financial assistance to a paper mill, in this case, Great Northern Paper, is indeed a transaction that will make the record books in conservation history.

What does this deal mean for Debsconeag and the surrounding region? It means that there will be no development on these protected lands in the future; public access is guaranteed for various recreation activities; more habitat areas will be preserved; a massive spread of contiguous forestland will be maintained; a commitment to sustainable forestry will be enforced; a more diversified economy will be established (which includes tourism); and this vital region will continue to be available to scientists who study the impacts of severe weather, climate change, pollution, disease, and the human impact on natural areas. It also means that remote wilderness areas that are becoming so scarce in the United States will have an opportunity to thrive and evolve. The pristine and shimmering lakes that are scattered across this stunning area in the shadow of Mount Katahdin are abounding with beauty, natural resources, and mature forests. And equally important, this critical corridor of conservation in north-central Maine is a lesson in how the economy and the environment do not have to be adversaries. A healthy alliance can be made between the most unlikely parties.

Further Reading

Austin, Phyllis, Dean Bennett, and Robert Kimber, eds. *On Wilderness: Voices from Maine*. Gardiner, ME: Tilbury House, 2003.

Lansky, Mitch. *Beyond the Beauty Strip: Saving What's Left of Our Forests*. Gardiner, ME: Tilbury House, 1992.

KENNEBEC HIGHLANDS

There are places in Maine that do not necessarily house a substantial number of rare and endangered species. They do not have extraordinary examples of natural communities. They might not be described as deep, remote wilderness areas, and yet the grassroots efforts to protect these areas suggest that they are quite special. The Kennebec Highlands region, which encompasses Rome, Vienna, New Sharon, and Mount Vernon in central Maine, is one of these places. What do the Kennebec Highlands have to offer? Breathtaking open space, undeveloped ponds, an important mountain range, wildlife habitat, and outstanding recreation opportunities for local residents and tourists.

The Kennebec Highlands are full of ponds and lakes. The Belgrade Lakes region is the famous location that inspired the writing of *On Golden Pond* by Ernest Thompson. Other ponds in the area include McIntyre Pond, Kidder Pond, Boody Pond, Round Pond, Beaver Pond, and Long Pond. Alpine club moss is a rare plant that appears near Watson Pond.

Kennebec Highlands does feature a noteworthy example of an unpatterned open basin fen ecosystem surrounding Beaver and Round Pond. This type of peatland ecosystem is strongly enriched with nutrients. It is open because water is still able to flow in and out of the system. The poison sumac grows in this wetland. Although this tree is common is southern states, it is uncommon for it to appear this far north. The blend of fen vegetation types and open water plant species create a diverse flora mix.

There is an abundance of wildlife in the Kennebec Highlands. While there is development in the region, it is not dense, which allows for animals with broad range habitats, such as bobcats, to roam the highlands. The lakes and ponds provide significant habitats for waterfowl and wading birds. Many birds, including the black-throated blue warbler, bald eagle, peregrine falcon, several species of hawks, great horned owl, and the common loon, can be found near the peaceful banks of the ponds in Kennebec. Additionally, the ponds are teeming with smallmouth bass, white perch, brook trout, golden shiner, brown bullhead, creek chub, and chain pickerel.

Kennebec Highlands is not without significant evidence of human activity. It is an area that is home to residential areas, shopping malls, timberlands, and blueberry fields. Much of the forest land has experienced recent timber harvesting. Hunting and fishing is quite popular in the area along with other activities such as hiking, snowmobiling, berry picking, camping, and horseback riding. One of the major tourist activities in Maine is to go sightseeing via car or bus.

Why have there been aggressive efforts made to protect this region? Encroaching development, illegal dumping, widespread timber harvesting, and unmanaged recreation are a few of the important reasons. Outdoor reaction tourism is essential to Maine's economy. Conservation projects that provide protection for the land and wildlife and also serve the tourism industry are an important goal for the Kennebec Highlands. The Belgrade Regional Conservation Alliance has worked to acquire more land for protection with more than 6,000 acres already acquired. The alliance also has helped to create designated trails to direct recreation use to certain areas and away from ecologically sensitive areas. Maintaining an adequate buffer zone around the ponds and wetlands and consistent stewardship is essential for conservation of these areas. The protection of the Kennebec Highlands started with just a few individuals who care about the natural heritage of their home region and grew into a successful conservation effort that protects large blocks of land for wildlife and keeps the banks of the glistening, clear ponds decked in trees and waterfowl rather than vacation homes.

Further Reading

Belgrade Regional Conservation Alliance. www.belgradelakes.org.

Maine Natural Areas Program. "Kennebec Highlands." http://www.mainenaturalareas. org/docs/program_activities/links/Landtrust/KennebecHighlands.pdf.

KENNEBUNK PLAINS AND WELLS BARRENS

In August and September, there is only one place in Maine that offers a sweeping view of a purple perennial called the northern blazing star. That place is the Kennebunk Plains and Wells Barrens natural area. This plant is critically imperiled in the state of Maine, it is rare for the entire New England region, and the population of the northern blazing star at Kennebunk Plains and Wells Barrens is the largest in the world. Unfortunately, the species is in decline. Although the presence of this state-endangered plant is more than enough reason to protect this natural area, there is another reason. The coastal sandplain grassland, especially on the Kennebunk Plains, is one of the most threatened natural communities in the northeast United States.

A sandplain grassland is comprised of native grasses and shrubs and is maintained by periodic burning. These grasslands were formed from melting glaciers many thousands of years ago when the glaciers dropped their sand and the streams from the melting water formed sandy plains. The deep sand deposits beneath the grassland allow water to percolate down quickly. Due to this high sand content of the soil, water and nutrients drain away easily, creating a climate that is perhaps prone to drought but also creating a very rare natural community. Plants that grow on these grasslands are the northern blazing star, lowbush blueberry, sand jointweed, stiff aster, poverty grass, and little bluestem. Rare animals in the area include the grasshopper sparrow, upland sandpiper, vesper sparrow, ribbon snake, wood turtle, and the northern black racer snake. The area is buffered on the north by the Kennebunk Plains Wildlife Management Area.

Other natural communities found at Kennebunk Plains and Wells Barrens are pitch pine heath barrens, pitch pine/scrub oak barrens, and a red maple alluvial swamp. Pitch pine heath barrens have little undergrowth and are dominated by pitch pine. They are also characterized by herbs and their open canopy. Pitch pine/scrub oak barrens are comprised of pitch pine, scrub oak, blueberry, and huckleberry. Red maple alluvial swamps have cinnamon fern, red maple, and skunk cabbage and occur next to the grasslands where water accumulates on the slopes.

To maintain the grasslands, the Nature Conservancy manages periodic burnings to reduce shrub growth, allow for the dispersal of rare plant seeds, foster nesting sites for grassland birds, and enhance the nutrient level in the soil. The curious existence of this prairie land in Maine suggests a long history of periodic burning by early Native American populations and later for blueberry production. Careful consideration is given to protecting the grasshopper sparrow nesting sites that are sensitive to disturbance. These appropriately named sparrows not only eat grasshoppers but sound like them as well. They are declining in numbers across their North American range due to habitat loss. Threats to the grasslands are dumping, encroaching residential development, gravel mining, recreation, and domestic pets. Roaming cats are a threat to the rare bird species in the grasslands. All-terrain vehicle traffic is also a major concern, particularly in the spring and summer months when the ground is soft and the vehicles can do extensive damage to nesting sites and vegetation.

In 2007, a 560-acre tract of land in the Wells Barrens was acquired by the Nature Conservancy in partnership with the local water district after 15 years of negotiation to protect the extraordinary natural communities and rare species of this area and secure for protection the headwaters of the Branch Brook, which cuts through the barrens and provides drinking water to nearby communities. This agreement will help reduce development in the area, which would compromise the drinking water, and it provides protection to a sizable portion of the Brook Branch watershed. Moreover, it is an example of how the needs of the people can be served as the needs of the wildlife and natural communities are also served.

Further Reading

Maine Department of Inland Fisheries and Wildlife. "Grasshopper Sparrow." http://www.state.me.us/ifw/wildlife/species/endangered_species/grasshopper_sparrow/index.htm.
Maine Natural Areas Program. www.mainenaturalareas.org/.
Nature Conservancy. "Wells Barrens." http://www.nature.org/wherewework/northamerica/states/maine/press/press3194.html.

Mount Agamenticus

Turtles love vernal pools. They can sit quietly for hours on a sunny rock or log until it is time to shuffle down to the surface of the water for a drink. The Mount Agamenticus region in southern York County in southern Maine has a high concentration of vernal pools, and it has a good number of turtles, some of which are rare. The problem for the turtles is that the region also has roads. Turtles cross roads on their way to one of the vernal pools to find food or if they are heading toward their nesting area. Turtle populations are in decline because these roads are seeing more and more traffic. The Mount Agamenticus region, which is treasured for being the only undeveloped coastal region in Maine between Acadia National Park and the Pine Barrens of New Jersey, is a high-priority conservation area for the state of Maine due to encroaching development that threatens the biodiversity and beauty of Maine's southernmost county.

Once populated by the Penacook tribe of the Eastern Abanaki Nation, Mount Agamenticus is an ecological oasis that is unique because of its transitional location. It is a mountain region, a wetland region, and a coastal region. It also straddles temperature zones so that it hosts the northernmost of certain southern plants, animals, and natural communities while also being home to southernmost populations of a variety of northern flora, fauna, and other ecological features. The dominant natural community types are the transitional hardwood forest and the oak-pine-hickory forest. Other more noteworthy communities for this region are the vernal pools, Atlantic white cedar swamp, perched-hemlock hardwood forest, and floating kettlehole bogs. The perched-hemlock forest has spicebush in its understory, which is a plant common in southern regions, but quite rare as far north as Maine. Other rare plants in the region include featherfoil, flowering dogwood, spotted wintergreen, wild leek, and white wood aster. Mount Agamenticus is home to 21 rare species of plants, 14 of which are classified as rare because it is the northernmost occurrence of that species.

The Mount Agamenticus region is a lively area for wildlife both common and rare. A few of the species identified as being of special concern are the spotted turtle, wood turtle, Blanding's turtle, scarlet bluet damselfly, New England bluet damselfly, and the ringed boghaunter dragonfly. The vernal pools provide a breeding ground for many amphibians and invertebrates.

Recognized by numerous organizations as a natural area of critical ecological significance, 10 local, state, and federal conservation agencies came together to form the Mount Agamenticus to the Sea Coalition to protect the lengthy list of rare plants and animals and the exemplary natural communities in the region. The initiative involves acquiring more natural areas by purchasing the lands or through donation. It also involves working with the six towns in the region—Wells, South Berwick, York, Eliot, Ogunquit, and Kittery—to promote low-impact development. In 2004, "A Conservation Plan for the Mount Agamenticus Region: A Community Plan for the Future" was drafted by more than 80 constituencies, including organizations, municipalities, and volunteers to protect the rich, natural heritage of this region. The people involved in developing this plan have seen the rapid growth that has occurred in the Mount Agamenticus region and fear losing it since development along coastal areas is in high demand. Hoping to preserve the rural character of the region, the exceptional opportunities for recreation, and the outstanding ecological qualities of Mount Agamenticus, the projects that are underway to preserve this area and the large number of people involved reveal an inspiring commitment to preserve one of Maine's beloved natural areas.

Further Reading

Mount Agamenticus Conservation Region. http://www.agamenticus.org.

Mount Agamenticus to the Sea Conservation Initiative. http://www.mta2c.org/.

SACO HEATH PRESERVE

Although this area's special features may not be readily apparent at first glance, a walk along the Saco Heath Preserve's one-mile self-guided trail and boardwalk is a walk through an ecologically unique woodland and peatland. Located in Saco, Maine, Saco Heath Preserve is over 1,000 acres and is an area of protection partly because of the Atlantic cedar bog and pitch pine bog, both of which have been ranked as critically imperiled in the state of Maine. The Saco Heath was created when two nearby ponds began filling up with decaying plant matter, or peat, until they grew together to form one large raised bog that sits above the groundwater level.

Bogs, or peatlands, are areas where the soil is comprised of only partly decomposed plant matter where the land is often moist and spongy. Ombrogenous raised peatlands, such as the Saco Heath, derive water from precipitation such as rain or snow, which creates harsh, acidic conditions. Peatlands that absorb nutrients from the ground can have a high nutrient level, but raised bogs that depend on nutrients from rain and the air have the poorest nutrient level. Many believe that the Atlantic white cedar bog that rests on this raised bog is the only one of its kind in the world. Saco Heath is the southernmost occurrence of this kind of peatland in Maine and home to a variety of endangered species.

Some of the state rare plants that grow in Saco Heath are Long's bulrush, smooth winterberry, wild ginger, and Wiegand's sedge. Hessel's hairstreak butterfly and the bog elfin butterfly are also rare and can be found at Saco. Hessel's hairstreak butterfly larvae feed on the Atlantic white cedar leaves, and the bog elfin survives on black spruce needles found in the preserve. Other varieties of vegetation that populate the area are sheep laurel, bog laurel, Labrador tea, leatherleaf, and rhodora. Sphagnum moss is abundant in the heath along with tamarack trees and cotton grass with its downy tips. The plant life that dresses the heath has evolved to do well in soil that is low in nutrients with a high acidic content. To protect the heath, careful management of its surrounding woodland and forest is essential. Trees found in the forest include beech, hemlock, white pine, red maple, sugar maple, red oak, yellow birch, and gray birch. Wildlife that inhabit the heath are moose, deer, snowshoe hare, and many others.

In the fall, blueberry bushes don their bright red color along the trail, and the boardwalk section of the trail meanders through peatland communities. In certain areas beneath the boardwalk, there can be seen an old all-terrain vehicle trail that caused damage to the heath by destroying the surrounding vegetation and compacting the heath, which disrupts the fragile drainage conditions that are necessary for a thriving peatland. Protection of this natural area's hydrology is essential to its conservation. Vehicles, foot traffic, nearby timber harvesting, and even clearing can damage this vulnerable area and therefore are highly discouraged.

The Saco Heath is one example of the exceptional biodiversity of the peatlands in Maine. There are some that have been lost, many that are threatened, and some peatlands in remote areas of northern Maine that are virtually untouched. As research continues to uncover the extraordinary scientific and ecological value of peatlands, greater effort is being directed toward their conservation. Whether they are called bogs, fens, or swamps, these spongy places have been under the influence of diverse perception. To some, they are useless, muddy swamps. To others, they are places to fear, as if one may walk into a bog and never come out. Stories of animal and human bodies buried in bogs and found centuries later are not uncommon. Some cultures valued bogs for their unusual plants that were prized for their medicinal qualities, while other cultures believe bogs were nothing short of temples, sacred places to commune with the divine. Regardless of one's idea of these in-between places that are not quite land and not quite water, what other natural landscape can stir the imagination like a bog at dawn when there is still a layer of fog hanging on the leaves of the tamarack?

Further Reading

Johnson, Charles W. *Bogs of the Northeast.* Hanover, NH: University Press of New England, 1985.
Nature Conservancy. "Saco Heath Preserve." http://www.nature.org/wherewework/north america/states/maine/preserves/art20273.html.

UPPER SACO RIVER

It is certainly an understatement to say that many plants, animals, and people depend upon the health of a river and its watershed. The Upper Saco River in western Maine is not only the source of drinking water and electricity for hundreds of thousands of people, its floodplain contains exceptional ecosystems and a host of rare and endangered species at both the state and local levels. The remarkably intact floodplain ecosystems along the Upper Saco are the most diverse and extensive in the region. The Saco River runs 134 miles from the White Mountains of New Hampshire through Maine to the Atlantic Ocean.

A few of the rare natural communities that occur in the floodplain are the riverwash sand barren, pitch pine/scrub oak barren, pitch pine bog, and pocket swamp. Blanding's

The Upper Saco River. (Courtesy of Stewart Scott Andrews)

turtle is a rare species that has been spotted along the Upper Saco River as well as the twilight moth, Edwards' hairstreak butterfly, and several species of rare dragonflies. The area also contains a substantial population of the globally rare plant Long's bulrush. The list of rare species that live within the exemplary natural communities along the Saco River is lengthy, making this river a high-priority preservation location.

The primary threats to the Upper Saco River are irresponsible recreation activities and unsustainable development. The ever-increasing interest in developing near the Saco threatens the floodplain's natural ability to filter and purify the water for drinking. More development means more polluted runoff that flows into the river, resulting in a reduction in water quality. Protecting the floodplain ecosystems is dependent upon keeping the natural hydrologic process intact. Dams, canals, poor forestry practices, and development all contribute to disrupting the Saco's drainage patterns, thus threatening the natural communities and rare species in the area.

Efforts are being made to return a salmon run to the Saco River. The nonprofit Saco River Salmon Club introduces salmon eggs into the Saco River each spring and monitors spawning areas and salmon populations. The group hosts tours of the hatchery to educate students and community members about the importance of restoring salmon to the river.

The Saco has a number of dams in its midsection that provide electricity to local residents. Unfortunately, these dams are the primary reason for the river's loss of salmon.

Also active in protecting the Saco is the Saco River Corridor Commission. One of the central goals of the commission is to carefully monitor the water quality of the Saco River by checking the water's turbidity, temperature, and acid and alkaline levels. Long-term testing helps the commission to monitor water quality trends for the benefit of municipalities along the Saco River that rely heavily on the Saco's clean water. Because rivers are constantly in flux, the water quality is tested on an ongoing basis to isolate potential areas of water degradation and take the next step toward restoration if necessary.

An important component in preserving the Upper Saco River water quality and the floodplain is education. All too often, recreation activities that take place along the river, such as canoeing, swimming, fishing, and camping, damage fragile ecosystems and habitats. Thousands of canoeists each summer paddle the cool waters of the Saco, and campsites are occasionally littered with trash. Educating visitors who would like to enjoy the beauty and serenity of the river about the extraordinary natural resources along this waterway will help to promote minimal-impact recreation practices. Additionally, numerous local, regional, state, and federal agencies are collaborating to secure more lands for protection and to foster sustainable forms of land use and forestry.

Further Reading

Barnes, Diane, and Jack Barnes. *Upper Saco River Valley: Fryeburg, Lovell, Brownfield, Denmark, and Hiram*. Portsmouth, NH: Arcadia, 2002.

Maine Natural Areas Program. "Upper Sacco River." http://www.mainenaturalareas.org/docs/program_activities/links/Landtrust/UpperSacoRiver.pdf.

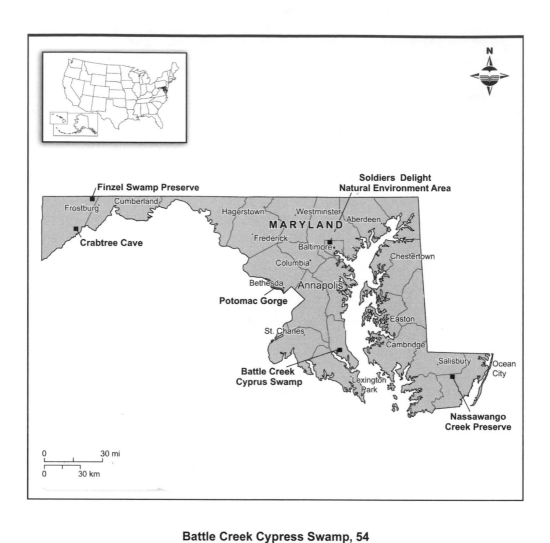

Battle Creek Cypress Swamp, 54

Crabtree Cave, 55

Finzel Swamp Preserve, 57

Nassawango Creek Preserve, 58

Potomac Gorge, 60

Soldiers Delight Natural Environment Area, 62

MARYLAND

aryland has a widely diverse landscape. From the eastern coastal plain to the central Piedmont and western Appalachian plateau, Maryland has wetlands, caves, frost pockets, shale barrens, coastal bogs, serpentine grasslands, forests, mountains, and cypress swamps. Although its coastal ecosystems have been greatly compromised by the pollution from commercial, industrial, and residential development, they still contain beaches, dunes, fields, and upland forests that are filled with wildlife. Maryland is a unique state where the north and the south come together to create a landscape that is reminiscent of the mid-Atlantic's ancient past. Its geographic location contributes to the state's population of rare and endangered plant and animal species and natural communities, because Maryland is often the southernmost occurrence for the northern species and the northernmost occurrence for southern species. Maryland shares the Delmarva Peninsula with Delaware and Virginia and attributes much of its economic vitality to its fishing industry, which is dependent upon one of the most important natural resources for the state: the Chesapeake Bay. Additionally, the Potomac Gorge in Maryland is just a short distance northwest of Washington, DC, but it is one of the most biologically diverse places in the national park system.

The Chesapeake Bay is a 200-mile estuary, the largest in the United States. It produces millions of pounds of seafood in one year. The bay receives its salt water from the Atlantic Ocean and fresh water from rivers and streams that empty into the bay. The largest freshwater contribution comes from the Susquehanna River that flows from Pennsylvania. The water quality of the Chesapeake is a barometer for the health of the waterways upstream, and, unfortunately, the toxic runoff from farmlands and industrial sites along the Susquehanna and other rivers have seriously degraded the bay's water quality. The Chesapeake Bay Program is a large state and federal effort designed to revitalize the bay by reducing the input of pollution into the bay, restoring habitats for plant and animal species, managing fisheries, and protecting the watershed region, which serves roughly 17 million people. The program is also interested in protecting and preserving the bay's historic and cultural heritages that tell the stories of its original indigenous inhabitants, its exploration and colonial settlement, shipwrecks, wars, and population boom.

In addition to bay restoration and other water quality programs, land conservation through waste management programs, air quality, forest stewardship, climate change, and controlling invasive species are focus areas in Maryland's environmental management plans. The Maryland Department of Environmental Resources and the Maryland Department of the Environment address Maryland's ecological challenges in partnership with other state and local organizations. Invasive species and their impact on ecosystems are directly related to habitat loss as birds and other wildlife that depend on the native plants have to find other places to nest and feed. Some of the invasive species of Maryland are zebra mussels, European water chestnut, virile crayfish, purple loosestrife, and water lettuce. Maryland is also actively researching the impact of climate change on the state's natural environment. The Maryland Commission on Climate Change investigates the existing and potential negative impacts of climate change to Maryland's ecology and economy. It also seeks to discover new ways to reduce the state's greenhouse gas emissions and explore ways to decrease Maryland's vulnerability to climate change, particularly along its coastal areas.

BATTLE CREEK CYPRESS SWAMP

South of Washington, DC, near Prince Frederick in Calvert County is one of Maryland's finest natural treasures. Battle Creek Cypress Swamp is a 100-acre sanctuary best known for its towering bald cypress trees and primeval splendor. Nestled between the Chesapeake Bay and the Patuxent River, Battle Creek is one of the few places where this magnificent tree can still be found in Maryland, and it contains the northernmost occurrence of the bald cypress. Considering Maryland's coastal development boom in the last century, it is a wonder that 100-foot-tall cypress trees still exist in the state. Some trees may even be 1,000 years old. The trees are said to be the offshoots of cypress tress that were abundant in the region many thousands of years ago. Because of the cypress, the sanctuary attracts many southern birds to Maryland, especially warblers. Recognizing the value of this natural area, the Nature Conservancy acquired this property in Maryland's Battle Creek Valley in 1957 to protect the bald cypress, the wildlife supported by these trees, and the swampy ecosystem within which they thrive. Battle Creek Cypress Swamp is also a site where large land animals such as mammoths used to roam before their extinction.

Occurring predominantly in the coastal Carolinas and Piedmont regions of the Southeast, the bald cypress tree is attractive to lumber companies because of its sturdy, erect stature and its ability to ward off insects and rotting. It is called "bald" because it loses its needles every fall, and it is easily identifiable by the reddish-brown knobby knees at its base that support its height in storms and high winds and that theoretically help the tree absorb oxygen. As late as the 1970s, massive cypress trees with a diameter of over 10 feet were still being logged in South Carolina, but very few of the giant trees still remain. Discussions of the bald cypress usually conjure images of this stately tree rising out of a misty bog, but evidence suggests that the tree can also do quite well in drier climates. For fruit, the bald cypress produces a hard cone that few animals can crack once it falls, contributing to its reduction in numbers. The Carolina parakeet would eat and disseminate the cypress seeds, but, in 1939, the parakeet was declared extinct. This colorful bird was hunted for its feathers or killed for invading orchards and crops.

In addition to these majestic trees, the sanctuary has tulip, red maple, gum, ash, poplar, oak, and holly trees to enhance the diversity of the area. Visitors can see deer, mink, muskrats, and turtles sunning themselves. Spring wildflowers burst in an array of colors in the swamp as violets, mayapple, and lady's slipper orchid yearly bloom. Although Battle Creek Cypress Swamp is not a large tract of land, it has a lot to offer. It is a unique area where north and south come together to create a memorable and peaceful experience in nature, and it is a place that reminds visitors of Maryland's ancient past.

Open to visitors during the warm season, the sanctuary contains a quarter-mile boardwalk trail for hiking through the tranquil swamp and a nature center with live animal exhibits and information about the sanctuary. It is supported by the Battle Creek Nature Education Society, a nonprofit organization dedicated to providing educational programs and financial assistance to the cypress swamp to ensure its preservation. The society offers volunteer opportunities and special events, workshops, and lectures for people of all ages in understanding herbs, wildflower identification, weather, wildlife, and bird-watching.

Further Reading

Battle Creek Cypress Swamp. http://www.calvertparks.org/Parks/CypressSwamp/CS home.htm.

Bowen, John. *Adventuring in the Chesapeake Bay Area*. 2nd ed. San Francisco: Sierra Club Books, 1999.

Ewel, Katherine, and Howard Odum, eds. *Cypress Swamps*. Gainesville: University Press of Florida, 2001.

Lippson, Alice Jane, and Robert L. Lippson. *Life in the Chesapeake Bay*. Baltimore: John Hopkins University Press, 2006.

CRABTREE CAVE

There are some natural areas in the Northeast where a green plant or a ray of sunshine cannot be found. These dark, ecological tombs are caves. In Garrett County of western Maryland, Crabtree Cave is so unique and fragile that only experienced scientists and cavers are permitted to enter its rocky depths.

Crabtree Cave was discovered in 1860 in a limestone quarry. Although the quarry closed around 1900, the cave has been frequently visited. Being the largest cave in Maryland, it is 4,200 feet of lightless, circuitous passages of Greenbrier limestone, a type of limestone that was highly valued and mined in the late 19th and early 20th centuries. The limestone was often burned to produce agricultural lime and was used for building stone.

Crabtree Cave is Maryland's largest habitat for bats and other cave-dwelling creatures. The rare and unusual Franz's cave amphipod and Franz's isopod are two aquatic invertebrates that meander through this world with no light. They have permanently lost their sight and color to adapt to the cave's pitch-black interior. To help protect these creatures, the Nature Conservancy maintains a gate that shields the invertebrates from harm and also keeps the bats from being aroused and agitated during hibernation. Caves are natural hibernacula or temporary roosting spots for bats. Several species that can be found in Crabtree Cave are little brown, big brown, Keen's bat, and the eastern pipistrel. Caves are highly fragile habitats and need protection from vandalism, chemical pollution in the groundwater, and the activities of scientists and explorers who disrupt the cave. These threats impact the traditional roosting sites and have contributed to a decline in the bat population.

Bats have received an undeserved bad reputation because of their association with nocturnal activities and dark, cavernous hiding places. But bats play a critical role in maintaining environmental health by keeping night insect populations in balance and for being natural pollinators. A decrease in bat populations often results in an increase in chemical pesticide use, particularly for mosquitoes and insects that are considered agricultural pests. But the ecological impact of this pesticide use is profound and far-reaching. These insects, through evolutionary processes, develop resistances to the pesticides. Therefore, the chemical poisons ultimately do more harm to their predators, such as fish and bats, and many other species. Eventually, stronger pesticides are used, which perpetuates the poisonous cycle. This ecologically destructive toxic spiral is referred to as the pesticide treadmill. Also, because of the loss of their traditional habitats in caves and tree hollows and the increasing difficulty of locating roosting sites needed for their survival, bats often end up taking roost in abandoned mines. Consequently, mine closures have been known to bury large numbers of bats.

The ecological value of caves is frequently underappreciated. To scientists called speleologists caves are important underground laboratories. Most caves with their winding tunnels and caverns are formed from slow-moving groundwater. Because of their ability to hold and filter water, limestone caves have a direct impact on underground water quality, and scientists are commonly concerned with the water circulation within caves. Many minerals are often found in caves, including calcite, aragonite, and gypsum. Stalactites and stalagmites, common features in a cave, are calcite deposits from slowly dripping water. Stalactites are tube- or cone-shaped deposits hanging down from the cave ceiling, and stalagmites grow upward from the cave floor.

There has always been considerable interest in caves as natural attractions and as places that provoke the imagination. But Crabtree Cave is considered difficult to explore and even quite dangerous by cavers because of its vertical climbs and tight crevasses. Two other smaller caves in Garrett County are Dead Man's Cave and Steep Run Cave. There is much speculation that western Maryland may have other unknown cave systems, making this a vital area for cave exploration and research.

Further Reading

Hurd, Barbara. *Entering the Stone: On Caves and Feeling through the Dark*. New York: Houghton Mifflin, 2003.

Moore, George, and Nicholas Sullivan. *Speleology: Caves and the Cave Environment*. Dayton, OH: Cave Books, 1997.

Palmer, Arthur N. *Cave Geology*. Dayton, OH: Cave Books, 2007.

FINZEL SWAMP PRESERVE

In western Maryland, in the central Appalachian Forest region, is a place reminiscent of some far northern tundra, where the winters are long and summers are short. But this is Garret County, Maryland, only hours from Baltimore. Finzel Swamp Preserve is a unique place located in a frost pocket, where the topography of the area and the surrounding hilly landscape hold moisture and cold air, forming a frosty terrain. Finzel is home to bobcats, smoky shrews, and woodland jumping mice. The saw-whet owl, sedge wren, Nashville warbler, Virginia rail, and alder flycatcher are state endangered birds that can be found at Finzel, and many other stunning birds such as the whippoorwill and the scarlet tanager fly within this chilly valley. Red spruce, bog ferns, and cotton grass are just a few of the plants that populate the preserve.

Finzel's mountainous landscape is a rare blend of three distinct communities: mountain peatland, palustrine wetland, and relict forest. Mountain peatlands, or mountain bogs, with their highly acidic, low-nutrient, water-saturated soils foster the growth of only certain kinds of plants that have adapted to these conditions. These bogs are becoming increasingly endangered and the plants along with them. Palustrine wetlands border lakes, ponds, rivers, and streams and are freshwater areas. They are also swampy areas where water fills in low areas or ground depressions. Finzel also has a relict forest community of spruce, alder, and tamarack. Relict forests are ecosystems that at one time covered a large amount of territory but are now confined to an isolated space.

The unusual ecological conditions at Finzel, including temperature, altitude, and precipitation, create a landscape that is biologically diverse and an attraction for hikers and photographers. The preserve is open year-round to visitors who want to experience Finzel's natural wonders.

The 326-acre preserve has been owned and maintained by the Nature Conservancy since 1970. The conservancy regulates the occurrence of invasive species while promoting the growth of swamp plants and the northern larch, or tamarack, which is uncommon as far south as Maryland. A similar frost pocket preserve in western Maryland is the Cranesville Swamp Preserve. While most of this natural area lies within the boundaries of West Virginia, Cranesville is an asset to Maryland for its superior wetlands and habitat for rare species.

Within the Finzel Swamp wonderland are the headwaters of the Savage River. Originating from cold mountain springs and flowing through the Savage River State Forest, this dancing river is one of the best trout streams in Maryland, and it is probably best known for being the location for the World Whitewater Championships and the Olympic Whitewater Trials.

Another important ecological aspect of Finzel Swamp Preserve is the role it plays in creating large greenways in western Maryland. The Savage River Greenway consists of a tract of land totaling 50,000 acres across several natural areas connecting Finzel, Big Run State Park, Savage River State Forest, and New Germany State Park. This extensive land mass helps to encourage and protect wildlife habitats in Garret County and the ecological integrity of all the parks and preserves involved. The greenways are also maintained for recreational and tourism activities, creating lengthy bicycle and hiking trails that extend several hundreds of miles. Greenways that connect urban areas to natural areas, parks, historic sites, and open spaces not only work to protect the cultural and natural heritages of Maryland but also provide sustainable options for visitors and residents to interact with their region and appreciate the beauty and history it has to offer.

Further Reading

Hurd, Barbara. *Stirring the Mud: On Swamps, Bogs, and Human Imagination*. Boston: Beacon Press, 2001.

Nature Conservancy. "Finzel Swamp." http://www.nature.org/wherewework/northamerica/states/maryland/preserves/art4786.html.

Nassawango Creek Preserve

Nassawango Creek Preserve near Snow Hill, Maryland, has much to offer the nature enthusiast as well as the history buff. Open to the public year round and providing a sampling of scenic canoeing and hiking experiences, Nassawango Creek Preserve is indeed a refuge for all who visit. It is Maryland's largest private nature preserve, and Nassawango Creek is considered to be the clearest and cleanest waterway in the state of Maryland. Frocked with towering bald cypress swamps, elegant orchids, and the remnants of an old 19th-century village, Nassawango is a place that the modern world seems to have left behind.

E. Stanton Adkins II donated 157 acres to the Nature Conservancy in 1978, and the preserve has grown 9,000 acres since its modest beginnings. It provides habitat to river otters, white-tailed deer, painted turtles, and the gray fox. It is home to more than 90 species of endangered plants and animals, 12 species of orchids, forests, and a rare plant called the wild lupine. Bird lovers can see many different species of warblers, ovenbirds, osprey, wild turkey, indigo bunting, blue grosbeak, red-shouldered hawk, and many species of waterfowl. The creek is home to more than 16 native species of fish and the mud sunfish, which is rare in the state of Maryland.

Concerns for the preserve include many of the common threats that exist for many natural areas. These threats are development, agricultural runoff, and alterations to the landscape. To address these challenges, the Nature Conservancy encourages comparible land use and helps to provide a buffer for the Nassawango Creek to protect its pristine waters.

The preserve has two hiking trails: the Francis M. Uhler Nature Trail and the Paul Leifer Nature Trail. From the trails, hikers can view the cypress swamps that help filter the water of the Nassawango before it eventually drains into the Chesapeake Bay. Wildlife and birds can be seen as visitors pass over boardwalks that bridge the wetlands.

Nassawango Creek Preserve. (Courtesy of Susan Henley)

A view from the Paul Leifer trail includes a 19th-century canal that was used to support a nearby iron industry.

Along the boundary of the preserve is the historic village of Furnace Town. From 1831 until 1850, Furnace Town was a bustling center for the production of iron. During these two decades, the sounds of smelting iron came day and night from the brick furnace named Nassawango as the furnace produced bars of iron that measured roughly two feet in length. Named after the creek, the furnace was used to smelt charcoal, shells, and the bog ore that came from bogs along the creek. Although the iron industry in Furnace Town produced large amounts of iron, the bog ore was of poor quality. When higher-quality and more economical iron was being produced in other parts of the country, the industry along the creek could not compete, and the Nassawango furnace was shut down. The bog ore in the area along the Nassawango was also depleted by this time. As the industry came to a close, the 300 people who resided in the area moved away, and many of the buildings and the furnace itself fell to ruin. The visitor's center in the Nassawango Preserve provides educational information about both the preserve and Furnace Town. Because the iron industry and the community of people who supported it along the creek had a significant influence on the landscape and its natural resources, Furnace Town is regarded as an important part of Nassawango's environmental and cultural history. The bogs along the Nassawango have, over time, regained their ore, and the Nassawango Creek Preserve is considered one of Maryland's most scenic natural areas.

Further Reading

Ewel, Katherine, and Howard Odum, eds. *Cypress Swamps*. Gainesville: University Press of Florida, 2001.

Furnace Town Heritage Museum. http://www.furnacetown.com/.

Moose, Katie. *Eastern Shore of Maryland: The Guidebook*. 2nd ed. Annapolis, MD: Conduit, 2005.

Nature Conservancy. "Nassawango Creek Preserve." http://www.nature.org/wherewework/northamerica/states/maryland/preserves/art21134.html.

POTOMAC GORGE

It is unusual when a wilderness area exists in close proximity to a major metropolitan area, but the Potomac Gorge in Maryland is just a short distance northwest of Washington, DC, and is one of the most biologically diverse places in the national park system. The gorge is a 15-mile corridor of the Potomac River spanning from above Great Falls to Theodore Roosevelt Island. A portion of the gorge is within the city limits of Washington, DC. The river is considered to be one of the healthiest river systems to exist so close to an urban center, and it is the primary source of water for people living in the Potomac region. Unfortunately, the gorge has lost roughly 113 of its 240 rare species and natural communities in the last century, making it an important site for protection by the national park system, the Nature Conservancy, and other state agencies.

The Potomac Gorge hosts more than 1,400 plant species and is home to some very unusual habitats. Within the gorge is the biologically rich Bear Island, a 96-acre nature preserve. Fifty state endangered species have been identified in this preserve, and it is the location for an exposed bedrock terrace natural community, which is very rare for this part of the country. Terrace communities exist at high levels along a river, often on outcrops and cliffs. Other natural communities in this area are riparian communities and upland forest blocks. Riparian communities exist along the river banks, and upland forest blocks are the rolling hills and wooded areas that occur in the valleys and highlands of the gorge. The Potomac Gorge is ecologically unique because it marks an area where the Piedmont meets the Atlantic coastal plain. The meeting place is known as the "fall line" landscape and is characterized by river rapids indicating that transition from ancient bedrock to the sandy coastal terrain. A few of the fascinating sights to be witnessed at Bear Island from the Billy Goat Trail are Virginia bluebells, Carolina tassel-rue, prickly pear, painted turtles, the tiger swallow-tail butterfly, wood frogs, warblers, great blue heron, and white-tailed deer. As with many natural areas along the East Coast, the gorge is also an important stopover site for migratory birds.

Of historical and environmental interest is the Chesapeake and Ohio (C&O) Canal that runs parallel to the Potomac Gorge and River. The C&O Canal was built in the

The Great Falls of the Potomac Gorge. (Courtesy of Patrick A. Rodgers)

mid-19th century and reaches 185 miles. It was built to enhance transportation and commerce trade routes because the Potomac was too hard to navigate and dangerous for ships. Today, the canal exists as the C&O Canal National Historic Park and offers much of the same ecological value and biodiversity of the wild Potomac. The construction of the C&O Canal is, no doubt, somewhat responsible for why the Potomac Gorge remains intact since the impact of travel and industry was transferred to this new water channel in the nineteenth century.

What is being done to protect the Potomac Gorge that harbors 15 globally endangered species and 100 state rare species? Protection involves the controlling of invasive species, tree planting, and more research of the gorge's flora and fauna. In summer 2006, the Nature Conservancy and National Park Service hosted a 30-hour BioBlitz that brought to the gorge more than 130 naturalists and biologists who surveyed the 15-mile stretch and found over 1,000 species, including two rare snail species and the black birch plant, which has never before been found east of the Appalachian Mountains.

In addition to being a haven for research and study, the Potomac Gorge is a place of refuge and recreation that is visited by millions of hikers, bicyclists, kayakers, fishers, canoeists, runners, and people looking to escape the bustle of city life.

Further Reading

Hyde, Arnout, and Ken Sullivan. *The Potomac*. New York: Gramercy, 1999.
Potomac Gorge. http://beta2.c-t-g.com/gorge/index_gorge.html.
Sabatke, Mark D. *Discovering the C & O Canal*. Rockville, MD: Schreiber, 2003.

SOLDIERS DELIGHT NATURAL ENVIRONMENT AREA

In central Maryland, west of Baltimore, lies a natural community that is the largest of its kind in the eastern United States. Soldiers Delight Natural Environment Area is 1,900 acres of serpentine barren and a critical habitat for 39 rare species that thrive in the unique conditions of this important conservation area. Its name dates back to the 1600s, when soldiers who patrolled the area enjoyed its open grassland beauty.

Occurring underground in this natural area is a geologic bedrock called serpentine. This magnesium-rich rock is greenish-gray in color and is accompanied by a natural community that is globally rare. At Soldiers Delight, this natural community is called a serpentine grassland. The soil in the grassland has a greenish color due to the high amount of magnesium and other metals. Serpentine gets its name from its resemblance to green-brown snakes of northern Italy, according to folklore. The soils are toxic to many species of plants, so those that grow in a serpentine community have adapted to the harsh soils. Many invasive species cannot survive in these soils, which helps to keep the plant community safe from most intruding plants. The high level of magnesium in the soil prevents the uptake of calcium, making it difficult for many plants to grow in these soils. Also, the presence of heavy metals such as chromium, cobalt, and nickel in serpentine soils are toxic to many plants. The presence of chickweed is a strong indicator of serpentine soils. Its hairy leaves protect it from the heat of sunlight while also holding in moisture. Plants need to be quite hardy to survive in dry, nutrient-poor serpentine soils. Despite being an inhospitable ecosystem for many plants, the Soldiers Delight grasslands have been threatened by the invasion of Virginia pines. One thousand acres are currently being monitored for invasive species, and measures are being taken to remove the Virginia pines from the area. Prescribed burnings are also taking place to help restore the grassland. The area is managed by the Maryland Department of Natural Resources and is assisted by the nonprofit group Soldiers Delight Conservation, Inc.

There are only four remaining serpentine communities in the state of Maryland where rare, threatened, and endangered species occur on serpentine grasslands. Some of the most endangered plants are the serpentine aster, sandplain gerardia, fringed gentian, and fameflower. Other species found in the grasslands are little bluestem, purplish threeawn, Indian grass, blazing star, and goldenrod. These prairielike ecosystems are not as diverse as other environments, but what species they do have are quite extraordinary.

While serpentine areas can be found scattered from Alabama to Canada, there are very few of them. The highest concentration of serpentine communities are in Pennsylvania and Maryland. Many thousands of acres along the eastern regions of these two states used to be covered in grassland before European settlement. Native Americans used to keep these prairie lands thriving with their burning practices, but once they were driven from their lands, the burnings discontinued, allowing for many of the areas to evolve into woodlands. Ultimately, mining and residential development are two significant causes for the loss of serpentine grasslands, making the conservation of such places as Soldiers Delight an ecological priority. This natural area was heavily mined for chromium ore in the 19th century, and a historic remnant of this mining can be found on the Choate Mine Trail. Just a little longer than one mile, this trail leads to the Choate Mine that was in operation until 1888. Other trails on the property are the Serpentine Trail, Red Run Trail, and Dolfield Trail. Like many preserved grassland areas, Soldiers Delight is a remnant of the open, windswept, tall-grass prairies that were once assumed barren, useless, or empty and only of value if they were developed, mined, or paved.

Further Reading

Anderson, Roger, C., James S. Fralish, and Jerry M. Baskin, eds. *Savannas, Barrens, and Rock Outcrop Plant Communities of North America*. New York: Cambridge University Press, 1999.

Maryland Department of Natural Resources. "Soldiers Delight Natural Environment Area." http://www.dnr.state.md.us/publiclands/central/soldiers.html

Cape Cod National Seashore, 66

David H. Smith Preserve and Fire Trail, 68

Mount Greylock State Reservation, 69

Reed Brook Preserve, 71

Walden Pond State Reservation, 73

MASSACHUSETTS

Massachusetts might be a small state, but the influence of its natural heritage and cultural history is unparalleled in New England. From east to west, the landscape varies widely from sandy beaches to rolling green hills to majestic forests in the west. It was the first state in the country to create a regional park system in 1893, when Boston conservationists became alarmed at the rapid urban growth and expansion of the city into the state's woodlands. To provide Boston residents with a retreat from urban congestion, a series of parklands were created around Boston for recreation and spiritual renewal.

Massachusetts is also the home state for Walden Pond, where Henry David Thoreau chronicled his exploration of a simplified life in the natural surroundings of Walden Woods, which culminated in the literary masterpiece *Walden*. First published in 1854, this work presented an environmental ethic of stewardship and a personal philosophy of social responsibility that grows more relevant and inspiring as environmental concerns become more urgent. He also authored *A Week on the Concord and Merrimack Rivers*, the essay "Natural History of Massachusetts," and essays that are important to the state's abolitionist history. His friend and neighbor Ralph Waldo Emerson published *Nature* in 1835, a collection of essays that shaped the central expression of American Transcendentalism and declared a divine interconnection between the human spirit and nature that continues to resonate with readers today.

Because of its extraordinary history and natural beauty, Massachusetts has a thriving tourism industry. With historical sites such as Plymouth Plantation and Bunker Hill, it is the location for a colonial history that has become deeply ingrained in the U.S. heritage. Places such as Cape Cod, Martha's Vineyard, and Nantucket attract visitors to the east, while western Massachusetts boasts the stunning Berkshires with Mount Greylock, the Mohawk Trail, and the Connecticut River pulsing through the central part of the state. In addition to the Connecticut River, the Blackstone, the Housatonic, the Hoosic, the Concord, and the Merrimack rivers flow through the state, creating rich river valleys.

Some of the exemplary ecosystems in Massachusetts are sandplain grasslands, heathlands, pitch pine/scrub oak forests, spruce-fir forests, wetlands, and serpentine outcrops. Two large reservoirs—the Quabbin and the Wachusett—provide drinking water for the Boston area. A conservation priority for Massachusetts is protecting native species and natural communities from invasive species. There are 66 invasive species that have been identified in the state that are not native to Massachusetts but grow rapidly and aggressively threaten native species. Invasive species kill native species and contribute to habitat loss, because birds and other wildlife that depend on the native plants must find other places to nest and feed. Some of the invasive species of Massachusetts are black locust, pale swallow-wort, Japanese knotweed, garlic mustard, purple loosestrife, Norway maple, and the common reed. In 2006, the state of Massachusetts issued a ban on the import and sale of the identified invasive species in order to gradually phase out these plants. Other key conservation issues for Massachusetts are open space and farmland protection, the cranberry and dairy industries, local food production, climate change, and water quality in the state.

CAPE COD NATIONAL SEASHORE

The Cape Cod National Seashore is a popular northeastern destination for people who love to be near the ocean. It is 44,600 acres of sandy beaches, seaside beauty, and awe-inspiring Atlantic sunrises. But this Massachusetts seashore is far more than just a tourist attraction. It is a natural area bubbling with diverse marine and freshwater ecosystems and home to globally rare species and habitats. Furthermore, it is a wellspring of stories from early American history.

Cape Cod is a 60-mile peninsula curling out into the Atlantic Ocean with a 40-mile seashore that has been protected by the National Park Service since 1961. The seashore is a repository of scenic beaches, salt marshes, tidal flats, and sand spits. Its freshwater system includes vernal pools, 20 permanently flooded kettle pools, bogs, and swamps. On shore are wispy dunes, sandplain grasslands, heathlands, and pitch pine/scrub oak forests. Cape Cod is essentially a long, narrow, dynamic glacial deposit. It is dynamic because wind, weather, surf, and other erosive forces are continuously changing the shape of the peninsula. In some areas, the changes are subtle, while in other locations, the changes are quite dramatic. This beach building and beach eroding are natural processes that occur along an ocean shoreline.

It is estimated that 370 species of birds can be spotted along the seashore; some nest on the beaches, and others stop at Cape Cod along their migratory routes. The roseate tern is an endangered species that can be found along the seashore, and the threatened piping plover is a beach-nesting bird that has a strong presence at this national seashore. The piping plover birds and their eggs rely on their camouflaged appearance for protection, but an increase in predators, loss of habitat, and human disturbance have significantly compromised this beautiful beach bird. Other birds that can be seen at Cape Cod are the common tern, least tern, Arctic tern, great black-backed gull, red-tailed hawk, great blue heron, cormorants, ospreys, and tree swallows.

Cape Cod National Seashore is abundant with coastal flora and fauna, and restoration projects to recover native and introduced species continue to be largely successful.

Dikes, roads, and railroads built a century ago have had devastating impacts on Cape Cod, altering marshland habitats and natural water regimes. Plants such as seablite, pickleweed, and spartina are native salt marsh plants that have been repopulating the wetlands due to restoration efforts.

The primary threats to the Cape Cod National Seashore are development, population growth, and climate change causing a rise in sea levels. An increase in pollutants compromises the quality of the fresh groundwater, and higher sea levels result in increased storm surge, flooding, increased erosion, and thus more saltwater intrusion upon freshwater sources. Of the many programs in place to safeguard this area is the National Park Service's Cape Cod National Seashore Prototype Long-Term Ecosystem Monitoring Program. This program provides close monitoring of the seashore's ecosystems and natural resources, conducts studies to analyze monitoring methods and results, and shares findings and relevant information with other coastal parks along the eastern seaboard.

Culturally, Cape Cod has been inhabited for many thousands of years. There is extensive archeological evidence that chronicles the stories of Native Americans who lived on the cape 10,000 years ago. The pilgrims also left their historical legacy during their brief stay on the cape before moving on to Plymouth. Now, Cape Cod is a mosaic of tourist attractions, artist gathering spots, shipwreck stories, and historic buildings and lighthouses. Evidence of an old whaling business and a commercial cranberry bog remind visitors of the cape's coastal industries. Cape Cod's rich history and its protected seashore hold enduring prominence as places of top priority for conservation efforts at the local, state, and federal levels. Climate change forecasts present a bleak future for places like

The Beach at Cape Cod National Seashore. (Courtesy of Melinda Applegate)

Cape Cod as rising seawaters threaten to submerge coastal regions and all that rests upon them. This forecast is a powerful reminder that global environmental challenges must be addressed for the protection of such important natural areas.

Further Reading

Materson, John P., and John W. Portnoy. *Potential Changes in Ground-Water Flow and Their Effects on the Ecology and Water Resources of the Cape Cod National Seashore, Massachusetts.* Washington, DC: U.S. Department of Interior: U.S. Geological Survey, 2005.

National Park Service. "Cape Cod. http://www.nps.gov/caco.

Schneider, Paul. *The Enduring Shore: The History of Cape Cod, Martha's Vineyard, and Nantucket.* New York: Holt Paperbacks, 2001.

Schwarzman, Beth. *The Nature of Cape Cod.* Lebanon, NH: University Press of New England, 2002.

DAVID H. SMITH PRESERVE AND FIRE TRAIL

On Martha's Vineyard and Nantucket, there is an ecosystem that is extraordinarily rare with only a few other small examples in existence worldwide. The coastal sandplain ecosystem in the David H. Smith Preserve on Martha's Vineyard is the most substantial of its kind on the island. Located in Edgartown, this 830-acre preserve features coastal grasslands and heathlands as well as the rare plants and animals that call this beautiful ecosystem home. The preserve is also known for its fire trail that educates visitors about the importance of prescribed burnings to restore and protect this threatened natural area. It is estimated that 80 percent to 90 percent of the world's coastal sandplain ecosystem is located on Massachusetts islands.

The coastal sandplain ecosystem includes sandplain grassland natural communities. A sandplain grassland is a flat area comprised of native grasses and shrubs and is maintained by periodic burning. These grasslands were formed from melting glaciers many thousands of years ago when the glaciers dropped their sand, and the streams from the melting water formed sandy plains. The deep sand deposits beneath the grassland allow water to percolate down quickly. Due to this high sand content of the soil, water and nutrients drain away easily, creating a climate that is perhaps prone to drought but also creating this very rare natural community. Wildflowers such as bluets, false indigo, asters, and field pussytoes often grow in this area. Coastal heathlands have grasses and some of these flowers as well, but they also contain shrubs such as blueberry, bayberry, huckleberry, and pasture rose. Rare animals such as the short-eared owl, northern harrier hawk, endangered moth species, hairy woodpeckers, and the grasshopper sparrow have recently made a comeback to Martha's Vineyard due to fire management.

Very little of this remarkable ecosystem exists in the world due to residential and commercial development. What does remain has been overwhelmed by nonnative species because of the lack of periodic burning to keep the prairielike coastal landscape open.

Until recently, wildfires and burning have been discouraged, because the fire would get too close to homes and businesses. The pitch pine/scrub oak forests have dominated the vegetation in the ecosystem, threatening to eradicate the plants that are characteristic of this ecosystem. The Nature Conservancy has worked with other partners to conduct safe and effective burnings to restore the coastal sandplains at David H. Smith Preserve. There are plans in place for the future to build a research facility at the preserve where further study of this rare ecosystem will take place in order to develop further strategies to restore and protect the coastal sandplains.

Restoring the native grassland and woodland habitats at David H. Smith Preserve continue as other progress is made to protect sandplain locations on Martha's Vineyard. Katama Plains Preserve is the largest parcel of sandplain grasslands on the island and is also located in Edgartown. It is closed to the public because of its highly sensitive habitat. The area is small—only 192 acres—but every acre of this natural community that can be protected is critical. The Marine Biology Laboratory and the Nature Conservancy are in the midst of a five-year plan to restore the sandplain ecosystem at Bamford Preserve on Herring Creek Farm. Once used for agricultural activities, Bamford Preserve is being restored to its native state as a sandplain grassland and heathland. Because rich agricultural soils differ substantially from the dry soils of a sandplain, adjusting the soil composition is necessary to support the vegetation that prefers the infertile soils and to discourage the growth of plants that thrive in fertile soils. Because Bamford Preserve connects to the Katama Plains Preserve, restoration of Bamford will safeguard a large tract of coastal sandplain grassland and heathland on Martha's Vineyard.

Further Reading

Dunwiddie, Peter. *Martha's Vineyard Landscapes: The Nature of Change*. Vineyard Haven, MA: Vineyard Conservation Society, 1994.

Mader, Sylvia S. *Martha's Vineyard Nature Guide*. Green Bay, WI: Mader Enterprises, 1985.

Nantucket Conservation Foundation. http://www.nantucketconservation.com/.

Nature Conservancy. "David H. Smith Preserve. http://www.nature.org/wherewework/northamerica/states/massachusetts/preserves/art5334.html.

MOUNT GREYLOCK STATE RESERVATION

Mount Greylock is the highest point in Massachusetts. It rises 3,491 feet above the nearby Berkshire Mountains, and views from the summit offer far-reaching vistas of the Green Mountains and other hilly landscapes. This state reservation is the first designated state park for Massachusetts, and its history is as interesting as its ecology. Within the reservation is a place called the Hopper. Designated a National Natural Landmark in 1987, the Hopper is a deep valley that contains within its slopes red spruce trees that are estimated to be more than 150 years old. The valley got its name from a grist mill's grain hopper. The mountain is geologically known for its old Greylock Schist formations that were pushed upward in the process of mountain building. The Greylock Schist, which has as its origins an ancient seabed, eventually folded over the young limestone and marble to create the mountain ridge.

The ecology changes dramatically from the lower slopes of the mountain to the summit region. The lower slopes are decked with the stunning northern hardwood forests characteristic of New England, but the higher ranges feature vegetation typical of a subalpine climate. This high-elevation boreal forest is the only one in the state of Massachusetts and includes red spruce, balsam fir, mountain ash, and yellow birch. The topographic extremes create a unique environment for a wide array of wildlife in the area as well. Close to 100 species of birds can be found on the reservation, along with moose, white-tailed deer, coyotes, fox, bobcat, and black bear.

The region of the Mount Greylock State Reservation extends across roughly 12,500 acres and was once hunting grounds for the Mahican tribe prior to English settlement. What is today called the Mohawk Trail was the footpath and passageway for various native peoples. Mount Greylock has its place in literary history as well as the snowy mountain view that inspired the description of the great white whale rising up from the sea in Herman Melville's *Moby Dick*. Other literary figures such as Nathaniel Hawthorne and Henry David Thoreau were inspired by the captivating Mount Greylock and the beauty of the Berkshires.

Mount Greylock State Reservation is within the spectacular Berkshire Taconic Landscape, which reaches across western Massachusetts, Connecticut, and New York. Its span encompasses the Berkshire and Taconic Mountains and connects them to the Appalachian Range. Covering more than 155,000 acres, there is no other place quite like it in southern New England. It is a lush wilderness, but not too intimidating for the occasional nature observer. Comprised of rich wetlands, northern hardwood forests, the Appalachian Trail, lakes, river systems, more than 150 rare and endangered species, and extraordinary views, the Berkshire Taconic Landscape is a conservation success story. Many organizations and landowners are involved in the preservation of this diverse area that is brimming with health and vitality.

The landscape, however, is not without its environmental challenges. Invasive species are a threat to the native flora and fauna; acid rain, storm runoff, climate change, and habitat destruction are all concerns that are being addressed by state, federal, and local agencies across the three states that share this beautiful woodland and wetland terrain. The Berkshire Taconic Landscape Program, an effective conservation collaboration effort, has been strategically addressing these threats since 1999. The Nature Conservancy has created the Weed-It-Now initiative that aims to reduce invasive plants on the Taconic Plateau. Other efforts include working with individual landowners to encourage sustainable land management practices, restoring the rare calcium-rich and high-alkaline wetlands, and linking the floodplain forest along the Housatonic River. By protecting the majestic mountains and lush wetlands, habitats for the rare timber rattlesnake and bog turtle will be preserved. Mount Greylock State Reservation and its surrounding Berkshire Taconic Landscape are being preserved as one of the last great wilderness areas in New England.

Further Reading

Kirby, Ed. *Exploring the Berkshire Hills: A Guide to Geology and Early Industry in the Housatonic Watershed*. Easthampton, MA: Earth View, 1996.

Kricher, John, and Gordon Morrison. *A Field Guide to Eastern Forests, North America*. Boston: Houghton Mifflin, 1998.

Massachusetts Department of Conservation and Recreation. "Mount Greylock." http://www.mass.gov/dcr/parks/mtGreylock/.

Strauch, Joseph. *Wildflowers of the Berkshire and Taconic Hills*. Woodstock, VT: Berkshire House, 1995.

REED BROOK PRESERVE

Although not an exceptionally large natural area, Reed Brook Preserve has a very special geologic feature that establishes the preserve as a critical conservation area in the state of Massachusetts. Tucked away in a hemlock ravine in the northwest corner of the state, Reed Brook Preserve is 101 acres of green forest and rocky terrain with a short, steep trail and the percolating brook (from which the preserve gets its name) that meanders through the property toward the northeast.

Occurring in this natural area is a geologic formation called a serpentine outcrop. This magnesium-rich rock formation is greenish-gray in color and is accompanied by a natural community that is globally rare. The soil near the outcrop has a greenish color due to the high amount of magnesium and other metals in the bedrock. Serpentine gets its name from its resemblance to green-brown snakes of northern Italy, according to folklore. The soils are toxic to many species of plants, so those that grow in a serpentine community have adapted to the harsh soils. Many invasive species cannot survive in these soils, keeping the plant community safe from intruding plants. The high level of magnesium in the soil prevents the uptake of calcium, making it difficult for many plants to grow in these soils. Also, the presence of heavy metals such as chromium, cobalt, and nickel in serpentine soils are toxic to many plants. Two that do grow at Reed Brook Preserve are maidenhair spleenwort and mouse-ear chickweed. Maidenhair spleenwort prefers the mossy rocks and outcrops at the preserve, and the mouse-ear chickweed plant is a strong indicator of serpentine soils. Its hairy leaves protect it from the heat of sunlight while also holding in moisture. Plants need to be quite hardy to survive in dry, nutrient-poor serpentine soils.

Reed Brook Preserve is situated within the Deerfield River watershed of northwest Massachusetts. The brook empties into the Deerfield River, which is considered one of the cleanest rivers in the region. Spanning partly into Vermont, the watershed is primarily a forested landscape with lakes, small towns, and several subwatersheds. The river is stocked with trout and is being used for the restoration of Atlantic salmon. The Deerfield River Watershed Association is a nonprofit organization that aims to safeguard and promote vitality of the natural resources within the Deerfield River watershed. This agency monitors and protects water quality, wildlife habitats, wetlands, and open spaces within the watershed. It also is very active in working with others to form educational programs to raise awareness about regional stewardship and to promote environmental education in schools. The major threats to the watershed include invasive species, habitat loss, chemical spills, and runoff from poor land use practices. As with many areas, the control of invasive species is a primary goal for many environmental organizations. In the Deerfield River region, measures are being taken to eradicate the Japanese knotweed. This invasive species has roots that can grow as deep as 6 feet and 23 feet horizontally, making it very difficult to control.

The Reed Brook Preserve has been owned by the Nature Conservancy since 1982 because of its interest in protecting the serpentine community. The conservancy continues

Reed Brook Preserve. (Dream-stime)

to maintain the trail and monitor the globally rare species at the preserve. While serpentine areas can be found scattered from Alabama to Canada, there are very few of them. The highest concentration of serpentine communities are in Pennsylvania and Maryland. Mining and residential development are two of the primary causes for the loss of serpentine grasslands and outcrops, making the conservation of such places as Reed Brook Preserve an ecological priority.

Further Reading

Anderson, Roger, C., James S. Fralish, and Jerry M. Baskin, eds. *Savannas, Barrens, and Rock Outcrop Plant Communities of North America.* New York: Cambridge University Press, 1999.
Deerfield River Watershed Association. http://www.deerfieldriver.org/.
Nature Conservancy. "Reed Brook Preserve." http://www.nature.org/wherewework/ northamerica/states/massachusetts/preserves/art5315.html.

WALDEN POND STATE RESERVATION

Massachusetts is considered the birthplace of the conservation movement by many, and the historic natural area of Walden Pond played the most significant role in fostering that reputation. As the location of Henry David Thoreau's famous trek into the woods "to live deliberately" for two years and two months from 1845 to 1847, Walden Pond is a designated National Historic Landmark that still resembles its original condition as Thoreau would have experienced it in his day.

Walden Pond is a kettle hole that in its deepest area is more than 100 feet deep. The pond was formed roughly 15,000 years ago by a glacier deposit when the last remaining glacier in New England was receding. Over time, sediments surrounded the large deposit, the ice chunk melted, and what remained was a large hole that filled with water and became the famous pond that inspired Thoreau and many others who have visited its banks.

The pond is surrounded by more than 2,600 acres of forest known as Walden Woods. This forest lies west of Boston in Concord and Lincoln and is comprised mostly of pitch pine, oak, and hickory. Historically, what saved Walden Woods is its acidic soil composition and sandy quality left behind by glaciers. This relatively infertile soil was not conducive for agricultural use in the 19th century and therefore remained untouched for quite some time. Much of the forest area was eventually cut down but has since regrown to resemble its original mosaic. White pine grows well in the sandy soils of Walden Woods and can be found throughout the forest. The white pine trees that Thoreau planted near his home on the property were destroyed by a hurricane in 1938.

Wildlife is abundant at Walden Pond. Red-tailed hawks, blackbirds, chickadees, and waterfowl can be seen in and around the pond, and red fox, coyote, deer, rabbits, chipmunks, squirrels, and other wildlife are attracted to the glistening waters. The pond is stocked each year with a variety of fish, but Walden was not teeming with fish even in Thoreau's time.

Ecologically, there are drawbacks for Walden Pond as the place linked to Thoreau's legacy of stewardship and environmental consciousness. Rough estimates indicate that close to 500,000 people visit the park each year. Swimming, fishing, hiking, and canoeing are permitted in the designated park area. To protect the natural resources of the pond and surrounding woods, the Massachusetts Department of Conservation and Recreation has placed a limit on how many people can be in the park at one time. When the park reaches its capacity, visitors are turned away. The park has been able to balance providing recreational opportunities for visitors while maintaining the ecological integrity of the area. Due to vigilant conservation activities, the water quality of Walden Pond has remained relatively clean and clear. While visitor use poses one threat to the area, other threats include invasive species, landfill toxins, and acid rain.

The educational value of Walden Pond State Reservation cannot be overstated. It is a place where visitors can learn the philosophies of Thoreau while absorbing the natural surroundings. It is also a place where visitors can ponder the idea of living with simplicity as the world becomes more complex and threatened by toxic overload and climate change caused by human activity. The call for environmental stewardship has never been more urgent, and places like Walden Pond can educate and inspire change. *Walden*, the American literary classic of nature writing penned by Thoreau, has shared with readers an environmental ethic and a way of being in the world that has been unparalleled

Walden Pond. (Flickr—Oranda)

since its publication in 1854. Although written in the 19th century, Thoreau's writings and the places that inspired them hold the key for a healthy, sustainable planet in the 21st century.

Further Reading

Massachusetts Department of Conservation and Recreation. "Walden Pond State Reservation." http://www.mass.gov/dcr/parks/walden/index.htm.

Maynard, W. Barksdale. *Walden Pond: A History*. New York: Oxford University Press, 2004.

Thoreau, Henry David. *Walden, Civil Disobedience, and Other Writings*. New York: Norton Critical Editions, 2007.

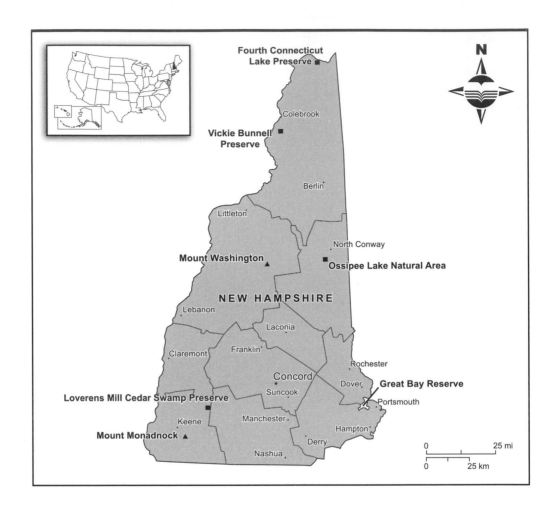

Fourth Connecticut Lake Preserve, 78

Great Bay Reserve, 80

Loverens Mill Cedar Swamp Preserve, 81

Mount Monadnock, 82

Mount Washington, 84

Ossipee Lake Natural Area, 86

Vickie Bunnell Preserve, 88

NEW HAMPSHIRE

New Hampshire is perhaps best known for its hardwood forests, north country, apples, maple products, White Mountain National Forest, and Mount Washington, which is the tallest mountain north of the Smoky Mountains and east of the Mississippi River. Known for its wild and dangerous weather that is in constant flux, Mount Washington is an important scientific laboratory for the study of New England's air pollution and its impact on climate change. New Hampshire is known as the granite state because of its granite quarries, and it is also known for its commitment to wildlife conservation. It is often referred to as the mother of rivers because of the rivers that have their headwaters in the state, including the Connecticut River. With its headwaters near the Canadian border, this ecologically rich and historic river meanders through New Hampshire, Vermont, Massachusetts, and Connecticut before emptying into the Long Island Sound and out to sea. The dominant ecoregion of the state is the Northeast Highlands. This thinly populated region is dominated by northern hardwood forests and spruce-fir forests. The Northeastern Coastal Zone ecoregion is located in southeast New Hampshire. This region is the most densely populated area of the state and is mostly comprised of pine, oak, and hickory forests.

New Hampshire is also often nicknamed the "Switzerland of America" because of the White Mountain National Forest, which contains six wilderness areas, nine scenic locations, and an abundance of wildlife. It features alpine natural communities, northern hardwoods, paper birch, and spruce hardwoods. The forest helps to restore 12,000 acres of wetlands, 35 watersheds, and many lakes and streams in the region while also hosting 160 miles of the Appalachian Trail Corridor. New Hampshire also has 18 miles of coastline that add to its ecological diversity.

In 1923, Robert Frost gave artistic expression to the rural character of the state in his book of poetry called *New Hampshire*, which features classics such as "Fire and Ice" and "Stopping by the Woods on a Snowy Evening." In 1924, Frost received his first Pulitzer Prize in poetry for *New Hampshire*, which established him as an American icon of poetry and an inspired voice rooted in the landscapes of New England.

One of the primary conservation concerns for New Hampshire is the natural resources of its coastal watershed region, which are under threat by sprawling development and destructive use of the land. In the last several decades, the landscape of southeastern New Hampshire has changed dramatically. There are few undeveloped lands remaining in this watershed that drains 46 towns and provides habitat to important plant and animal species. Current strategies to promote conservation and sustainability in the coastal region include land acquisition and conservation easements, public outreach for education and input, regulating development in the region, and protecting the region's biodiversity, natural communities, and water quality. The strategies are being implemented by the Nature Conservancy, the state of New Hampshire, and numerous other regional organizations that support the state's coastal environmental health.

The state is also addressing the issue of climate change. In 2007, a Climate Change Policy Task Force was created to develop action projects designed to promote energy efficiency and the use of renewable energy resources while also supporting the state's economy. Public listening sessions were held to allow citizens to voice their concerns and make suggestions to the New Hampshire Department of Environmental Services regarding what measures should be taken to reduce New Hampshire's carbon footprint.

FOURTH CONNECTICUT LAKE PRESERVE

In the northern tip of New Hampshire are a series of Connecticut lakes. The southernmost lake is First Connecticut Lake, the Second Connecticut Lake is nearby to the north, the Third Connecticut Lake is a little more to the north, and then there is the Fourth Connecticut Lake. This Connecticut Lakes Region is characterized by spectacular wilderness and undeveloped northern countryside. But what makes the Fourth Connecticut Lake particularly special is that it is the headwaters of the magnificent Connecticut River, the most significant river in New England, impacting four states and embedded with cultural history.

The Connecticut Lakes Region is also known as the Great North Woods of New Hampshire, where sparkling, pristine rivers and lakes are teeming with fish, and opportunities for solitude in remote forests are abundant. The Great North Woods span Maine, New Hampshire, Vermont, and New York. The Connecticut River has its beginnings here where the water is cool and pure. It makes its way down through the lakes and travels along the New Hampshire–Vermont border before bisecting Massachusetts and Connecticut and emptying into the Long Island Sound and out to sea.

Although the Connecticut River has seen its share of challenges in the last century, the 1972 passing of the Federal Clean Water Act put to an end over a century of the Connecticut River being used as a garbage and sewage dump. In the last few decades, improvements in the water quality and overall health of the Connecticut River, which is the largest river system in New England, have been remarkable. Its watershed covers more than 11,000 square miles, and the river travels 410 miles from its headwaters to the Long Island Sound. Its name was derived from the Native American word *quenticut,* which means "the long tidal river."

The Fourth Connecticut Lake Preserve contains more than 70 acres of red birch, American mountain ash, spruce, and balsam fir forest with the small Fourth Lake shining in the midst. There is a moderately challenging trail that is used to access the lake where deer, river otter, moose, and waterfowl can be seen. Insect-eating plants such as the sundew and pitcher plant are near the lake, and within the lake's waters is bladderwort. The lake is ringed with a floating bog mat decked with mosses and grasses. The forest undergrowth is comprised of creeping snowberry, bluebead lily, goldthread, and a stunning array of wildflowers.

The preserve is protected by the Nature Conservancy after the Champion International Corporation donated the property to the organization in 1990. The conservancy built the trail five years later for the purpose of nature observation and study. The preserve is roughly 22 miles from the village of Pittsburg, New Hampshire, and falls just below the Canadian border. The trail follows the international boundary line between the United States and Canada. The area around the preserve is significant as well. A large tract of land known as the Connecticut Lakes Headwaters Natural Area, is owned by the New Hampshire Fish and Game Department and is held as a conservation easement by the Nature Conservancy. Much of the forest surrounding the Fourth Connecticut Lake was cut down in the early 20th century, but since it has been able to regenerate. Fearing development would alter the natural integrity of northern New Hampshire, the Connecticut Lakes Headwaters Partnership brought together many individuals and organizations for the purpose of developing conservation strategies for the Connecticut Lakes Region. In 2003, the partnership won the Wildlife Management Institute's Touchstone Award that recognizes sound leadership and innovative conservation efforts in the United States.

Further Reading

Bessette, Alan E., Arleen R. Bessette, William K. Chapman, and Valerie Conley Chapman. *Wildflowers of Maine, New Hampshire, and Vermont.* Syracuse, NY: Syracuse University Press, 2000.

Kricher, John, and Gordon Morrison. *A Field Guide to Eastern Forests, North America.* Boston: Houghton Mifflin, 1998.

Marchand, Peter J. *North Woods: An Inside Look at the Nature of Forests of the Northeast.* Boston: Appalachian Mountain Books, 1987.

Nature Conservancy. "Fourth Connecticut Lake Preserve." http://www.nature.org/wherewework/northamerica/states/newhampshire/preserves/art6129.html.

GREAT BAY RESERVE

While it may be true that New Hampshire does not have much of a coastline, it has its share of important mudflats and tidal waters that deserve attention. The Great Bay is a large, inland estuary fed by tidal waters from the salty Atlantic Ocean that mix with the fresh water that drains into the bay from several rivers, one of which is the Piscataqua River. Formed from glacier melt waters 14,000 years ago, the Great Bay has more than 150 known species of plants, birds, and fish residing in the reserve and estuary, and 23 of those are listed as threatened or endangered.

The Great Bay Reserve is 10 miles inland and is composed of eelgrass beds, mudflats, salt marshes, upland forests, channel bottom, and rocky intertidal habitats. Eelgrass is a flowering plant that grows underwater. It serves several very important functions. It provides habitat and a place to hide for young fish and other aquatic life; it helps to filter water, improving water quality and clarity; and it helps to keep sediments on the bay floor in place. At low tide, mudflats are widespread in the Great Bay. Birds, snails, crabs, and clams feed and burrow in the nutrient-rich mudflats. Channel bottom habitats provide refuge for aquatic life when the tide is low. Oysters thrive very well in these habitats. Rocky intertidal habitats are known for their seaweeds, barnacles, and mussels. The salt marsh areas are rich wetlands areas with smooth cord grass, salt meadow hay, and hosts of fish and animal life hiding in the wetland tangle of plants. Salt marshes are common in estuaries because they need low-energy tides and areas where fresh water and salt water come together.

The forest areas contain red maple, red pine, red oak, white pine, quaking aspen, shagbark hickory, black gum, and sweet pepper bush. At home in the estuary are shrimp, mud snails, green crabs, and soft-shelled clams. Harbor seals have been spotted in the estuary, and many types of fish are commercially harvested. Great Bay Estuary is known for being the most significant winter nesting spot for bald eagles in the Northeast, and osprey nests have been observed in the reserve.

In addition to bald eagles, many other endangered species live in the Great Bay. Common loons, pied-billed grebes, common terns, northern harriers, sedge wrens, and Henslow's sparrows can be seen. Plants considered rare in the state of New Hampshire— such as robust knotweed, hairy brome grass, and lined bulrush—can be found at a place called Adams Point. Other state rare plants in the estuary include marsh elder, large salt marsh aster, prolific knotweed, salt marsh gerardia, and dwarf glasswort.

The reserve covers more than 10,000 acres and is managed by the New Hampshire Department of Fish and Game. A group called the Great Bay Stewards assist with fundraising endeavors that support educational opportunities for visitors and local residents. Much research is being conducted at the reserve, some of it being carried out by the University of New Hampshire's Jackson Estuarine Laboratory. Since 1982, the New Hampshire Department of Environmental Services has directed a coastal program that is responsible for the restoration and protection of New Hampshire's natural resources while also serving the economic needs of the people who live in the state's coastal region.

The program emphasizes controlling water pollution and fostering citizen stewardship activities. There are also many volunteer opportunities available for people who want to help protect this magnificent New Hampshire coastal region.

The importance of the Great Bay Estuary and Reserve cannot be overstated. In addition to its natural resources that are critical for New Hampshire, this area offers a respite from urban living for people who live in the region; it provides economic vitality through its fishing industry; and it helps to support the larger Gulf of Maine watershed.

Further Reading

Great Bay National Estuarine Research Reserve. http://www.greatbay.org/.

National Estuarine Research Reserve System. "Great Bay Reserve, New Hampshire." http://www.nerrs.noaa.gov/GreatBay/.

U.S. Department of Commerce, National Oceanic and Atmospheric Administration. "Ocean and Coastal Management in New Hampshire." http://coastalmanagement. noaa.gov/mystate/nh.html.

LOVERENS MILL CEDAR SWAMP PRESERVE

In Antrim, New Hampshire, at the north branch of the Contoocook River, there is a nature preserve that is quite unusual. Loverens Mill Cedar Swamp Preserve provides a home for the rare Atlantic white cedar and is an excellent example of a boreal swamp that is more typical of climates farther north. At 1,040 feet, Loverens Mill receives channeled cold air from the surrounding hills, prompting the presence of more northern species such as black spruce and tamarack. This area also boasts remarkable diversity in plant and animal life and is a preserved page of human history.

Atlantic white cedar swamps are rare and extraordinary natural communities. Perhaps one reason why Atlantic white cedar trees have become rare is because they grow very slowly. Trees that are hundreds of years old may only be one foot in height. This slow growth makes them susceptible to invasive trees and plants within the swamp. Water levels in the swamp must be ample since the tree's roots are submerged for quite some time, but many swamp areas are drying out due to human activity. Interrupting natural water patterns in the region surrounding the swamp will impact the area's water level. Atlantic white cedar can thrive in a variety of water depths, but too much fluctuation will kill the trees. Atlantic white cedar swamps are extremely valuable for their ability to remove toxins from water, but they require buffer zones due to the negative impact of development on the community. These swamps have a high level of organic peat and are usually highly acidic. Examinations of the pollen within the peat have determined that Atlantic white cedar has been growing in the swamp for 4,000 years.

What else is growing at Loverens Mill Cedar Swamp? Sphagnum moss, red maple, mountain holly, sheep laurel, cinnamon fern, maleberry, and smooth winterberry are some of the wetland plants thriving at the preserve. Yellow loosestrife adorns the bog mats in the summer. Also known as swamp candles, this handsome plant with fiery golden-yellow blossoms is hardy with creeping roots. It is sometimes viewed as invasive because of its ability to spread, but its captivating flower makes it hard not to admire.

The presence of bright green Hessel's hairstreak butterfly is a strong indicator that Atlantic white cedar is nearby. This lovely butterfly only feeds on Atlantic white cedar, so if the tree is lost as a species, the butterfly will be lost as well. Other noteworthy creatures stirring in the swamp are ebony jewelwing damselflies, otter, mink, muskrat, beaver, coyote, moose, white-tailed deer, and black bear. Birds that frequent the swamp include Louisiana waterthrush, veery, white-throated sparrow, hermit thrush, wild turkey, and black-capped chickadee.

Most natural areas have a story to tell about the people who live or have lived within their boundaries. Loverens Mill Cedar Swamp Preserve was once the site of a saw- and grain mill in the late 1700s. Originally built by Samuel Dinsmore, the mill had had several owners until Joseph Loverens bought the mill in 1864. For more than a century, this mill produced important wood products, such as barrels, buckets, and shingles for houses. Remnants of mill activity are still present at the preserve as a reminder of early settler use of the land.

A three-mile trail in the preserve allows visitors to observe all that the area has to offer including a boardwalk that passes through a stunning stand of Atlantic white cedar, boulders dropped by glaciers 15,000 years ago, and the glistening waters of the Contoocook River. Owned by the Nature Conservancy, the preserve was recently expanded to 1,268 acres of high-priority conservation in New Hampshire.

Further Reading

Kricher, John, and Gordon Morrison. *A Field Guide to Eastern Forests, North America.* Boston: Houghton Mifflin, 1998.

Nature Conservancy. "Loverens Mill Cedar Swamp." http://www.nature.org/wherewework/northamerica/states/newhampshire/preserves/art956.html.

New Hampshire Department of Environmental Services Atlantic White Cedar Communities. http://des.nh.gov/organization/commissioner/pip/factsheets/cp/documents/cp-20.pdf.

MOUNT MONADNOCK

There are places considered so sacred and captivating that poets feel moved to write about them, painters are inspired to capture their beauty, and musicians write songs to capture the emotions stirred by such places. Mount Monadnock in Chesire County, New Hampshire, in the towns of Jaffrey and Dublin is just a little more than 22 miles east of the Connecticut River and 10 miles north of the state border. Many people believe that it is the most hiked mountain in the United States and that it holds worldwide hiking popularity, ranking second to Mount Fuji in Japan.

Monadnock rises above sea level to about 3,165 feet. It is mostly bald at its summit due to fires, but the open space allows for scenic, far-reaching vistas to the peaks of Vermont and Massachusetts. Vegetation on the mountain includes blueberries, mountain cranberries, trillium, lady's slippers, and devil's paintbrush. Wildlife such as moose, deer, black bear, falcons, wood turtles, and hawks live on the mountain. Geologically speaking, a monadnock is an isolated area that is much higher than its surrounding landscape due to erosion. The higher hills, being made of a strong, erosion-resistant bedrock such as quartzite, become isolated as the surrounding rock erodes away. The mountain is also known for its mineral spring.

Mount Monadnock has a long history of human involvement. Once covered with red spruce, the bald summit is a result of burnings implemented to clear the area so it could be used as pastureland, but also to destroy wolf dens. Wolves that lived on the mountain were feeding on the sheep owned by nearby farmers. Because of its popularity, visitors who are looking for solitude may not be satisfied with a hike on one of Mount Monadnock's many trails, but citizens and conservations groups have been fighting for and protecting this mountain for a very long time with much success as the mountain has been an attractive site for developers for the last century. The mountain is owned by the Society for the Protection of New Hampshire Forests, the state of New Hampshire, and the town of Jaffrey.

Many paintings have been inspired by the majestic beauty of Monadnock from as early as 1840 with a lithograph drawing by Charles T. Jackson called *Mount Monadnock from Jaffrey* to a 2007 pastel rendering of the mountain by Donna Allen called *Monadnock Reflections in Perkins Pond*. The mountain has been eloquently described in the poetic writings of Ralph Waldo Emerson, John Greenleaf Whittier, H. P. Lovecraft, and in Amy Lowell's "Monadnock in Early Spring," where the poet describes the mountain as "Cloud-topped and splendid, dominating all / The little lesser hills which compass thee." An excerpt from the poem "Monadnock in October" by Civil War poet Edna Dean Proctor captures the mountain's colors:

> Along its slope, where russet ferns were strewn
> And purple heaths, the scarlet maples flamed,
> And reddening oaks and golden birches shone,-
> Resplendent oriels in the black pines framed

There are locations on the mountain that are called Thoreau's Seat and Emerson's Seat after the visionary Transcendentalist writers of 19th-century American literature, but there is no evidence that the authors visited those particular locations. The names of the seats were likely created in honor of the philosophical writings of these New England authors who valued a deep, spiritual connection with the nonhuman natural world.

Making Mount Monadnock all the more intriguing is a cave shrouded in mystery, called Pumpelly Cave. The location of the cave is unmarked, and legend suggests that those who wanted to visit the cave in the 19th century were blindfolded so they couldn't reveal its location. Even today, park rangers will not reveal the cave's location.

Few places in the northeast have inspired, mystified, and mesmerized as many people as Mount Monadnock. The cultural history of the mountain is as rich as its natural wonders, and the people who have been fighting for its preservation know that the mountain is far more valuable than anything that could ever be built upon it. Sometimes referred to as the Grand Monadnock, the mountain inspired a poem called "Monadnock Mountain and Its Surroundings" by Amos A. Parker around 1870. The first stanza reveals how many people feel about the Monadnock.

> In Southern Cheshire
> The mountains appear
> Scattered around with a liberal hand,
> But one looms up tall
> Far above them all
> And long since was christened the Grand.

Further Reading

Brandon, Craig. *Monadnock: More than a Mountain*. Keene, NH: Surry Cottage Books, 2008.

Mount Monadnock. http://www.monadnockmountain.com/.

Timlow, Elizabeth Weston. *The Heart of Monadnock*. Keene, NH: Surry Cottage Books, 1922.

MOUNT WASHINGTON

In the heart of the White Mountain National Forest stands a mountain that is not only the highest peak in New Hampshire, but it is also the highest peak north of the Smoky Mountains and east of the Mississippi River. Towering at 6,288 feet, Mount Washington is a place that inspires awe in everyone who sees it. Known for its wild and dangerous weather that is in constant flux, the mountain is an important scientific laboratory for the study of New England's air pollution and its impact on climate change.

Once called Agiocochook, Mount Washington's first early colonist to reach the mountain's summit was Darby Field in 1642. Two more centuries passed before there was any known activity on the mountain. Later, Mount Washington became so popular that the summit was called the "City among the Clouds." The Great Fire of 1908 changed this bustling activity as dry climate and high winds caused a raging fire that turned every structure into ash and rubble except for the Tip Top House, which still stands on the summit today. The Mount Washington Observatory was established in 1932, and, ever since, the erratic weather of the mountain has been daily documented.

The Mount Washington Observatory is a nonprofit organization that is committed to conducting research at Mount Washington for the purpose of studying the mountain's cloud constitution and atmospheric composition. The observatory also explores regional air quality, weather changes at the summit, ice physics, and climate change. In the 1990s, a project called AIRMAP was created to monitor air pollutants in New England and their impact on the region's climate. Housed at the University of New Hampshire's Climate Change Research Center, AIRMAP scientists keep daily records of atmospheric conditions in order to analyze trends and make predictions about future climate variability. In the spring of 1934, a wind gust measured at the summit of Mount Washington set a record for the highest surface wind speed ever documented anywhere on earth. Due to the convergence of several weather systems, a super hurricane developed that created the 231-miles-per-hour wind that still holds the record today.

On a clear day, views from the summit of Mount Washington can reach as far as 100 miles, but at least half the time, the summit is shrouded in dense cloud cover. The mountain is part of the New Hampshire Presidential Mountain Range that is about 12 miles in length with its peaks named after U.S. presidents. Mount Monroe, Mount Jefferson, and Mount Eisenhower are a few examples. Naming the mountain peaks after presidents has not been widely embraced by everyone. Reverend Thomas Starr King in 1860 openly expressed that the mountains should have retained their original descriptive names given by the Native Americans in the region. But perhaps what is most extraordinary about this mountain range from an ecological standpoint is that above the tree line is the largest U.S. contiguous alpine area east of the Mississippi. This area, which is above 4,500 feet, is decked with dazzling alpine plants, fir scrub, and low spruce. With the frequent icing, high winds, and dramatically fluctuating weather conditions, only a few special plants can survive above the tree line.

The White Mountain National Forest where Mount Washington is located is a New England treasure. With six wilderness areas, nine locations protected because of their remarkable scenery, endless recreational opportunities, and an abundance of wildlife that includes moose and black bear, White Mountain National Forest is a natural wonder that spans central New Hampshire and into Maine. It features alpine natural communities, northern hardwoods, paper birch, and spruce hardwoods. The forest helps to restore 12,000 acres of wetlands, 35 watersheds, and many lakes and streams in the region. A 160-mile stretch of the Appalachian Trail and many other trails for hiking and snowmobiling cross through this remarkable forest, and yet the forest has remained healthy and relatively intact.

Further Reading

AIRMAP. http://airmap.unh.edu/.

Marchand, Peter J. *North Woods: An Inside Look at the Nature of Forests of the Northeast.* Boston: Appalachian Mountain Books, 1987.

Mount Washington Observatory. http://www.mountwashington.org/.

U.S. Forest Service. "White Mountain National Forest." http://www.fs.fed.us/r9/forests/white_mountain/.

Ossipee Lake Natural Area

L ike other natural areas that have been classified as barrens, Ossipee Pine Barrens in New Hampshire was deemed useless by early settlers who found the area's acidic soils ill suited for agriculture. This misunderstanding protected Ossipee Barrens from being turned into farmland, but, as with many barrens, it could have easily been targeted for development prior to the 1980s when efforts to protect the barrens by the Nature Conservancy took a foothold. Now, Ossipee Pine Barrens is the last intact pitch pine/scrub oak forest remaining in New Hampshire.

More than 2,000 acres of this preserve are protected for their biodiversity and for their ability to filter water and provide clean water to people who live in the Ossipee region. Home to the globally rare pitch pine/scrub oak forest, Ossipee Pine Barrens hosts rare moths and butterflies as well as bird species that are being observed less and less in New Hampshire. Roughly 900 acres of the preserve is comprised of this pitch pine/scrub oak forest. There are several hiking trails in the preserve and wild blueberries that visitors can pick near the end of summer.

Nearby is the state-owned Ossipee Lake Natural Area of 400 acres. Recognized by conservationists as one of the most important natural areas in New Hampshire, Ossipee Lake has significant pond shore natural communities and several rare plant species such as hairy hudsonia, sand cherry, and fine grass-leaved goldenrod. It is also identified as an important archeological site due to the numerous findings that shed light on the Native American populations that once lived in the region. One of the biggest threats to the shoreline and sandplain communities of Ossipee Lake is recreation. This activity has threatened the fragile vegetation and habitats and has called into question Ossipee Lake's designation as a natural area.

In spring 2007, the Nature Conservancy published an update that details progress that has been made and future plans for restoring the Ossipee Pine Barrens. Through generous donations and grants, hundreds of additional acres of land have been acquired for protection. One of the primary methods of restoring the barrens is through prescribed burnings. These burnings not only help to promote growth of the unique plant communities in the barrens but they also help to protect local residents from uncontrolled wildfires. As woodland debris such as branches, leaves, twigs, and vegetation builds up on the barrens, it acts as fuel that could spark wildfires. Either through lightning or human initiation, these wild fires have historically been the way the pine barrens have been naturally maintained until nearby residential and commercial development suppressed the burnings. As a result, much debris has accumulated, and the flora and fauna of the barrens have become threatened. Species such as white pine that do not tolerate fire very well have been growing in the barrens and overtaking the pitch pine/scrub oak community. Pitch pine's thick bark protects the tree during fire, and its seeds disseminate and sprout most successfully in burning areas. Scrub oak and blueberry thrive after burnings, and butterflies and moths are strongly attracted to their vegetation.

An important step in safeguarding nearby homes and businesses from fire is to create fire protection buffer zones of 200 to 300 feet. By thinning out the trees, clearing

Ossipee Lake. (Courtesy of John Thomas)

the brush, and keeping the areas mowed, the likelihood of fire in these zones is greatly reduced. With the help of state and local agencies, the Nature Conservancy will conduct numerous prescribed burnings within the barrens in future years during appropriate weather conditions in order to support the restoration of the pine barrens' natural communities. This will help to ensure the survival of the plants and animals that have adapted to the conditions of burned regions while also protecting the barrens as a fantastic filtering system that will provide clean water to people who live in the Silver Lake watershed.

Further Reading

Anderson, Roger, C., James S. Fralish, and Jerry M. Baskin, eds. *Savannas, Barrens, and Rock Outcrop Plant Communities of North America.* New York: Cambridge University Press, 1999.

Forman, Richard T. T. *Pine Barrens: Ecosystem and Landscape.* New Brunswick, NJ: Rutgers University Press, 1998.

Nature Conservancy. "Your Land, Your Water, Your Future." http://www.nature.org/wherewework/northamerica/states/newhampshire/files/opbcampbroch.pdf.

VICKIE BUNNELL PRESERVE

North of the spectacular White Mountain National Forest and south of the Con-necticut Lakes Region of New Hampshire is another natural area significant to the granite state. The Vickie Bunnell Preserve is a wellspring of biodiversity with old-growth forests, a cranberry bog wetland complex, northern hardwood forest, alpine habitats, rocky cliffs, and 28 miles of meandering streams. There are 13 mountain peaks higher than 3,000 feet in this area, one being the elegant Bunnell Mountain that stands at 3,723 feet. Furthermore, the 10,330-acre Vickie Bunnell Preserve holds a high elevation balsam fir and spruce fir forest that is considered the best of its kind north of the White Mountains.

Named after Vickie Bunnell, a former local judge and nature enthusiast, the preserve is part of the larger Vickie Bunnell Tract, and it is connected to the Nash Stream State Forest in order to protect an expansive natural corridor for wildlife. Other properties in the area that add to this conservation block are the Lake Umbagog National Wildlife Refuge and the West Mountain Wildlife Management Area in Vermont. Wildlife roam-ing the area include bobcat, black bear, moose, deer, coyote, mink, pine marten, north-ern red-belly dace, black-backed woodpecker, and Bicknell's thrush. Rare plants can also be found in the preserve, such as green-bracted orchid, yellow-rattle, boreal bentgrass, lily-leaf twayblade, and millet grass.

The high-elevation balsam fir and spruce fir forests usually occur on slopes within the range of 3,000 to 4,000 feet. Red spruce tends to dominate this natural community, although high-elevation areas have been experiencing a decline in red spruce due to the acid in the clouds that often cloak the summits. This acid fog strips the nutrients from the trees, making them more susceptible to harsh winds and weather. Another challenge for this rare natural community is the budworm. The balsam fir is the tree that is the pri-mary host for the budworm in the northeast, although other trees such as the red spruce and black spruce are also hosts. A balsam fir and red spruce forest is the most likely site to find a budworm infestation.

The nearby Lake Umbagog National Wildlife Refuge is an important area as well, spanning 7,000 acres and providing diverse waterfowl spawning grounds and a vital wet-land complex. In 1972, a place in the refuge called Harper's Meadow was designated a Floating Island National Natural Landmark to emphasize the significance of the rich floating bog natural community of Harper's Meadow. The refuge includes the same wild-life that traverses the Bunnell Tract, and the fish swimming in Lake Umbagog provide food for the bald eagles, ospreys, and common loons that soar over its glassy surface.

This area of New Hampshire has seen its share of timber harvesting, and half of the Nash Stream Forest is still managed for the acquisition of timber. At 18,680 acres, the Bunnell Tract has been undergoing restoration projects to protect its abundant natural resources. One aspect of the restoration includes removing old logging roads and cul-verts to help bring back natural water patterns that will encourage forest and vegetation growth in the area. In some cases, water bars are being used that cross over the old road bed to promote water flow. Some of the roads are at high elevations, creating major erosion problems.

To protect the balsam fir and spruce fir forests that are so important to the Vickie Bunnell Preserve, more research is being conducted to study the impact of atmospheric conditions, climate change, and budworm outbreaks on this natural community. But the fact that the preserve and the Bunnell Tract forestlands are relatively unfragmented is a good sign that this natural area is in good health, and the current conservation efforts and restoration projects will help to keep it that way.

Further Reading

Kricher, John, and Gordon Morrison. *A Field Guide to Eastern Forests, North America.* Boston: Houghton Mifflin, 1998.

Marchand, Peter J. *North Woods: An Inside Look at the Nature of Forests of the Northeast.* Boston: Appalachian Mountain Books, 1987.

Nature Conservancy. "Vickie Bunnell Preserve." http://www.nature.org/wherewework/ northamerica/states/newhampshire/preserves/art6158.html.

Sweetwater Trust. http://www.sweetwatertrust.org/.

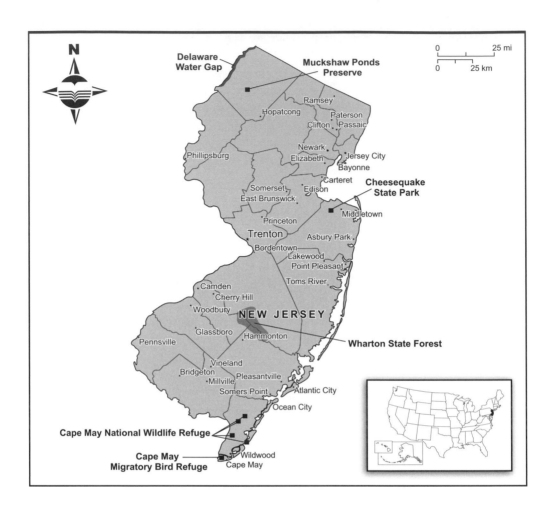

Cape May Migratory Bird Refuge, 92
Cap May National Wildlife Refuge, 93
Cheesequake State Park, 95
Delaware Water Gap, 97
Muckshaw Ponds Preserve, 98
Wharton State Forest, 99

NEW JERSEY

New Jersey is not well known for its natural areas, but the criticism that New Jersey has little to offer in terms of its natural resources is not fair. The negative reputation stems from the state's dense population, its industrial past, and its location along the highly populated eastern seaboard with two major cities not far away. In fact, many of the counties are considered to be suburban areas of either New York to the north or Philadelphia to the south. But New Jersey has a thriving tourism industry as people flock to its beaches each year to enjoy the seashore, and Cape May is the stopover site for thousands of birds migrating along the Atlantic Flyway. In the state's northwest Highlands (or Skylands) lies the Delaware Water Gap National Recreation Area, which is 67,000 acres of forest, lakes, ponds, ridges, valleys, and floodplain that stretch across western New Jersey and eastern Pennsylvania. It is the largest natural area in the national park system between Virginia and Maine.

Perhaps the most important natural area is the New Jersey Pine Barrens. Covering a vast one million acres in the state's coastal plain region, the area was designated the Pinelands National Reserve in 1978. It is an area abundant in wildlife and rare, native plant species while also being rich in cultural history and folklore. The Pine Barrens are maintained by encouraging natural fire regimes, discouraging potentially damaging development, and educating visitors to promote appropriate recreational activities. To illustrate the global significance of the Pine Barrens, in 1983, the area was designated a United Nations International Biosphere Reserve. The reserve was initially created to protect open lands and discourage further development, but it now safeguards some of the state's most valuable natural resources, one of which is the Kirkwood-Cohansey Aquifer that contains more than 17 trillion gallons of water. The pinelands are also used for blueberry and cranberry production.

New Jersey's conservation programs address air quality, water quality, the protection of open spaces, and the cleanup of brownfields. Climate change is a concern for the state because of its coastal location and the potential impact of rising seawaters along its shoreline that may threaten protected areas and create hazards along the highly developed beachfronts. A program that was created to minimize the state's greenhouse gas emissions is the New Jersey Clean Energy Program. This initiative encourages the use of renewable energy sources and energy-efficient home and business practices through financial incentives. Also to address the issue of climate change and to promote environmental health, the New Jersey Cool Cities Initiative was implemented to plant thousands of trees in urban areas to reduce energy costs, improve air quality, and enhance the general environmental health of the state's cities.

New Jersey is also one of the few states to acknowledge environmental justice as an issue for its citizens. Environmental justice concerns refer to areas that have low-income and racially segregated communities that are often targets for landfills, waste dumps, or environmental neglect. These communities often lack the political and economic power to implement environmental policies in their communities and are at greater risk of suffering health conditions related to the air, water, and land qualities of their neighborhoods. According to the New Jersey Department of Environmental Protection, "various studies show communities of color and low-income communities are exposed to a disproportionate amount of industrial pollution and other environmental hazards." The state's Environmental Justice Program is designed to restore and revitalize these communities to promote ecological and public health.

Cape May Migratory Bird Refuge

Along the New Jersey shoreline, it is hard to find a stretch of beachfront that hasn't been overtaken by development, but on the southwest tip of the Cape May Peninsula, the Cape May Migratory Bird Refuge preserves one mile of New Jersey's coastal biodiversity and is the stopover site for thousands of birds migrating along the Atlantic Flyway. The refuge, owned by the Nature Conservancy since 1981, attracts bird enthusiasts and researchers from around the world who get the chance to see species that fly many thousands of miles from the Arctic to their southern feeding grounds. The refuge is also a nesting site for some birds, including the threatened piping plover and least tern. Piping plovers during the 19th century were plentiful along the Atlantic coastline until hunting for the millinery (hat making) trade devastated the species. Numbers recovered due to the Migratory Bird Treaty Act of 1918 but then dramatically declined again during the second half of the 20th century because of extensive development and recreational use along the beaches. While most of the year the beach is open to public access, some areas are closed during the spring season to protect these beach-nesting birds.

Totaling 229 acres in West Cape May Borough off Bayshore Road, the Cape May Migratory Bird Refuge is a resting spot for birds all year-round. In May, the refuge is visited by the largest number of migratory and unusual species; during the summer months, the piping plover chicks, warblers, and shorebirds populate the refuge. In the colder months, the peregrine falcon, Cooper's hawk, and other raptors frequent the area.

Locally known as The Meadows, the area's ponds, marshes, meadows, dunes, and coastline host aquatic and plant communities important to the region, and the refuge's coastal waters hold an interesting history. The remains of a town named South Cape May rests scattered about the ocean floor just offshore from the refuge. Once a Victorian resort town, South Cape May was pummeled by a storm in the 1950s and is now buried under the sea. The lost town is a testament to the importance of dunes, which protect inland communities from storm surge.

In June 2007, the refuge reopened to visitors after undergoing an extensive restoration project. Being heavily impacted by shoreline erosion, the refuge was showing significant signs of wetland degradation from salt water encroaching upon freshwater marshes, allowing for prominent growth of invasive plants and threats to freshwater species. This multimillion-dollar restoration project was necessary to protect an area that is considered one of the top avian viewing locations in the world. The New Jersey Department of Environmental Protection, the Army Corps of Engineers, and the Nature Conservancy of New Jersey worked in partnership to create a one-mile dune in the refuge, replenish the beach, inhibit the growth of phragmites (tall, reedy plants), and improve drainage patterns. They also built two ponds that would support the endangered piping plover, five ponds for the southern gray tree frog, islands for gulls and terns, levees to protect the area from flooding, and a 60-foot-wide channel to allow the Nature Conservancy to manage water levels in the refuge. For visitor education and enjoyment, a new trail, viewing platform, visitor's booth, and improved parking conditions have been added. Reports from the Nature Conservancy indicate that the restoration efforts showed signs of success almost immediately as birds and other species began to populate and utilize the restored areas. It is estimated that more than one million seabirds and 60,000 raptors migrate through the Cape May Migratory Bird Refuge each year, making it a high-priority area for preservation by state, private, and federal agencies.

Further Reading

Stone, Witmer, and Roger Tory. *Bird Studies at Old Cape May: An Ornithology of Coastal New Jersey*. Mechanicsburg, PA: Stackpole Books, 2000.

Sutton, Clay, and Pat Sutton. *Birds and Birding at Cape May*. Mechanicsburg, PA: Stackpole Books, 2006.

CAPE MAY NATIONAL WILDLIFE REFUGE

Established in the mid-1970s, the Ramsar Convention, known as the Convention on Wetlands of International Importance, is an international treaty formed to recognize and protect wetland areas due to their ecological, scientific, and cultural importance. The Ramsar agreement calls for a sustainable use of fragile wetlands and commitment to conservation of these areas. In 1992, the Cape May National Wildlife Refuge was designated a Ramsar site. The refuge is on the Ramsar list because it provides habitat for thousands of migratory birds, including songbirds, woodcock, raptors, and shorebirds. While the refuge hosts about 317 bird species, it is also home to 42 mammal species and 55 reptile and amphibian species.

Part of the Delmarva Coastal Area Ecosystem, the refuge has three units: the Delaware Bay Division, the Great Cedar Swamp Division, and Two Mile Beach area. The Delaware Bay Division, located on the western coastal regions of the Cape May Peninsula, has numerous important habitats, including grasslands, vernal pools, forest wetlands, and salt marshes, and it is an important breeding ground for the horseshoe crab.

The Great Cedar Swamp is home to a large contiguous forest, bogs, marshes, hardwood swamps, and Atlantic white cedar stands. The area is part of the Pinelands National Reserve and Great Egg Harbor National Scenic and Recreational River. The Two Mile Beach area is comprised of beachfront, maritime forest, tidal ponds, as well as migratory and beach-nesting birds throughout the year.

The refuge, founded in 1989, currently protects 11,000 acres with future plans to significantly expand. As suburban sprawl continues to grow in New Jersey, with housing developments and shopping plazas being built on a regular basis, the refuge becomes increasingly critical to the ecological health of the Cape May Peninsula. Wetlands not only provide protection from storm surge, but they also act as a filter for the water supply by removing toxins and impurities. They regulate river flow; provide spawning zones and habitats for plants, insects, and birds; support the region's biodiversity; and offer flood protection for inland communities. The marshes and waterways in the refuge provide important breeding and feeding resources for crabs, summer flounder, and striped bass, which are important species to the local recreational and commercial fishers in Cape May.

Two Mile Beach is a confirmed nesting site for the endangered piping plover. Bald eagles and the peregrine falcon, both on the federal list of endangered and threatened animals, use the refuge during their migration, while species listed as endangered on the New Jersey state list include ospreys, several species of owls and herons, mud salamanders, and corn snakes. A rare species of lily called the swamp pink also lives on the refuge in addition to roughly 34 state-listed endangered plants.

As Cape May County continues to be developed, there are few places where people can go to enjoy nature and experience the peace and quiet of a forest canopy and fresh air. The importance of natural areas to the physical and psychological health of the local community in these highly developed regions cannot be underestimated. In addition to the restorative qualities, the refuge is perhaps one of the few remaining places where a sense of Cape May's ecological history can be found, where people can connect to the Cape May that existed before the landscape became valuable primarily for its commercial use. The refuge continues to implement area management plans to preserve this remnant of the old Cape May while also improving upon trails and visitor accommodations for those who seek the Cape May National Wildlife Refuge, whether for research, education, birding, solitude, or exercise.

Further Reading

Beans, Bruce E., and Larry Niles, eds. *Endangered and Threatened Wildlife of New Jersey.* New Brunswick, NJ: Rutgers University Press, 2003.
Lomax, Joseph L. *The Wildlife of Cape May County, New Jersey: A Habitat Guide to the Vertebrate Fauna.* Stone Harbor, NJ: Wetlands Institute, 1980.

CHEESEQUAKE STATE PARK

Some natural areas deserve special attention not only for what they are but also for what they have overcome. Cheesequake State Park in Middlesex County is one of those places. Situated in northeast New Jersey, just south of New York City, Cheesequake has seen its share of urban and suburban industrial pollutants. Originally, this land was a hunting and fishing area for the Lenni Lenape Indians. It was then used as a port for ships and commerce by early colonists. The wreckage of an old dock still exists on Cheesequake Creek. The land was then the site of a ceramics factory before being purchased in 1938 and established as a park in 1940. Today Cheesequake is next door to a massive landfill, surrounded by development, downstream from the largest metropolitan area in the United States, split by the busy Garden State Parkway, and still it finds a way to be a prized location of biodiversity and a combination of ecosystems significant to the state. Cheesequake, feeling the pressure of development on all of its boundaries, is an oasis in the middle of bustle and industry. The interpretive center in the park is useful for visitors who want to learn more about human interaction with the nonhuman natural environment.

Cheesequake, as a natural area, is important for being a transitional zone, a place where the southern New Jersey hardwood forests and pine barrens meet the northern coastal salt marshes and wetlands. This zone creates a climate that is rich with vegetation and is appealing to hikers and bicyclists, who experience moving from one ecosystem to another on a relatively short trail system. Trails meander through white cedar groves, pitch pine forests, and salt marshes.

There are other unique aspects of Cheesequake State Park. It has been said that this park's curious name comes from *cheseh-oh-ke,* a Lenni Lenape word meaning "upland." Also, because of the pitch pines at Cheesequake, there are amber formations in the park. Due to a strong storm in 1993 that caused flooding in the area, plant debris around the salt marsh carrying large amounts of plant and tree resin was pushed ashore in ball formations, making Cheesequake a useful location for the study of amber deposits. Central New Jersey has been a prime location for the study of fossilized amber dating back to the Cretaceous age, between 135 and 65 million years ago. Many insects, plants, and flowers have been collected fossilized within this bronze gem.

Cheesequake State Park rests on the west end of the Raritan Bay. Once a vibrant fishing area in the 19th and early 20th centuries, Raritan is currently used primarily for recreation. The second half of the 20th century saw Raritan become an ecological

A Swamp in Cheesequake Park. (Courtesy of Miguel Vieira)

disaster due to pollution from the densely populated surrounding development. The old ceramic factories left behind substantial amounts of chemical waste in the ground that have filtered into the land and bay. DDT that was once sprayed to control mosquitoes has been found in high doses; runoff from landfills; and a wide array of toxins from household, sewer, and construction near the bay have turned the water into a chemical and waste reservoir. But there is hope. Several citizen and state agencies work to preserve and protect the ecological integrity of Raritan.

Despite the pollution of the bay, recreational fishing is popular, and many local residents go to Cheesequake to swim along the bay shoreline. Cheesequake is a testament to nature's insistence to survive even under the most challenging circumstances humanity has created for it. The park remains a botanical preserve with a wide assortment of wildflowers, several miles of scenic trails, a meeting place for New Jersey's distinct ecosystems, and an opportunity to study the devastating impact human activity can have on the environment.

Further Reading

Brown, Michael. *New Jersey Parks, Forests, and Natural Areas.* Piscataway, NJ: Rutgers University Press, 2004.

New Jersey Department of Environmental Protection. "Cheesequake State Park." http://
www.state.nj.us/dep/parksandforests/parks/cheesequake.html.

DELAWARE WATER GAP

The Delaware Water Gap National Recreation Area is 67,000 acres of forest, lakes,
ponds, ridges, valleys, and floodplain that stretch across western New Jersey and
eastern Pennsylvania. It is the largest natural area in the national park system between Virginia and Maine. Slicing through the Appalachian Mountains and creating
the scenic gap are 40 miles of the Delaware River, which, in total, is 330 miles long
and forms some of the most spectacular waterfalls in New Jersey and Pennsylvania.
Because of the size of the area and the wide range of habitats, many different kinds of
plants and animals can be seen when visiting. Black bears, otters, fox, wild turkeys,
beavers, and coyotes can be found here as well as more than 260 species of birds and
61 species of fish, 10 of which have been identified as rare. The rivers and streams in
the park have exceptional water quality, and the area supports a diversity of plant life,
including hemlock ravines, hickories, hardwood forests, wildflowers, ferns, rhododendrons, and even cactus barrens with the occasional prickly pear. The hemlock trees
are currently under threat by an insect from Asia called the hemlock woolly adelgid.
This insect harms the trees by sucking out all of the sap, thus killing it. The hemlock
trees are extremely important to the region's ecosystem because they provide necessary shade for native plant species to thrive.

The Delaware Water Gap was initially designed in 1965 to be primarily a recreational area for local residents. Hiking, fishing, painting, and canoeing are popular activities in the area. Some of the most breathtaking vistas can be seen while hiking the
Appalachian Trail that runs along the Kittatinny Mountain ridge in New Jersey. At the
end of the Kittatinny ridge is Mount Tammany, 1,527 feet above sea level, from which
spectacular panoramic views of the gap can be seen. But the gap is no longer valued
just for its recreational opportunities. As development and threatening environmental
degradation became more pronounced, the area became protected as an important conservation area not only for its natural resources but also for its cultural and historical
significance.

The Delaware Water Gap has a controversial history. The park was initially established in 1965 with the intention of having it located in a proposed area surrounding a
reservoir that would be created with the construction of a dam called the Tocks Island
Dam over the Delaware River near Smithfield Beach. The decision to build the dam was
overturned, but many historic homes and buildings were destroyed in preparation for
building the dam. Because of this decision, the Delaware River is one of a few remaining
major rivers in the United States that does not have a dam or some other structure to
control water flow, and, therefore, special effort has been made to preserve existing buildings that tell the stories of the history and cultures that influenced the area. To share the

rich history of the area, a newsletter called *Spanning the Gap* was created and written by park rangers for visitors and researchers.

Some other interesting facts are that, in the 19th century, the Delaware Water Gap was considered a Wonder of the World and was even then a tourist attraction. The area was also once the site of the French and Indian War, and numerous historic colonial settlements in New Jersey are still intact. The area is considered important for its archeological treasures. Archeologists have found evidence of prehistoric populations that once lived in the area, which has shed considerable light on studies attempting to identify and understand Native American tribes that lived along the eastern seaboard.

Further Reading

Brodhead, L. W. *The Delaware Water Gap: Its Scenery, Its Legends, and Early History.* Ann Arbor: University of Michigan Scholarly Publishing Office, 2005.

National Park Service. "Delaware Water Gap National Recreation Area." http://www. nps.gov/dewa/.

MUCKSHAW PONDS PRESERVE

Muckshaw Ponds is a 412-acre preserve located in Andover Township in Sussex County, which was established in 1988 in New Jersey's environmentally sensitive northwestern hills and valleys. Muckshaw, considered a Natural Heritage Site, is a marvel of sinkholes and ponds. Managed by the Nature Conservancy, this natural area is a rich botanical resource. The highly alkaline soil, formed by slowly dissolving bedrock beneath the ponds and surrounding ridges, promotes ideal conditions for certain state threatened plants, including white-grained mountain rice, small bedstraw, and rush aster. The rare longtail salamander also makes this preserve its home. Muckshaw's vernal ponds, which are temporary pools of water, fill up with water in winter and spring and then dry out in the summer and fall. The plants in the region have done well in adapting to wet conditions for half the year and dry conditions for the rest of the year. While the preserve has many small ponds, there is one larger pond trimmed in a limestone ridge and a hardwood forest. The preserve also has sinking streams that go underground and then reemerge anywhere from a yard to several miles away. This unique combination of ridges, forest, ponds, sinkholes, and rock outcrops makes Muckshaw a wetland of topographical and geological wonder.

Muckshaw Ponds Preserve is of historical interest as well. Lt. James Moody was a Revolutionary War loyalist spy, a North American who provided military services for Britain. Born in 1744 in Sussex County, Moody was a farmer who did not take much interest in the war until his farm was attacked by rebels in 1777. There are many legends surrounding Moody's persona, but he apparently risked his life freeing prisoners, seeking intelligence by impersonating a rebel, and recruiting other loyalists. Referred to as "that villain Moody" by George Washington, Moody made Muckshaw his hideaway by living in one of its large rock shelters while supporting the British cause during the Revolutionary War.

The Nature Conservancy has been working hard to protect and expand Muckshaw Ponds Preserve. In 2005, the conservancy purchased a substantial tract of land that connects the preserve to the nearby 1,900-acre Whittingham Wildlife Management Area. Without this purchase, it is likely that this tract of land would have been developed for residential housing. With the expansion connecting Muckshaw to the Whittingham area, a long greenway was created that helps further support plant and wildlife in the region, as well as protect water quality for millions of people in the region.

At another area in the preserve, the Nature Conservancy is working with a tenant farmer to balance agricultural demands with preserving the wetland community at Muckshaw that helps maintain the region's water purity. Valley View Farms has reduced some of its cropland in order to provide a buffer zone to protect Muckshaw's sinkhole ponds. This forest buffer zone has been restored by the Nature Conservancy through cultivating native plants and a new irrigation system designed to put less stress on the ponds at Muckshaw.

Muckshaw Ponds Preserve is part of the larger New Jersey Skylands region. Morris, Somerset, Sussex, Huntingdon, and Warren counties in Northwest New Jersey are all considered part of the Skylands. This region of New Jersey is a popular tourist and recreation area because of its 60,000 acres of state parkland, two national parks, ridges, valleys, bustling towns and villages, orchards, back roads, and rivers. The Appalachian Trail crosses through the Skylands at the Delaware Water Gap, and this region is teeming with history of the American Revolution. The Skylands region of New Jersey, with its hidden treasures such as Muckshaw Ponds Preserve, is a significant place indeed for a state that has received harsh criticism for its overdevelopment and perhaps unfair reputation as an industrial land of turnpikes and factories absorbing the pollution of New York City.

Further Reading

Cunningham, John T. *This Is New Jersey*. New Brunswick, NJ: Rutgers University Press, 1994.

Shenstone, Susan Burgess. *So Obstinately Loyal: James Moody, 1744–1809*. Montreal, Quebec: McGill-Queen's University Press, 1999.

WHARTON STATE FOREST

Originally inhabited by the Lenni Lenape Indians, the Pine Barrens of New Jersey are dark, lush, dense, and beautiful landscapes. The old, abandoned sandy roads and the ancient visage of the pines, swamps, and bogs make the pinelands a place of legend and folklore. The Batsto River with its meandering water percolating the color of tea only enhances the mystery of this extraordinary area. The most notable legend is that of the New Jersey Devil. According to the legend, Deborah Smith Leeds, pregnant with her 13th child, was so tired of being pregnant that she cursed the birth of her 13th child, claiming that she would rather give birth to the devil's child than to give another child to her conceited husband. It is said that Leeds gave birth to a creature that has the head of horse, wings like a dragon, and a four-foot-long serpentine torso. While there are many variations to the story, the Jersey Devil is said to still be living in the New Jersey pinelands, and seeing the creature is a bad omen forecasting imminent disaster and tragedy.

Wharton State Forest is part of the larger New Jersey National Pinelands Reserve. The Pine Barrens, which span more than one million acres in central New Jersey, represent the largest undeveloped area between Boston and Richmond, Virginia. Wharton State Forest stretches from the southern border of the Pine Barrens region and into the heart of what is considered the largest representation of pitch pine worldwide.

The Pine Barrens are maintained by encouraging natural fire regimes, discouraging potentially damaging development, and educating visitors to promote appropriate recreational activities. Wharton is home to the Annie M. Carter Nature Interpretive Center,

Batona trail in the Wharton State Forest. (Courtesy of Mark Reynolds)

which is committed to educating students and researchers about the fragile nature of the pinelands and the cost of human impact.

Spreading over 110,000 acres that reach into Camden, Atlantic, and Burlington Counties, Wharton State Forest is the largest in the New Jersey State Park System. The forest includes over 500 miles of unpaved, sandy roads, historic buildings, a pineland ecosystem, cranberry and blueberry farms, rivers, streams, numerous lakes, ponds, trails, impenetrable scrub pine, and a diversity of wildlife and plant species. The land was initially acquired by the industrialist Joseph Wharton. The land remained in the Wharton family until 1954, when the state of New Jersey purchased the land.

Within Wharton Forest are three smaller natural areas: Batsto Natural Area, Oswego River Natural Area, and Atsion Recreation Area. Batsto Natural Area borders the Mullica and the Batsto rivers and includes pine and oak forest communities representative of the pinelands. A shallow aquifer beneath the sandy pinelands is said to contain a substantial amount of pure glacial water. When it bubbles up, it paints the Batsto River the color of tea. What is perhaps more well known about this area is Batsto Historical Village, a restored collection of 33 buildings that were once part of an iron works community that dates back to 1766. The Iron Works Company supplied many wartime products during the American Revolution, including kettles, ammunition, and weaponry. This area was also a glassmaking industrial center and includes buildings such as the post office, sawmill, and the general store, preserved to maintain the 19th-century feel of this historical and industrial center. The Oswego River Natural Area and Preserve is a freshwater wetland that is home to several rare species, including the bog asphodel, pine barrens tree frog, and pine barren boneset. The Oswego River Preserve, managed by the Nature Conservancy, is protected because of its diversity and because its streamside corridor is comprised of cedar swamps, hardwood swamps, and pine barren savannas, all of which are threatened wetlands. Atsion, once a small intentional village like Batsto, is now primarily a public beach and recreation area.

One of Wharton Forest's main attractions is the 50-mile Batona Trail, which stretches from the adjacent Bass River State Forest, north through Wharton, and into the Lebanon State Forest. Created as a wilderness trail in 1961, the name *Batona* stands for BAck TO NAture. A hike along the Batona Trail is a hike through New Jersey's most precious resource: the pinelands ecosystem. The trail is primarily a forest canopy path where a stop at Apple Pie Hill renders a panoramic view of the pinelands region.

Further Reading

Burger, Joanna. *Whispers in the Pines: A Naturalist in the Northeast*. Oklahoma City, OK: Rivergate, 2006.

Forman, Richard T. T. *Pine Barrens: Ecosystem and Landscape*. New Brunswick, NJ: Rutgers University Press, 1998.

Maher, Neil M., ed. *New Jersey's Environments: Past, Present, and Future*. New Brunswick, NJ: Rutgers University Press, 2006.

Mason, Robert J. *Contested Lands: Conflict and Compromise in New Jersey Pine Barrens*. Philadelphia: Temple University Press, 1992.

Adirondack Park, 104

Albany Pine Bush Preserve, 106

Atlantic Double Dunes, 108

Chaumont Barrens Preserve, 109

Finger Lakes, 111

Sam's Point Preserve, 113

Southern Lake Champlain Valley, 114

NEW YORK

In the summer of 1858, one of the most important intellectual gatherings took place at Follensby Pond in the northern Adirondack Mountains. Philosopher, nature luminary, and celebrated literary figure Ralph Waldo Emerson met with nine other intellectuals for what was called the Philosopher's Camp at Camp Maple. This historic meeting gave birth to the Transcendentalist movement and helped to fuel the wilderness preservation movement. According to Christopher McGrory Klyza, "Just as the forests and moose are returning to their homes in the landscape of the region, so too should the wilderness discussion return to the home of its first advocate and the country's first protected wilderness areas in the Adirondacks and Catskills of New York." It was an ideal location for a discussion that brought nature and the arts together in a state that is quite possibly the most diverse state in the northeast United States. Largely forested and rich with diverse natural communities, New York is abundant with natural, historic, and cultural resources. The Adirondacks have wetlands, pinelands, alpine and subalpine communities, spruce and fir slopes, northern hardwood forests, lakes, and mixed wood forests. New York also contains the Catskill Mountains, Shawangunk Mountains, Niagara Falls, Atlantic Ocean beach ecosystems, Great Lakes ecosystems, and the Finger Lakes region known for its water recreation and landscape well suited for wine production. New York's geography is defined by eight ecoregions as defined by the U.S. Environmental Protection Agency. The two main ecoregions are the Eastern Great Lakes/Hudson Lowlands, which is a predominantly agricultural region that spans from the Great Lakes to the Hudson Valley, and the Northeastern Highlands, which include the mountains, forest, and lakes of the Adirondacks and Catskills. Other important ecoregions are the Erie Drift Plains, the Northeastern Coastal Zone, the Northern Appalachian Plateau, the North Central Appalachians, the Ridge and Valley Region, and the Atlantic Coastal Pine Barrens.

Of the environmental threats to the state of New York, controlling invasive species and pollution impacting the water quality of the state's coastal waters, Great Lakes, Finger Lakes, wetlands, and river systems are priorities. Organizations such as the New York State Department of Environmental Conservation, the New York chapters of the Nature Conservancy and Audubon Society, and numerous local organizations are working to monitor the effects of acid rain, particularly in the Adirondacks and Catskills, where the already nutrient-poor soils are unable to neutralize acid deposition. Certain areas of the state are addressing the issue of high levels of mercury in the water sources. In 2006, collaborative efforts involving conservation groups in the Great Lakes basin implemented a program to reduce mercury in products and in waste. This program came after the 2004 New York State law that was passed that bans the sale of certain mercury-loaded products and requires the responsible disposal and labeling of products that contain mercury.

Because of the rapidly growing problem of invasive species in New York State, in 2003, an invasive species task force was created to make recommendations for conservation action toward species that are aggressive and destructive to native species. While some action is being taken to eradicate species that threaten the biodiversity of New York's natural areas, much more funding is needed, particularly from federal sources. According to the New York State Department of Environmental Conservation, "there is no overarching federal legislation that recognizes the magnitude of invasive species as an issue. Thus, there is no dedicated funding stream available for their management." Invasive species and their impact on ecosystems are directly related to habitat loss as birds and other wildlife that depend on the native plants have to find other places to nest and feed, and sometimes are pushed to extinction. Some of the invasive species of New York are zebra mussels, European water chestnut, Eurasian water milfoil, purple loosestrife, and the giant hogweed, which is also a threat to human health.

ADIRONDACK PARK

No other natural area in the northeast United States is home to so many natural communities as Adirondack Park. There are bogs, swamps, marshes, mixed wood forests, pinelands, northern hardwood forests, spruce and fir communities, and subalpine and alpine communities. Additionally, there are a staggering number of lakes, roughly 3,000, and more than 30,000 miles of streams and rivers. The Adirondack Mountains were formed by glaciers millions of years ago. Created in the shape of a dome that is roughly 160 miles wide and 1 mile high, these mountains are quite different from the Appalachian Mountains that form a long stretch of peaks from Georgia to Maine. Spanning a vast six million acres, this diverse park is hard to miss when looking at a New York State map. In fact, Adirondack is the largest protected natural area in the United States.

The New York State Adirondack Park Agency has identified areas within the park that are critical environmental areas. These critical sites tend to be wetlands and high-elevation areas. One exceptionally diverse and rich area within the Adirondack wetland system is Spring Pond Bog Preserve. Varieties of vegetation that populate the area are sheep laurel, bog laurel, Labrador tea, leatherleaf, and rhodora. The plant life that thrives

Along Mt. Jo Trail, Adirondack Park. (Courtesy of Ross Barclay)

in the bog has evolved to do well in the soil that is low in nutrients and highly acidic. To protect the bog, careful management of its surrounding woodland and forest is essential. Trees found in the forest include beech, hemlock, white pine, red maple, sugar maple, red oak, yellow birch, and gray birch.

The high-elevation balsam fir and spruce fir forests of Adirondack usually occur on slopes within the range of 3,000 to 4,000 feet. Red spruce tends to dominate this natural community, although high-elevation areas have been experiencing a decline in red spruce due to the acid in the clouds that often cloak the summits. This acid fog strips the nutrients from the trees, making them more susceptible to harsh winds and weather. Another challenge for this rare natural community is the budworm. The balsam fir is the primary host for the budworm in the Northeast, although other trees such as the red spruce and black spruce are also hosts. A balsam fir and red spruce forest is the most likely site to find a budworm infestation.

Adirondack is a mosaic of public land and privately owned land, which adds to the extraordinary diversity of the region, but human impact on the park is not to be underestimated. In fact, when the park was created in 1892, it was because the region was being heavily exploited for its timber and water resources. In 1971, the Adirondack Park Agency was created to develop land use plans that would protect the park's natural, cultural, and historical resources while promoting recreational opportunities for residents and visitors. Controlling invasive species and restoring native flora and fauna to the park is a priority for the conservation agencies working to protect Adirondack. In 2007, the Adirondack Chapter of the Nature Conservancy made a landmark purchase of 161,000 acres of pristine, intact forest in the geographic and biological center of Adirondack Park that was once owned and carefully managed by the Finch, Pruyn, and Company paper mill. This glorious landscape of 90 mountains, 70 lakes and ponds, and miles of rivers and streams adjoins the Adirondack Forest Preserve to form a vast and seamless tract of protected land. It is the most biologically diverse area in the park, hosting 95 species that are rare or of ecological significance.

Today, there are thousands of miles of remote designated wilderness areas at Adirondack along with open spaces, meadows, hiking and snowmobile trails, camping grounds, and ski slopes. Mount Marcy, New York's highest peak, towering more than 5,300 feet, graces the sky within the High Peaks region of the park and dazzles hikers with its breathtaking views. In 1932 and 1980, Adirondack's Lake Placid took the worldwide stage as the region's snowy mountain slopes and scenery were ideal for the Olympic Winter Games.

Further Reading

Adirondack Park Agency. http://www.apa.state.ny.us/index.html.

Schneider, Paul. *The Adirondacks: A History of America's First Wilderness*. New York: Henry Holt, 1997.

Terrie, Philip G. *Contested Terrain: A New History of Nature and People in the Adirondacks*. Syracuse, NY: Syracuse University Press, 1997.

ALBANY PINE BUSH PRESERVE

There are only a handful of inland pine barrens ecosystems left in the world, and one of the largest is located at the Albany Pine Bush Preserve in Albany, New York. Pitch pine/scrub oak barrens are often comprised of pitch pine, scrub oak, wildflowers, prairie grasses, and huckleberry. At the preserve, there is a sandplain grassland natural community and a wetland area known as the pine barrens vernal ponds that hosts a number of interesting aquatic species. This unique and diverse ecosystem provides habitat for rare species that have adapted themselves to this sandy, well-drained, prairielike environment.

A sandplain grassland is comprised of native grasses and shrubs and is maintained by periodic burning. These grasslands were formed from melting glaciers many thousands of years ago when the glaciers dropped their sand and the streams from the melting water formed sandy plains. The deep sand deposits beneath the grassland allow water to percolate down quickly. Due to this high sand content of the soil, water and nutrients drain away easily, creating a climate that is perhaps prone to drought but also creating rare natural community. Plants that grow on these grasslands are the buttonbush, bulrush, pink lady's slipper, shadbush, wild blue lupine, Indian grass, and little bluestem. Animals in the area include the prairie warbler, great blue heron, eastern coyote, eastern towhee, great horned owl, and the spotted turtle. Some of the more rare species are the eastern spadefoot toad, inland barrens buckmoth, and the Karner blue butterfly.

The curious existence of this inland pine bush suggests a long history of periodic burning by early Native American populations who used the fires to replenish plants that provided nuts and berries. The Mohawk Iroquois lived to the west of the pine bush, while the Mahicans lived to the east. The first European settlers were the Dutch and English, who feared the pine bush because it provided a hiding place for criminals. Despite its dangerous reputation in the 19th century, settlers gathered blueberries, huckleberries, and elderberries in the pine bush. Trees were used for shingles, fences, and firewood; animal pelts were harvested; and the damming of Patroon Creek created Rensselaer Lake, which provided fresh drinking water to residents of Albany.

Threats to the pine bush are invasive species, encroaching residential development, and the lack of natural wildfires. To maintain the grasslands, the Albany Pine Bush Preserve Commission in cooperation with other organizations manages periodic burnings to reduce shrub growth, to allow for the dispersal of rare plant seeds, foster nesting sites for grassland birds, and enhance the nutrient level in the soil. In 1978, a grassroots effort called Save the Pine Bush worked to stop development in the area, and today more than 3,000 acres have been protected to preserve the pine bush for its biodiversity. The pine bush provides extraordinary research and educational opportunities for local schools, colleges, and universities to conduct studies on rare species and their habitats.

The Pine Bush Nature Preserve. (Courtesy of Mike Carey)

Some of the invasive species that are currently threatening the pine bush are garlic mustard, black locust trees, and aspen trees. Although aspen trees are native to the pine bush natural community, the lack of wildfires allows for the aspens to thrive too aggressively, threatening other pine bush vegetation, such as the wild blue lupine. The survival of the federal endangered Karner blue butterfly is largely dependent on wild blue lupine, making this lovely wildflower a conservation priority at the preserve.

The preserve has a trail system that allows for recreational use of the area, and it contains a Discovery Center that includes exhibits and informational items for visitors. The Albany Pine Bush Preserve Commission continues to acquire more land to provide an appropriate buffer zone for pine and to ensure the long-term protection of this rare ecosystem.

Further Reading

Albany Pine Bush Preserve Commission. http://www.albanypinebush.org/main.htm.

Forman, Richard T. T. *Pine Barrens: Ecosystem and Landscape*. New Brunswick, NJ: Rutgers University Press, 1998.

Colvin, Roderick. "Community-Based Environment Protection, Citizen Participation, and the Albany Pine Bush Preserve. *Society & Natural Resources* 15, no. 5 (May/June 2002): 447–54.

ATLANTIC DOUBLE DUNES

A double dune geologic formation is a unique coastal occurrence that contains an ecosystem that is quite rare in the state of New York. One of the best remaining examples of this formation is Atlantic Double Dunes located in East Hampton, Long Island. This 200-acre area contains the primary dune that lies closest to the sea, and further inland is the secondary dune that was formed by waves crashing into the shore thousands of years ago. What lies in between, in the interdunal zone, is a wetland area of exceptional biodiversity.

Formed by thousands of years of erosion and beach building, the Atlantic Double Dunes ecosystem is so fragile that visitation is possible only through guided tours with the Nature Conservancy. Common plants such as American beachgrass and seaside goldenrod thrive in the primary dune area, where the conditions are harsh, but the interdunal zone is a rich habitat for rare species. Roundleaf boneset, southern arrowwood, orchids, and pine-barren sandwort are a few of the rare plants that can be found in the wetland. Other plants located at the site are beach heather, wild indigo, horseweed, and many others. The secondary dune contains growths of oak and pitch pine.

In addition to its coastal biodiversity, Atlantic Double Dunes is the stopover site for birds migrating along the Atlantic Flyway. Studies suggest that the threatened piping plover and least tern have attempted to nest on the beaches of this natural area but with little success due to storm tides and recreational vehicles. Piping plovers during the

19th century were plentiful along the Atlantic coastline until hunting for the millinery trade (hat making) devastated the species. Numbers recovered due to the Migratory Bird Treaty Act of 1918, but then dramatically declined again during the second half of the 20th century because of extensive development and recreational use along the beaches. Other birds that visit this area include swallows, cedar waxwings, hawks, shorebirds, songbirds, and waterfowl. A rare toad called the eastern spadefoot resides in the interdunal wetland as well as the eastern hognose snake, which has steadily been declining in numbers on Long Island.

Recreation or increased human activity would be devastating to the Double Dunes. While it is a site for the research of coastal plant and wildlife communities, increased development in nearby surroundings, recreational vehicles, or the construction of boardwalks and trails would result in fragile habitat loss. The best protection for this irreplaceable habitat and ecosystem is to minimize land disturbance as much as possible.

A second occurrence of the double dune system exists on Long Island at the Amagansett National Wildlife Refuge. Although this protected area is much smaller, the ecosystem is just as diverse and fragile as the Atlantic Double Dunes. Many of the same plants and animal species are present in both places. Amagansett is also an important stopover site for raptors migrating along the Atlantic coast. Peregrine falcons, hawks, and American kestrels have been documented in sizable numbers at the refuge. The Amagansett National Wildlife Refuge is carefully managed to protect the unusual beach and dune habitat. Beach-nesting birds are monitored, human disturbance and nonnative species are controlled, and protecting the dune system is a priority for the U.S. Fish and Wildlife Service. Both Amagansett National Wildlife Refuge and Atlantic Double Dunes are undeveloped beaches on Long Island, and these natural areas are scarce for that reason alone. As with all coastal areas, wind, storms, and tides shape the beaches into what they are, and allowing the natural processes to do their work is an important part of conserving their value.

Further Reading

U.S. Fish and Wildlife Service. "Long Island National Wildlife Refuge Complex." http://www.fws.gov/northeast/longislandrefuges/.

Nature Conservancy. "Atlantic Double Dunes." http://www.nature.org/wherewework/northamerica/states/newyork/preserves/art10986.html.

CHAUMONT BARRENS PRESERVE

Alvar barrens are rare grassland areas that have a thin layer of soil and occur over limestone or dolostone bedrock. Chaumont Barrens Preserve in Jefferson County, New York, is one of a number of alvar ecosystems that exists in the Great Lakes region of the United States. These ecosystems contain imperiled habitats for rare plant species along with moss gardens, shrubs, wildflowers, and woodlands. Most of North America's alvar landscapes are located along the Great Lakes, where they form an arc from New York to Michigan. Chaumont Preserve is considered the most exemplary alvar ecosystem in New York State and one of the best of its kind worldwide.

The term *barren* is somewhat of a misnomer. It is a term that came about to describe prairies or grasslands that seemed to have no agricultural value. But these ecosystems are rich in plant and animal diversity. Alvar barrens are places accustomed to the extreme. Spring floods lead to summer droughts in these rocky grasslands. Plants that grow on this harsh landscape include bloodroot, yellow lady's slipper, prairie smoke, white cedar, white pine, reindeer lichen, and early buttercup. Animals that can be seen from the 1.7-mile self-guided trail are porcupine, coyote, whippoorwill, bobcat, prairie warbler, scarlet tanager, and ruffed grouse.

Alvar ecosystems have been discovered only recently. The first alvar sites in North America were discovered in the mid-1960s, and it was not until the mid-1980s that the alvar communities in New York were identified. Because of their relative newness within the scientific and conservation communities, very little was known about their ecological importance, and there were no organized programs in place to protect them.

In the late 1990s, the International Alvar Conservation Initiative was formed to research, restore, and protect the diminishing alvar landscapes in the Great Lakes basin. Working in cooperation with the Great Lakes Program of the Nature Conservancy as well as other organizations and universities, this initiative identified high-priority alvar sites, improved the information available regarding the ecological significance of these areas, promoted acquisition of high-priority alvar lands, implemented means of restoring alvar communities, increased public awareness of the need for alvar conservation, and formulated a plan to monitor the restoration progress of these sensitive ecosystems. Now there are many alvar sites that have been identified as critical areas in the Great Lakes basin. In New York, the Jefferson County Alvar Megasite includes Chaumont Barrens, Limerick Cedars, Lucky Star, and Three Mile Barrens. There are also important alvar communities in Michigan, Ohio, and Ontario.

One of the primary methods to restore barrens communities is through prescribed burnings. These burnings not only promote growth of the unique plant communities in the barrens but they also help to protect local residents from uncontrolled wildfires. As woodland debris such as branches, leaves, twigs, and vegetation builds up on the barrens, it acts as fuel that could spark wildfires. Either through lightning or human initiation, these fires have historically been the way the barrens have been naturally maintained until nearby residential and commercial development suppressed the burnings. Other conservation activities that have taken place to restore the alvar lands include controlling nonnative invasive species. Chaumont is currently under threat by an extremely invasive plant called the pale swallow-wort. Preferring limestone based soils, the swallow-wort has wreaked havoc on alvar communities and has the potential to infest an area and choke rare and native plant communities. For visitors, boardwalks and interpretive trails exist at the preserve to promote public awareness and enjoyment of the unique alvar landscape and its captivating wildflowers.

Further Reading

Anderson, Roger, C., James S. Fralish, and Jerry M. Baskin, eds. *Savannas, Barrens, and Rock Outcrop Plant Communities of North America.* New York: Cambridge University Press, 1999.

United State Environmental Protection Agency. *Conserving Great Lakes Alvars: Final Technical Report of the International Alvar Conservation Initiative—March, 1999.* Compiled by Carol Reschke, Ron Reid, Judith Jones, Tom Feeney, and Heather Potter on behalf of the Alvar Working Group. Chicago: Nature Conservancy Great Lakes Program, 1999. http://www.epa.gov/ecopage/shore/alvars/.

FINGER LAKES

The Finger Lakes region of New York consists of 11 long, narrow lakes that resemble fingers spanning out over the landscape to form the Finger Lakes basin. This large drainage basin contains more than 400 lakes and ponds and is well known for its wine industry. Precipitation into this predominantly rural area flows into the Oswego, the Oneida, the Seneca, and the Clyde rivers that ramble around dairy farms and through forests. This region also is home to an extraordinary silver maple–ash swamp and an Appalachian oak-hickory forest where shagbark hickory, maples, oaks, and eastern hemlocks abound. The 11 Finger Lakes are Cayuga, Otisco, Owasco, Skaneateles, Canadice, Canandaigua, Conesus, Hemlock, Honeoye, Keuka, and Seneca.

The two most undeveloped lakes in this unique region are Hemlock Lake and Canadice Lake. Hemlock Lake is located 25 miles south of Rochester in Livingston County and is roughly 7 miles in length and 91 feet deep. Vegetation at the lake largely consists of beds of milfoil, a submerged aquatic plant that is sometimes defined as an invasive species because of its aggressive ability to choke native aquatic plants. Canadice Lake, the smallest of the lakes, is in Ontario County about 30 miles south of Rochester. It is 3 miles long, and its maximum depth is 95 feet. Plant life along the lake includes milfoil, pondweeds, and eelgrass. Both Hemlock and Canadice contain an abundance of fish, particularly trout and salmon populations. Other wildlife that can be found in the region include river otters, native salmonids, black bear, bald eagles, woodland salamanders, the rare timber rattlesnake, and migrating birds.

These pristine lakes and their surrounding forests that lie within the Finger Lakes region largely define the character of central New York and are therefore considered an ecological priority. Hemlock and Canadice lakes are major sources of water for the Rochester area, making water quality enhancement programs an important part of conservation activities in the region. The Finger Lakes are subject to a number of pollution threats. Past and present industrial activities from urban centers and residential development threaten the water quality of some of the lakes, particularly Onondaga Lake. Agricultural runoff is the primary source of toxic pollutants for lakes that lie in more

Watkins Glenn Gorge in Finger Lakes. (Courtesy of Pamela L. DePalma)

rural regions, and incompatible forest management has made a negative impact as well. The Nature Conservancy has been working for last decade in the western Finger Lakes region by acquiring sensitive lands near the lakes to help protect the picturesque wooded shorelines and water quality of the western lakes.

There are other natural areas that are extremely important to this region of New York. In the northern tier of the Finger Lakes region at the north end of Cayuga Lake is the Montezuma Wetlands Complex and the Montezuma National Wildlife Refuge. Montezuma is regarded as one of the best wetlands areas and stopover sites for migratory birds in the northeast. Every season, flocks of birds descend upon Montezuma to rest, feed, or nest. Some of the birds that can found at Montezuma are sandpipers, dowitchers, trumpeter swans, cerulean warblers, ducks, geese, killdeer, herons, egrets, chickadees, and sandhill cranes. Wildflowers in the wetland include trillium, mayapples, vetches, iris, mallow, and white water lily. The refuge contains an extensive trail system for hiking and wildlife observation.

Also of critical ecological importance is a large swamp system at the south end of Honeoye Lake. This wetland complex contains an exemplary silver maple–ash community for the state of New York that filters impurities from the water and helps to keep the waters of Honeoye at a high quality. Honeoye and the other 10 Finger Lakes create a unique and remarkable landscape in the northeast United States and are a treasure for the natural heritage of central New York.

Further Reading

Engeln, Oscar Diedrich. *Finger Lakes Region: Its Origin and Nature*. Ithaca, NY: Cornell University Press, 1988.

Mohler, Charles L., Peter L. Marks, and Sana Gardescu. *Guide to Plant Communities of the Central Finger Lakes Region*. Ithaca, NY: Cornell Internet-First University Press, 2006.

New York's Finger Lakes. http://www.fingerlakes.org/.

SAM'S POINT PRESERVE

East of the Catskill Mountains in southeast New York is one of the rarest places on earth. It is one of the most important natural areas in the Northeast and in the entire United States. Sam's Point Preserve, located in the northern Shawangunk Mountains, sits on top of the Shawangunk Ridge at its highest point. Once called Ellenville Ice Caves, Sam's Point contains a unique geologic occurrence of ice caves, waterfalls, cliffs, vistas that reach into five states, historical remnants of a huckleberry culture, and an extremely rare ecosystem known as the ridgetop dwarf pine barrens.

Owned by the Open Space Institute and managed by the Nature Conservancy, Sam's Point is a wellspring of biodiversity and home to close to 40 rare plant and animal species. Walking along one of the seven hiking trails, visitors may see unusual plants such as clustered sedge, arctic rush, rhodora, and mountain spleenwort. Other plants include sheep laurel, wintergreen, and sweet fern. Wildlife sometimes encountered at the preserve include timber rattlesnakes, foxes, black bears, bobcats, hawks, falcons, and warblers. Hundreds of migratory birds nest at Sam's Point amid the pitch pine trees and feed from the blueberry and huckleberry bushes.

The dwarf pine barrens are comprised of stunted pitch pine trees that are less than 16 feet tall. The thin, rocky soils of Sam's Point provide the foundation for this globally rare community. The pitch pine trees need fire because the cones of the tree are serotinous, which means they require fire to open. The heat of fire opens the pine cones and allows the seeds to disseminate over the soil that has been enriched by the burning.

Therefore, one of the primary methods to replenish pine barrens communities is through prescribed burnings. These burnings not only promote growth of the unique plant communities in the barrens but they also help to protect local residents from uncontrolled wildfires. As woodland debris such as branches, leaves, twigs, and vegetation builds up on the barrens, it acts as fuel that could spark wildfires. Either through lightning or human initiation, these fires have historically been the way the barrens have been naturally been maintained until nearby residential and commercial development suppressed the burnings. Restoring a natural fire regime is a priority in the conservation efforts that aim to maintain pine barrens communities.

The huckleberry pickers used to start wildfires to enrich the summer harvest of berries. The huckleberry pickers were part of a culture within the Shawangunk Mountains that has vanished. From the 1920s to the 1960s, people from the surrounding regions used to come to Shawangunk during the summer months and earn a fair amount of money by picking and selling huckleberries. Sam's Point was dense with berry bushes that would sometimes yield 25 to 30 quarts a day for one person, who would then sell the berries to the general store, where the berries would be shipped to other markets in New York and the Northeast. The berry pickers enjoyed a sense of community as people from various locations would come together to work the land and share their experiences over dinner. The culture began to deteriorate as a changing economy brought fewer people to the mountains in the summer, leaving only their shacks as a reminder of those communal summers and campfire conversations.

In addition to the rich cultural history and ecological significance of this natural area, Sam's Point has much to offer visitors. People visit the preserve for bird-watching and hiking the trails that feature Verkeerderkill Falls and cliffs called Gertrude's Nose and Margaret Cliff. Visitors also enjoy the cold air coming from the ice caves, where fractures in bedrock receive snow and ice in the winter. But the cold air cannot escape in the summer, and the caves act as natural refrigerators as the snow and ice often remains in the caves all summer long, emitting a refreshing, cool air amid the hot pine barrens.

Further Reading

Forman, Richard T. T. *Pine Barrens: Ecosystem and Landscape*. New Brunswick, NJ: Rutgers University Press, 1998.

Friends of the Shawangunk Mountains. http://shawangunks.org/.

Nature Conservancy. "Sam's Point Preserve." http://www.nature.org/wherewework/ northamerica/states/newyork/preserves/art12207.html.

Open Space Institute. http://www.osiny.org/site/PageServer.

SOUTHERN LAKE CHAMPLAIN VALLEY

To the east of Lake Champlain are the Green Mountains of Vermont. To the west of the lake are the glorious peaks of the Adirondack Mountains. And to the south of the lake are the Catskill Mountains of New York. Nestled amid these three mountain ranges is the scenic and ecologically diverse Southern Lake Champlain Valley. Cliffs, forests, rivers, wetlands, and a remarkable array of rare species live in this impressive valley, including clayplain forest plant communities.

Clayplain forests used to dominate the Champlain Valley, but they are now considered endangered and only occur in small fragments. Valley clayplain forests contain a wide variety of trees, including white pine, white oak, red maple, red oak, shagbark hickory, white ash, and bur oak. This forest type contains a greater variety of tree species than any other forest community in the northern New England region. There is an abundance of plant and herbaceous communities that are supported by the fertile clay soil of the clayplain forest. Some of these species are more common in southern regions, but they thrive in the warmer, Champlain Valley climate. Additionally, many animal species call the clayplain forest home because of the number of nut-producing trees that provide them with food.

Animals that inhabit the valley are bobcats, black bears, timber rattlesnakes, and peregrine falcons. The Poultney River boasts rich aquatic life, including 12 species of native freshwater mussels. The river also is home to the eastern sand darter. This small fish is on New York's list of threatened species. The primary reason for the decline of the eastern sand darter is loss of habitat. It prefers sandy stream bottoms, but damming and other river activities have greatly disrupted the clean, sandy floor of many rivers and streams.

Threats that are compromising the region are development, invasive species, agricultural pollution, and practices that negatively impact water quality, poaching of rare species, and disease. The eastern New York, Adirondack, and Vermont chapters of the Nature Conservancy as well as many other conservation groups are working to restore the clayplain forests, control invasive species, and encourage community stewardship and conservation. Additional work to help protect the clayplain forest region is being undertaken by the Chaplain Valley Clayplain Forest Project. This program promotes the research, education, and stewardship of the valley clayplain forest ecosystem to foster understanding of the critical importance of this forest type and to encourage sustainable land use practices that help to preserve this important link to the Champlain Valley's ecological history. Activities include controlling invasive species (particularly honeysuckle), tree planting, and educational events that teach local residents about the unique and complex characteristics of the forest in their region. Because of the warmer climate of the southern Champlain Valley region, agriculture has been the dominating force that has disrupted the natural cycles and native species in this region. Only roughly 10 percent of the original valley clayplain forest ecosystem still remains in fragments throughout the landscape.

There are many opportunities for local residents to volunteer to help with conservation efforts in the Southern Lake Champlain Valley. For the last two decades, volunteers have helped to control water chestnut populations in Southern Lake Champlain because of the damage this invasive species can do to ecologically sensitive wetlands. Thousands of pounds of water chestnut plants are pulled each year by dedicated volunteers. The Champlain Valley Plant Restoration Nursery located in Whitehall, New York, also accepts help from volunteers and interns who help to manage seeds for their native plant restoration project. The nursery began in 2002 with the Poultney-Mettowee Watershed Partnership and the Nature Conservancy's Southern Lake Champlain Valley Program to plant trees that will reduce erosion along stream banks, improve water quality, and regenerate native plant communities in the region.

Further Reading

Champlain Valley Clayplain Forest Project. http://www.clayplain.org.

Lake Champlain Committee. http://www.lakechamplaincommittee.org/lake/natural. html.

Lake Champlain Region. http://www.lakechamplainregion.com/.

Winslow, Mike. *Lake Champlain: A Natural History*. Bennington, VT: Images from the Past, 2008.

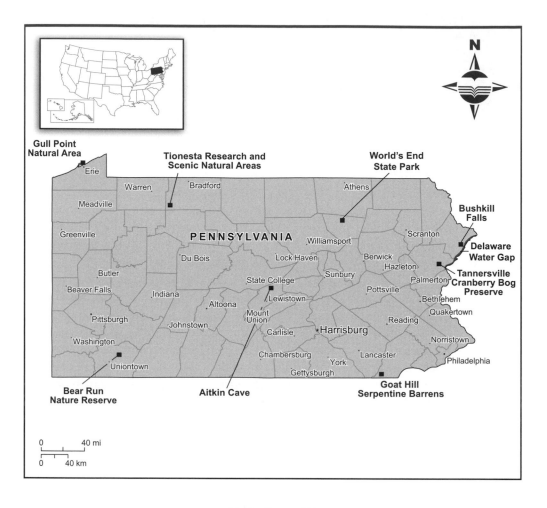

Aitkin Cave, 118

Bear Run Nature Reserve, 120

Bushkill Falls, 121

Delaware Water Gap, 122

Goat Hill Serpentine Barrens, 124

Gull Point Natural Area, 125

Tannersville Cranberry Bog Preserve, 127

Tionesta Research and Scenic Natural Areas, 128

World's End State Park, 129

PENNSYLVANIA

Before European settlement, Pennsylvania was a vast, lush forestland. Like many states in the northeast United States, Pennsylvania's ecological identity has been partly formed by an unrestrained exploitation of its natural resources—particularly timber, coal, iron, and steel. Events in Pennsylvania's history that have made a powerful impact on the state's ecology also helped to shape this identity. Events such as the Johnstown Flood of 1889, Hurricane Agnes in 1972, the nuclear accident at Three Mile Island in 1979, the discovery of radon gas in 1984, and Pennsylvania's long coal-mining history, which has left as its legacy thousands of acres of abandoned mines and their toxic runoff, while towns, such as Centralia, struggled for years with an uncontrolled mine fire.

Despite these challenges, Pennsylvania has been remarkably resilient. From the Delaware Water Gap National Recreation Area and the Pocono Mountains in the east to Lake Erie and the Allegheny National Forest in the west, and all the verdant Pennsylvania wilds in between, Pennsylvania is blanketed in state parks, forests, wild lands, and natural areas. Efforts to restore Pennsylvania from the timber industry that ravaged the state in the 19th century began in 1898 when the state began to purchase conservations lands. The result of this land acquisition 100 years later is that Pennsylvania forestland now totals more than two million acres, helping to restore the state to a time when its natural abundance inspired author Rebecca Harding Davis to write, "Nowhere in this country from sea to sea, does nature comfort us with such assurance of plenty, such rich and tranquil beauty as in those unsung, unpainted hills of Pennsylvania."

Pennsylvania's natural wonders have been an inspiration for many, including the legendary ecologist, writer, and biologist Rachel Carson, who was born in Springdale in Allegheny County and attended what is now Chatham College. Carson's groundbreaking *Silent Spring* challenged the country's pesticide abuse and presented the writer's passionate plea for the understanding that all life forms on earth are interconnected and that the impacts of pesticide use are far reaching. Carson was deemed by many as hysterical in the 1960s after the publication of *Silent Spring* for perspectives that are now considered common knowledge within scientific communities.

Since Pennsylvania is roughly 60 percent forest, protecting the state's woodlands is central to the conservation efforts taking place in the state. But other critical conservation priorities for the state include improving air quality, addressing issues related to abandoned mines, mine safety, subsidence and acid drainage, improving water quality across the state and the Chesapeake Bay, and developing alternative, cleaner energy programs.

Ecologically speaking, Pennsylvania has been struggling with its coal history for a long time, and conservation activities geared toward addressing the environmental hazards related to mining are ongoing. The Surface Mining Control and Reclamation Act of 1977 places limitations on active mining, funds abandoned mine reclamation, prevents abuse within the industry, and protects natural and cultural resources from destruction through mining. The act was amended in 2006 so that funding could be acquired to clean up land and water sources polluted by past coal mining to assure public health and safety. Acid mine drainage is a serious problem in the state of Pennsylvania and arguably its biggest source of water pollution.

In recent years, Pennsylvania has invested millions of dollars toward initiatives that reduce energy costs to consumers and promote renewable energy sources in what is called the Energy Independence Strategy. In 2008, Governor Edward Rendell signed into law a $650 million fund package that is designed to reduce energy costs to residents and businesses, create jobs in renewable energy industries, and reduce dependence on foreign sources of energy. The package also provides loans and grants for renewable energy projects and rebates for the installation of solar energy technology, funds for wind and geothermal projects, green buildings, and pollution control.

AITKIN CAVE

If it were not for their dark, enclosed, rocky tunnel nature, caves might have the reputation for showcasing some of the best scenery on earth. Aitkin Cave is located on the Richard O. Rowlands Preserve in central Pennsylvania and is home to a wide diversity of bats, some of which are considered rare. Despite the fear often associated with these earthen passageways, plenty of human footfalls have impacted Aitkin Cave, which resulted in cave disturbance and a decline in bat populations. Caves are highly fragile habitats and are in need of protection from heavy recreation, vandalism, chemical pollution in the groundwater, and the activities of scientists and explorers who disrupt the cave. These threats impact the traditional roosting sites and have contributed to a decline in the bat population.

Caves are natural hibernacula, or temporary roosting spots, for bats. Several species that can be found in Aitkin Cave are the little brown bat, the big brown bat, Keen's bat, the Indiana bat, and the rare small-footed bat. This tiny bat, also called the small-footed myotis, is only three inches long. It likes to roost near the entrances of caves and mines, which might make it more vulnerable to disturbance than other bats. Listed as a threatened species by the Pennsylvania Game Commission, this petite tunnel dweller is still somewhat mysterious to scientists.

Bats have received an undeserved bad reputation because of their association with nocturnal activities and dark, cavernous hiding places. But bats play a critical role in maintaining environmental health by keeping night insect populations in balance and for being natural pollinators. A decrease in bat populations often results in an increase in chemical pesticide use, particularly for mosquitoes and insects that are considered agricultural pests. But the ecological impact of this pesticide use is profound and far reaching. These insects, through evolutionary processes, develop resistances to the pesticides. Therefore, the chemical poisons ultimately do more harm to their predators, such as fish and bats, and many other species. Eventually, stronger pesticides are used, which perpetuates the poisonous cycle. This ecologically destructive toxic spiral is referred to as the pesticide treadmill. Also, because of the loss their traditional habitats in caves and tree hollows and the increasing difficulty of locating roosting sites needed for their survival, bats often end up taking roost in abandoned mines. Consequently, mine closures have been known to bury large numbers of bats.

The ecological value of caves is frequently underappreciated. To scientists called speleologists caves are important underground laboratories. Most caves with their winding tunnels and caverns are formed from slow-moving groundwater. Because of their ability to hold and filter water, limestone caves have a direct impact on underground water quality, and scientists are commonly concerned with the water circulation within caves. Many minerals are often found in caves, including calcite, aragonite, and gypsum. Stalactites and stalagmites, common features in a cave, are calcite deposits from slowly dripping water. Stalactites are tube- or cone-shaped deposits hanging down from the cave ceiling, and stalagmites grow upward from the cave floor.

Aitkin Cave and the surrounding preserve are owned and managed by the Nature Conservancy. In 1987, the entrance to the cave was gated to prevent recreational use during the bat hibernation period from September to April. The bats can come and go through the gate, but human visitors cannot. Because of this effort, the bat population at Aitkin Cave has experienced a dramatic increase, ensuring the survival of these underground inhabitants that play an immeasurable role in keeping an ecosystem in balance.

Further Reading

Gillieson, David S. *Caves: Processes, Development, and Management.* Boston: Blackwell, 1996.
Nature Conservancy. "Richard O. Rowlands Preserve at Aitkin Cave." http://www.nature.org/wherewework/northamerica/states/pennsylvania/preserves/art4333.html.

BEAR RUN NATURE RESERVE

I n western Pennsylvania, near the Maryland border, there is a region called the Laurel Highlands that is quite literally a land of falling water. The largest natural area in this region is Ohiopyle State Park, a white-water oasis for nature photographers and experienced boaters. Within the park is the Ferncliff Peninsula National Natural Landmark, which is a botanical wonder amid the bubbling Youghiogeny River, and next door to Ohiopyle is Bear Run Nature Reserve and Frank Lloyd Wright's architectural masterpiece appropriately named Fallingwater. This region is also home to Pennsylvania's highest point, Mount Davis, a peak along the 30-mile Negro Mountain ridge in the center of the Allegheny Plateau.

Northeast of Ohiopyle is Bear Run Nature Reserve and Frank Lloyd Wright's Fallingwater. This home is one of the most famous works of architecture in the United States. In an article in the *New York Times* in 1986, Paul Goldberger states that "Fallingwater is Wright's greatest essay in horizontal space; it is his most powerful piece of structural drama; it is his most sublime integration of man and nature." The structure is striking because it rises over a waterfall rather than facing it. The house was built between 1936 and 1939 for Edgar Kaufmann and his family, who often spent their summers at Fallingwater. The home is surrounded by the 5,061-acre Bear Run Nature Reserve, which is managed by the Western Pennsylvania Conservancy. Bear Run Reserve is known for its high-quality streams, plant diversity, and second-growth hardwood and hemlock forests. There are more than 20 miles of hiking trails in the reserve as well as rare plants species such as the buffalo nut and the single-headed pussytoes. There is an area designated as an important bird area by the National Audubon Society, and Bear Run Reserve encompasses a significant portion of both the Bear Run watershed and Laurel Run watershed. In 2007, the Western Pennsylvania Conservancy developed a conservation plan for Bear Run Reserve that involves close monitoring of aquatic habitats, studying the impact of acid rain on the streams and forests, restoration of a hardwood forest that is native to this region, controlling invasive species, and maintaining hiking trails.

The mountain laurel, Pennsylvania's state flower, flourishes at Bear Run Reserve. Mountain laurel is a heath shrub similar to rhododendron. It has dark green, glossy leaves that are beautiful all year long, and its vibrant spring and summer floral display adds a dramatic flare to Bear Run Reserve. This evergreen shrub's flowers vary in color from white to pink, and it thrives in this rocky woodland.

Ohiopyle State Park's impressive list of waterfalls, rocky ledges, scenic overlooks, and tumbling river currents can be explained geologically. The park is situated where the Laurel Ridge meets the Youghiogeny River, creating a landscape that combines the rugged and rocky with the flowing riverine. Highlights of Ohiopyle are waterfalls cascading 20 and 30 feet and a gorge that is 14 miles long. Ferncliff Peninsula is also very important in the park. This 100-acre botanical reserve receives seeds from Maryland and West Virginia that are often deposited by the northbound Youghiogeny. The low elevation of the peninsula allows these plants to grow north of their range, creating a biodiverse ecosystem.

The Laurel Highlands region encompasses three counties—Somerset, Westmoreland, and Fayette—and is considered a high-priority preservation area for the Western Pennsylvania Conservancy. Limestone caves, sandstone outcrops, waterfalls, healthy forests and streams, and biodiversity make this region captivating. What is unforgettable to most visitors is the sound. The gurgling rush of the Bear Run or the Youghiogeny falling over mossy boulders and tumbling into crystalline pools can be heard well before they come into view.

Further Reading

Pennsylvania Department of Conservation and Natural Resources. "Ohiopyle State Park." http://www.dcnr.state.pa.us/stateParks/parks/ohiopyle.aspx.

Western Pennsylvania Conservancy. "Bear Run Nature Reserve." http://www.pacon serve.org/e-conserve/spring-07/trail.htm.

Wright, Frank Lloyd, and Robert McCarter. *Fallingwater: Frank Lloyd Wright*. London: Phaidon, 1994.

BUSHKILL FALLS

In the rolling, green Pocono Mountains of eastern Pennsylvania, a natural spring percolates and rises up through the rocks to form the headwaters of a creek called Bushkill. From there, the pristine water makes its way down toward the Delaware River picking up speed and volume as it tumbles over rocks and ledges, creating one of the most scenic and breathtaking waterfall displays in Pennsylvania.

Nicknamed the Niagara of Pennsylvania, Bushkill Falls is a series of eight misty waterfalls, some of which cascade 100 feet over cliffs tucked away in lush forest. Trails of different lengths take visitors through the forest to view the eight falls from a variety of angles. A walk through the Bushkill Falls property is marked by the roaring sound of falling water, the bubble of small creeks, and a colorful bloom of wildflowers in the warm season. Ferns, mosses, boulders, and a gorge make the beauty of the area even more dramatic, while a network of bridges hovers over the ravines. In its larger context, the falls are located in Bushkill, Pennsylvania, where the Pocono Mountain range is home to an abundance of wildlife, streams, lakes, and rich vegetation.

The Pocono Mountains are considered to be one of the world's "last great places," according to the Nature Conservancy. Shaped by its glaciated history, the Poconos are still significantly influenced by water and ice. The landscape hosts a remarkably diverse array of natural communities that include boulder fields, wetlands, heath lands, oak barrens, and hardwood forest. The most significant threat to the Pocono region is development due to its proximity to surrounding metropolitan areas such as New York, Philadelphia,

Harrisburg, and Scranton. Development that continues to close in on the area will increase the risk of the Pocono region losing its rich, natural heritage. Many local, state, and federal partnerships are helping to conserve the area through land acquisition, conservation easements, public education and outreach, scientific research, and the removal of invasive species.

Bushkill Falls is next to the Delaware Water Gap National Recreation Area, which is 67,000 acres of forest, lakes, ponds, ridges, valleys, and floodplain that stretch across western New Jersey and eastern Pennsylvania. It is the largest natural area in the national park system between Virginia and Maine. Slicing through the Appalachian Mountains and creating the scenic gap are 40 miles of the Delaware River, which, in total, is 330 miles long and forms some of the most spectacular waterfalls in Pennsylvania. Because of the size of the area and the wide range of habitats, many different kinds of plants and animals can be seen when visiting. Black bears, otters, fox, wild turkeys, beavers, and coyotes can be found here as well as more than 260 species of birds and 61 species of fish, 10 of which have been identified as rare. The rivers and streams in the park have exceptional water quality, and the area supports a diversity of plant life, including hemlock ravines, hickories, hardwood forests, wildflowers, ferns, rhododendrons, and even cactus barrens with the occasional prickly pear. In the 19th century, the Delaware Water Gap was considered a Wonder of the World and was even then a tourist attraction.

The primary threat to Bushkill Falls is the recreational impact. Because of its scenic beauty, the area hosts a large number of visitors each year who want to take in the extraordinary splendor of the falls. This threat is also apparent in the Delaware Water Gap, which bears the impact of roughly five million recreational visits each year. Bushkill Falls receives protection through the private ownership of the Charles E. Peters family. The area has been open to the public since 1904.

Further Reading

Oplinger, Carl, and Robert Halma. *The Poconos: An Illustrated Natural History Guide*. New Brunswick, NJ: Rutgers University Press, 1988.

Ostrander, Stephen. *Great Natural Areas in Eastern Pennsylvania*. Mechanicsburg, PA: Stackpole Books, 1996.

National Park Service. "Delaware Water Gap National Recreation Area." http://www.nps.gov/dewa/.

DELAWARE WATER GAP

The Delaware Water Gap National Recreation Area is 67,000 acres of forest, lakes, ponds, ridges, valleys, and floodplain that stretch across western New Jersey and eastern Pennsylvania. It is the largest natural area in the national park system between Virginia and Maine. Slicing through the Appalachian Mountains and creating the scenic gap are 40 miles of the Delaware River, which, in total, is 330 miles long and forms some of the most spectacular waterfalls in New Jersey and Pennsylvania. Because of the size of the area and the wide range of habitats, many different kinds of plants and animals can be seen when visiting. Black bears, otters, fox, wild turkeys, beavers, and coyotes can be found here as well as more than 260 species of birds and 61 species of fish, 10 of which have been identified as rare. The rivers and streams in the park have exceptional water quality, and the area supports a diversity of plant life, including hemlock ravines, hickories, hardwood forests, wildflowers, ferns, rhododendrons, and even cactus barrens with the occasional prickly pear. The hemlock trees are currently under threat by an insect from Asia called the hemlock woolly adelgid. This insect harms the trees by sucking out all of the sap, thus killing it. The hemlock trees are extremely important to the region's ecosystem because they provide necessary shade for native plant species to thrive.

The Delaware Water Gap was initially designed in 1965 to be primarily a recreational area for local residents. Hiking, fishing, painting, and canoeing are popular activities in the area. Some of the most breathtaking vistas can be seen while hiking the Appalachian Trail that runs along the Kittatinny Mountain ridge in New Jersey. At the end of the Kittatinny ridge, is Mount Tammany, 1,527 feet above sea level, from which spectacular panoramic views of the gap can be seen. But the gap is no longer valued just for its recreational opportunities. As development and threatening environmental degradation became more pronounced, the area is now protected as an important conservation area not only for its natural resources but also for its cultural and historical significance.

The Delaware Water Gap has a controversial history. The park was initially established in 1965 with the intention of having it located in a proposed area surrounding a reservoir that would be created with the construction of a dam called the Tocks Island Dam over the Delaware River near Smithfield Beach. The decision to build the dam was overturned, but many historic homes and buildings were destroyed in preparation for building the dam. Because of this decision, the Delaware River is one of a few remaining major rivers in the United States that does not have a dam or some other structure to control water flow, and, therefore, special effort has been made to preserve existing buildings that tell the stories of the history and cultures that influenced the area. To share the rich history of the area, a newsletter called *Spanning the Gap* was created and written by park rangers for visitors and researchers.

Some other interesting facts are that, in the 19th century, the Delaware Water Gap was considered a Wonder of the World and was even then a tourist attraction. The area was also once the site of the French and Indian War, and numerous historic colonial settlements are still in tact. The area is considered important for its archeological treasures. Archeologists have found evidence of prehistoric populations that once lived in the area, which has shed considerable light on studies attempting to identify and understand Native American tribes that lived along the eastern seaboard.

Further Reading

Brodhead, L.W. *The Delaware Water Gap: Its Scenery, Its legends, and Early History.* Ann Arbor: University of Michigan Scholarly Publishing Office, 2005.

National Park Service. "Delaware Water Gap National Recreation Area." http://www. nps.gov/dewa/.

GOAT HILL SERPENTINE BARRENS

Near the Pennsylvania-Maryland border is a protected natural area called the State-Line Serpentine Barrens, which is the most significant example of a serpentine barren natural community in the eastern United States. Serpentine barrens are extremely rare and because of their unusual occurrence, and plants that populate these barrens are also rare. Goat Hill Preserve is 600 acres of serpentine ecology that lies within the State-Line Barrens in Chester County, Pennsylvania. It has served as an important research location for botanists and it is a treasure for Pennsylvania's natural heritage.

Goat Hill contains a natural community that is called a serpentine grassland. The soil in the grassland has a greenish color due to the high amount of magnesium and other metals. Serpentine gets its name from its resemblance to green-brown snakes of northern Italy, according to folklore. The soils are toxic to many species of plants, so those that grow in a serpentine community have adapted to the harsh soils. Many invasive species cannot survive in these soils, which helps to keep the plant community safe from most intruding plants. The high level of magnesium in the soil prevents the uptake of calcium, making it difficult for many plants to grow in these soils. Also, the presence of heavy metals, such as chromium, cobalt, and nickel in serpentine soils are toxic to many plants. The presence of chickweed is a strong indicator of serpentine soils. Its hairy leaves protect it from the heat of sunlight while also holding in moisture.

Goat Hill contains rare plants that can only be found in serpentine communities of Pennsylvania and Maryland. Some of these plants are the serpentine aster, round-leaved fameflower, prairie dropseed, chickweed, and a number of different species of fern, including Christmas, maidenhair, and hay-scented. The serpentine aster is particularly rare in that the daisylike plant has its origins in serpentine soils, unlike other plants that migrated from other habitats and adapted to the serpentine conditions. The harsh environment of the barrens, much like a desert or prairie, produces plants that have a high tolerance for dry, hot conditions. The pitch pine forests and meadows sprinkled with wildflower blossoms attract whippoorwills, warblers, the bobwhite quail, and a host of moths and butterflies. Other important serpentine barrens in Pennsylvania with a similar selection of species are Chrome Barrens, Nottingham Barrens, and the New Texas Barrens.

Although Goat Hill is managed by the Pennsylvania Department of Natural Resources, the Nature Conservancy, and other local organizations, the preserve is still undergoing succession and is in danger of losing its native vegetation. Development in surrounding areas prohibits fire that is needed to maintain barrens communities. Therefore, woodland vegetation is moving into the barrens habitat and threatening the serpentine community. Illegal dumping is also a concern for the preserve. Steps being taken to address these threats include cutting down woodland trees, scheduling prescribed burnings, and replanting serpentine plants. At one time, Native American populations periodically burned the serpentine areas to keep the woody vegetation from entering the grasslands. When forced removals, smallpox, and the encroachment of settlers dramatically reduced the Native American populations, livestock grazing and trampling helped to keep the grasslands maintained. Livestock is no longer permitted on serpentine areas, requiring conservation projects that will reduce the woodland plants.

The fact that Goat Hill Preserve still exists at all is a conservation success story. At one time, Goat Hill was heavily mined for its chromium and magnetite. An organization called Concerned Citizens of West Nottingham Township was created when news spread that an excavating company wanted to quarry in the area. This grassroots effort saved the serpentine barrens from further exploitation. Today, dedicated volunteers who are familiar with serpentine plant communities offer their time to remove woodland vegetation so the prairie grasses can thrive.

Further Reading

Anderson, Roger, C., James S. Fralish, and Jerry M. Baskin, eds. *Savannas, Barrens, and Rock Outcrop Plant Communities of North America*. New York: Cambridge University Press, 1999.

Maryland Department of Natural Resources. "Natural Communities—Serpentine Grasslands." http://www.dnr.state.md.us/wildlife/serpentine.asp.

GULL POINT NATURAL AREA

Presque Isle State Park is located on a sandy peninsula that stretches out into the vast waters of Lake Erie in the far northwest corner of Pennsylvania. On Presque Isle is a fragile ecological environment and haven for migratory birds called Gull Point Natural Area. Because of its proximity to Lake Erie, Gull Point and the larger Presque Isle area contain bird and plant species (particularly at Gull Point) that can be found nowhere else in the state, making this natural area a critical habitat for endangered and threatened species.

Because of its fragile ecosystem, the 67-acre Gull Point is closed to the public from April through November. One reason for this diligent protection is to safeguard the feeding and nesting areas for the federally endangered piping plover. In the early 1950s, piping plovers were regular inhabitants of Presque Isle's outer beaches until habitat loss forced the birds to seek nesting areas elsewhere. Piping plovers seemed to all but disappear at Presque Isle until 2005, when they were observed at Gull Point. At that time, it seemed that they were just passing through, but their presence at the natural area during the summer, their nesting season, provoked stronger conservation efforts to make the area an attractive and suitable nesting site for them. The Pennsylvania Game Commission, Presque Isle State Park staff, and the U.S. Fish and Wildlife Service work cooperatively to try to restore the piping plover's population numbers by 2020. Their presence has been slowly increasing along the Great Lakes shorelines, but 150 pairs of plovers will need to be present on Gull Point and at Presque Isle for at least five years for this shy bird to be removed from the endangered species list.

Presque Isle, which means "almost an island" in French, is still a hot spot for migratory birds despite the several million visitors that arrive at its beaches each year. More than 330 species of birds have been documented at Presque Isle, and more than 30 of them are species that are declining in numbers. Some of the birds that can be seen on Presque Isle are the Baltimore oriole, eastern towhee, great horned owl, great heron, belted kingfisher, and least bittern. Presque Isle also has an abundance of plant life, including switch grass, Carolina rose, bull thistle, cardinal flower, lupine, wild grape, fringed gentian, yellow iris, and the New England aster that attracts monarch butterflies.

Presque Isle is a place that is always evolving. The lake was once a deep valley that filled with water from a large melting glacier. As the glacier retreated, it dropped sediments that eventually became what is now the Presque Isle Peninsula. Past storms that have flooded the neck of the peninsula have transformed it into an island on several occasions. Beach erosion is a substantial part of Presque Isle's history. Wave action is continuously moving the peninsula eastward. Beach nourishment and 58 breakwaters are currently being used to try to control beach movement.

Presque Isle has a fascinating human history as well. The Eriez Indians once populated the area until French settlers arrived in the 1700s. A bay at Presque Isle, once called Little Bay, was a refuge where ships were constructed for the War of 1812. In the Battle of Lake Erie, after defeating the British in the *Brig Niagara*, Commodore Oliver Hazard Perry and his crew returned to Little Bay to tend to the wounded. The following winter was so harsh that many of the crew members died, and the bay was renamed Misery Bay in their honor. The peninsula also hosts the Presque Isle Lighthouse, the North Pier Light, and the Tom Ridge Environmental Center for learning more about the peninsula's unique natural and cultural history.

Further Reading

Ostrander, Stephen. *Great Natural Areas in Western Pennsylvania*. Mechanicsburg, PA: Stackpole Books, 2000.

Platt, Carolyn. *Birds of the Lake Erie Region*. Kent, OH: Kent State University Press, 2001.

Tom Ridge Environmental Center. http://www.dcnr.state.pa.us/trecpi/index.html.

TANNERSVILLE CRANBERRY BOG PRESERVE

Bogs, or peatlands, are areas where the soil is comprised of partly decomposed plant matter where the land is often moist and spongy. Tannersville Cranberry Bog in eastern Pennsylvania is not technically a bog. Rather, it is an acid fen. Bogs are replenished by precipitation, while fens have as their water source a stream or a spring. The term *bog* is often used to refer to a variety of different kinds of peatlands, because the plant life that thrives in them is often the same. But this 900-acre boreal bog is strikingly unique. It is the southernmost occurrence of a low-altitude fen that has vegetation that is more akin to an ancient northern forest.

The Tannersville Cranberry Bog is located in the Pocono Mountain region of Pennsylvania near Stroudsburg. It is a glacial swamp formed from the Wisconsinan glacier that covered the area 15,000 years ago. As the glacier melted, ice chunks broke off from the larger glacier and settled into holes, creating lakes, bogs, and other landforms. Peat accumulates very slowly in bogs. Since the peat is roughly 50 feet deep at this site, it is estimated that the Tannersville fen is close to 6,000 years old.

Vegetation that flourishes in the area includes sheep laurel, bog laurel, Labrador tea, leatherleaf, and rhododendron. Sphagnum moss is abundant in the fen along, with tamarack trees and cotton grass with its downy tips. The plant life that dresses the fen has evolved to survive in a soil that is low in nutrients with a high acidic content. Gorgeous native orchids can be found in this area such as the rose pogonia and the heart-leaved twayblade, which is endangered in the state of Pennsylvania. Other botanical fascinations in this fen are the calla lilies and the insect-eating sundew and pitcher plants. To protect the Tannersville fen, careful management of its surrounding woodland and forest is essential. Trees found at the preserve include black spruce, tamarack, hemlock, white pine, red maple, poison sumac, and yellow birch. Wildlife in the preserve includes black bear, otter, snowshoe hare, and many others.

The Tannersville Cranberry Bog Preserve stands as an anomaly amid its surrounding hilly landscape. The Pocono Mountains are considered to be one of the world's "last great places," according to the Nature Conservancy. Shaped by its glaciated history, the Poconos are still significantly influenced by water and ice. The landscape hosts a remarkably diverse array of natural communities that include boulder fields, wetlands, heath lands, oak barrens, and hardwood forest.

Whether they are called bogs, fens, or swamps, these spongy places are perceived in many different ways. To some, they are useless, muddy swamps. To others, they are places to fear, as if one may walk into a bog and never come out. Stories of animal and human bodies buried in bogs and found centuries later are not uncommon. Some cultures valued bogs for their unusual plants that were prized for their medicinal qualities, while other cultures believe bogs were nothing short of temples, sacred places to commune with the divine. Regardless of one's idea of these in-between places, these scenes that are not quite land and not quite water, what other natural landscape can stir the imagination like a bog at dawn when there is still a layer of fog hanging on the leaves of the tamarack?

The marvelous function of the Tannersville Cranberry Bog, in addition to its vegetation display, is that the thick layer of peat absorbs and filters rainwater and runoff helping to cleanse and purify the water in the Pocono Creek watershed.

Further Reading

Harding, John. *Marsh, Meadow, Mountain*. Philadelphia: Temple University Press, 1986.

Ostrander, Stephen. *Great Natural Areas in Eastern Pennsylvania*. Mechanicsburg, PA: Stackpole Books, 1996.

TIONESTA RESEARCH AND SCENIC NATURAL AREAS

The Tionesta Research Natural Area is located in the Allegheny National Forest in northwest Pennsylvania. Adjacent to this site is the Tionesta Scenic Area. Both of these extraordinary forests contain an old-growth hemlock-beech community where some of the trees are estimated to be more than 300 years old. The two areas combined comprise more than 4,000 acres of lush Pennsylvania woodland on the Allegheny Plateau. The areas became federally recognized in 1973 when they were designated national natural landmarks for containing North America's largest hemlock–white pine northern hardwood forest.

Established in 1940, the Tionesta Natural Areas showcase a landscape that is characterized by sweeping steep hills and stream valleys. The elevation ranges from 1,550 feet to 1,980 feet keep the temperatures cool. In addition to the hemlock-beech community, other trees that thrive in the areas are black cherry and sugar maple. The West Fork Run and East Fork Run streams percolate clear water through the areas and provide drinking water for the forest wildlife. Some of the more common species found at Tionesta are black bear, white-tailed deer, bobcats, and porcupines. Common birds include kingfishers, herons, owls, hawks, woodpeckers, and warblers. Two rare species living in the Tionesta areas are Swainson's thrush and yellow-bellied flycatcher. Swainson's thrush is a medium-sized bird with an olive-brown colored back. Its breeding locations are primarily in Alaska and Canada, but its numbers seem to be on the decline. The yellow-bellied flycatcher is a small olive green bird with a yellowish breast and white and yellow stripes on its wings. This bog-loving bird is most commonly seen in Maine and Minnesota, but it occasionally appears in the cool, moist forests of Pennsylvania, New York, and West Virginia.

Weather and other disturbances have taken their toll on the Tionesta forests. Ice storms and tornadoes have caused widespread damage to the areas in the last century. Diseases such as beech bark disease, elm spanworm, and chestnut blight have infected the forests, and the hemlock trees are currently under threat by an insect from Asia called the hemlock woolly adelgid. This insect harms the trees by sucking out all of the sap, thus killing it. The hemlock trees are extremely important to Tionesta's ecosystem not only because of their old growth but also because they provide necessary shade for native plant species to thrive.

The Tionesta Natural Areas are located within the spectacular Allegheny National Forest and within the larger north-central region of the state known as the Pennsylvania Wilds. Established in 1923, this forest covers roughly 513,000 acres and includes within its boundaries many scenic areas in addition to the Tionesta tracts. One of these places is the Allegheny Islands Wilderness, which encompasses seven islands in the Allegheny River. The total area is 368 acres of willow, sycamore, and silver maple forest trees. Several of the islands, some of which host exceptional riverine forests, are Crull's Island, Thompson's Island, Baker Island, No Name Island, and King Island.

The Forest Service publishes a document called Schedule of Proposed Action, which details the current problems facing the Allegheny National Forest and the projects that are being implemented to address those challenges. The Forest Service embraces the phrase "land of many uses" to describe its approach to forest management. This approach promotes ecosystem, wildlife habitat, and watershed protection, while also supporting recreation and timber harvesting as long as it is conducted in a sustainable manner. The Allegheny National Forest does have a substantial logging history. Planting and nurturing tree seedlings were the primary goals of the Forest Service in the early 20th century. By the 1940s, the majority of the forest began to evolve into a diverse and vital second-growth forest. Only small pockets of old-growth forest remain at places like the Tionesta areas and at Hearts Content National Scenic Area.

Further Reading

Fergus, Charles. *Trees of Pennsylvania and the Northeast.* Mechanicsburg, PA: Stackpole Books, 2002.

MacDonald, Samuel. *The Agony of an American Wilderness: Loggers, Environmentalists, and the Struggle for Control of a Forgotten Forest.* Lanham, MD: Rowman & Littlefield, 2005.

U.S. Forest Service. "Allegheny National Forest." http://www.fs.fed.us/r9/forests/allegheny/.

WORLD'S END STATE PARK

Because of the unique geology of this natural area, World's End literally inspires a feeling of being at the ends of the earth. The primary force that is responsible for creating the valleys and gorge at World's End is Loyalsock Creek, a tributary of the West Branch Susquehanna River. Through the process of erosion, this powerful creek has been carving its way through the Endless Mountains landscape of Pennsylvania for millions of years.

Resting atop the Allegheny Plateau in Sullivan County known as the Sullivan Highlands, World's End is an S-shaped valley that affords spectacular scenery down into the valley where the cold Loyalsock Creek runs and across the hills where mountain laurel and fall foliage are at their finest in Pennsylvania. Wrapped around this winding valley are seven mountains that, layered upon one another, give the area an impression of endlessness. Logging devastated the area in the early 20th century until 1928, when an organization called the Department of Forest and Waters bought the property to prevent further destruction of its forests and natural beauty. Then, in 1933, President Roosevelt created the Civilian Conservation Corps, which employed workers to take on conservation efforts that would construct parklands, restore forests, and create trails. Now, World's End State Park is a scenic, rustic, rocky terrain cloaked in hemlock, maples, oak, and other hardwoods. Hemlock trees in the Northeast are currently under threat by an insect from Asia called the hemlock woolly adelgid. This insect harms the trees by sucking out all of the sap, thus killing it. The hemlock trees are extremely important to this area not only because of their old growth but also because they provide necessary shade for native plant species to thrive.

World's End is located in the larger Endless Mountains, which encompass four counties—Sullivan, Susquehanna, Wyoming, and Bradford—in northeast Pennsylvania. This region contains other natural areas (in addition to World's End) and nine mountain ranges that seem to go on forever. One of these areas is the Woodbourne Forest and Wildlife Preserve that contains the largest old-growth forest that remains in northeastern Pennsylvania. This forest is comprised of white pine, ash, maples, hemlock, oaks, and other hardwoods. Woodbourne also contains bog ecosystems, making it treasured for its biodiversity. Black bear, coyote, owls, hawks, mink, southern bog lemming, and river otter are some of the wildlife in the area, and the bog plants growing in the preserve include leatherleaf, pitcher plants, and sundew.

Another popular natural area in the Endless Mountains landscape is the scenic Rickett's Glen. Designated a national natural landmark in 1969, this area has 22 waterfalls, one of which falls 94 feet. There are trees that are estimated to be more than 500 years old at Rickett's Glen; towering white pine and hemlock abound along hiking trails that weave around waterfalls.

The most significant threat to the Endless Mountains and the handful of discrete natural areas is development due to proximity to surrounding metropolitan areas such as New York, Philadelphia, Harrisburg, and Scranton. The Pocono Mountain region, which is nearby to the east, faces the same challenges. Development that continues to close in on the area will increase the risk of this landscape losing its rustic, natural heritage. Many local, state, and federal partnerships are helping to conserve the area through land acquisition, conservation easements, public education and outreach, scientific research, and the removal of invasive species. These conservation plans that foreground fostering local stewardship communicate that a better future can be created for these natural areas through the unified efforts of organizations, concerned residents, and government agencies who come together to preserve the natural heritage of the place they call home.

Further Reading

Fergus, Charles. *Trees of Pennsylvania and the Northeast.* Mechanicsburg, PA: Stackpole Books, 2002.

Stacy, Bonnie. *Heritage of the Endless Mountains, Pennsylvania.* Portsmouth, NH: Arcadia, 1999.

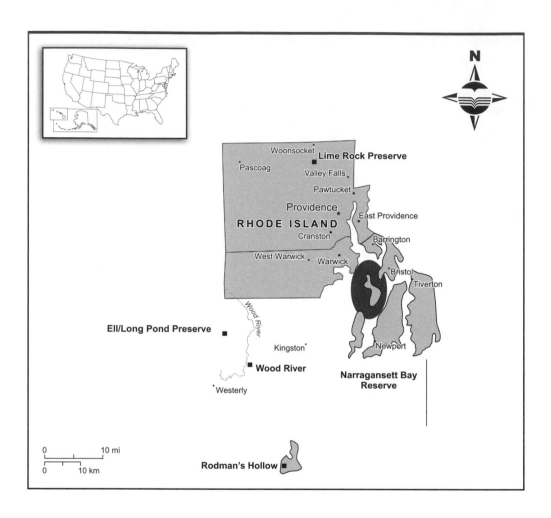

Ell/Long Pond Preserve, 134

Lime Rock Preserve, 136

Narragansett Bay Reserve, 137

Rodman's Hollow, 139

Wood River, 140

RHODE ISLAND

Although Rhode Island is the smallest state in the country and, at the same time, one of the most developed, it contains an abundance of wildlife refuges, diverse coastal ecosystems, and a rich maritime heritage. Known as the ocean state, Rhode Island has a coastal landscape that includes freshwater wetlands, grasslands, barrier beaches, salt marshes, sea grass beds, a high migratory bird population, shrubland ecosystems, shoreline bluffs and dunes, and magnificent ocean vistas. Perhaps one of Rhode Island's most valued natural areas is Block Island. This 6,200-acre island was formed by glaciers many thousands of years ago, and what exists today is an island protected by state, local, and federal environmental management agencies as well as the stewardship of its residents.

While some locations on Block Island are developed to support its summer tourism industry, it contains nature and wildlife preserves, broad sweeping views of open space, a glacial depression called Rodman's Hollow, morainal grasslands, and is home to endangered species. Perhaps one of the greatest assets to Block Island is its people. The year-round residents are committed to preserving the natural and cultural heritage of their home. Other islands important to the state are Patience, Prudence, Hope, and Dyer Islands—all protected within the Narragansett Bay Reserve.

Because Rhode Island is largely defined by its coastal region, water quality and the health of its wetlands is a conservation priority for the state. Many of the state's rivers and estuarine water sources are contaminated by bacteria, residential and urban runoff, and high levels of mercury. The primary threat to lakes and ponds is the presence of nonnative invasive species. The degradation of Rhode Island's waters has resulted in a significant loss of biodiversity, because fish and birds rely on these habitats for nesting and feeding. Maintaining the integrity of the state's coastal waters is important to the state's economic vitality due to the commercial and recreational fishing industries that bring millions of dollars to the state, and also because the scenic beauty of these areas promotes a strong tourism industry. The State Coastal and Estuarine Habitat Restoration Strategy developed by the state's Coastal Resources Management Council identified critical coastal habitat areas that are impaired and developed goals for restoring these habitats. Some of the strategies include removing nonnative invasive species, planting native vegetation, restoring natural water regimes, improving water quality by controlling pollution input, and creating buffer zones around sensitive areas.

Rhode Island is also strongly committed to wildlife and species conservation. The Audubon Society of Rhode Island has many wildlife refuges across the state and there are currently five national wildlife refuges managed by the U.S. Fish and Wildlife Service. The state's Department of Environmental Management also maintains thousands of acres of wildlife management areas for recreational purposes. The Rhode Island Division of Fish and Wildlife is currently developing a Wildlife Conservation Strategy that aims to identify what wildlife species inhabit the state, if the species are in decline, to detect threats that are compromising the wildlife and their habitats, and to develop the appropriate conservation actions for protecting the wildlife.

Ell/Long Pond Preserve

Ell/Long Pond Preserve is one of the most diverse natural areas in Rhode Island. The preserve supports a stunning display of rhododendron and mountain laurel in the summer as well as a white cedar swamp, an oak-pine community, bogs, mossy boulders, and red maple trees. As a habitat for wildlife, the preserve is home to squirrels, deer, fox, opossum, warblers, snakes, and bobcats. The 268-acre area is jointly owned by the Audubon Society of Rhode Island and the Nature Conservancy.

Located in southwestern Rhode Island in Hopkinton, Ell/Long Pond Preserve is a series of valleys and ridges that create breathtaking views and rugged hiking terrains. One of the most fascinating aspects of this preserve is the Ell Pond wetland area. Ell Pond is not open to public access, but for good reason. The pond's ecosystem is a fragile and unique example of classical succession with concentric rings that reveal stages of the wetland's development. At the center is the open water of the pond. Surrounding the pond is a quaking bog mat where cranberries, leatherleaf, pitcher plants, and sundews grow. The next ring is a bog comprised of Atlantic white cedar. The final ring is a swamp area of red maple. This wetland is then surrounded by a rhododendron and mountain laurel forest area. Because this area is a priority preservation site for the state of Rhode Island, for the Audubon Society, and the Nature Conservancy, Ell Pond will be able to continue to naturally evolve and be a wetland of vital interest to researchers and home to plants and animals that thrive in its layered communities.

As part of the Pawcatuck Borderlands, Ell Pond and Long Pond belong to a larger network of natural areas that are protected in the state of Rhode Island. This borderlands region is a large forest system that crosses the Rhode Island–Connecticut border stretching from Boston to Washington, DC. This incredible east coast conservation effort continues to grow through land acquisitions and land management initiatives

Long Pond. (Courtesy of Steve Metcalf)

that recognize the ever-increasing threats that compromise the health of New England's coastal areas. The Pawcatuck Borderlands includes important wetland areas such as Ell/Long Pond Preserve as well as several important rivers and hardwood forests. It also contains substantial yet unique pitch pine forest natural communities that are common for coastal areas but have been decreasing due to high demands for commercial and residential development. But the borderlands region is most notably known for its giant rhododendron forest and Atlantic white cedar. Classified as a cypress tree, the Atlantic white cedar in Pawcatuck is a wetland tree that is home to the Hessel's hairstreak, a globally endangered butterfly, and an equally rare dragonfly called the banded boghaunter.

Ell Pond and Long Pond are the only national natural landmarks in Rhode Island. Ell Pond is managed by the Nature Conservancy, and Long Pond is managed by the Audubon Society of Rhode Island. The Long Pond portion of the preserve includes most of the hiking trails from which a grove of Hemlock trees called The Cathedral and rock outcrops can be observed. Just south of Ell/Long Pond Preserve is Canonchet Brook Preserve, a 600-acre natural area that contains a blend of old-growth and new-growth forest where oak trees, tulip poplars, white pine trees, hickory, maple, witch hazel, blueberry bushes, and mountain laurel can be seen among the slopes and rocky terrain. The Ell/Long Pond Preserve is a special place in and of itself, and its place nestled within the

Pawcatuck Borderlands will help to ensure its protection as a federally recognized natural landmark.

Further Reading

Borderlands Project. http://www.borderlandsproject.org.

Henshaw, Carol. *Natural Wonders of Connecticut & Rhode Island: Exploring Wild and Scenic Places*. New York: McGraw-Hill, 2000.

Nature Conservancy. "Ell/Long Pond Preserve." http://www.nature.org/wherewework/ northamerica/states/rhodeisland/preserves/art4091.html.

LIME ROCK PRESERVE

Just a short drive from Providence, Lime Rock Preserve may not be the wildest location in Rhode Island, but it is certainly unique. Home to 30 rare plant species, the dolomitic marble that characterizes this preserve influences the quality of the soil, which in turn creates a fertile foundation for plants that are unusual for Rhode Island. Red oak, hickory, ferns, horse balm, violets, red and white baneberry, bellwort, nodding trillium, trout lily, and jack-in-the-pulpit all can be found in this 130-acre preserve. Although the preserve is close to a metropolitan area, it still hosts an abundance of wildlife. It is a fascination for botanists and naturalists, and its network of hiking trails makes it a scenic getaway from urban life year-round.

Created in 1986, Lime Rock Preserve is part of a geologic region that is very different from the granite-based geologic makeup common for New England. The distinguishing feature at Lime Rock is the ledges of marble that are made of recrystallized dolomitic limestone. Similar to limestone, dolomite is a sedimentary rock that is comprised of calcium magnesium carbonate that can be found all over the world. It is more common to find the mineral in quarries of the Midwest than in New England. Dolomite typically forms rhombohedrons, although different-shaped crystals have been found. It is frequently clear, pearly white, or pink.

The calcareous soil, which contains calcium carbonate, provides the rich nutrients for plants and wildflowers. Horse balm, for example, with its scented lemon-yellow flowers, prefers the fertile, moist soils at Lime Rock. Jack-in-the-pulpit is another plant more common for the woods of Illinois than Rhode Island, but it finds the soils of Lime Rock quite suitable for growth. Soil becomes calcareous through the weathering of calcareous rocks, which, in this case, is the dolomitic limestone. Calcareous soil is also often present in coastal regions from the breakdown of shells.

Lime Rock Preserve is located in the town of Lincoln, which is within the Moshassuck River watershed. The headwaters of the Moshassuck River are located within the preserve among the oak trees. The headwaters are relatively clean and clear, but, as the river meanders south toward Providence, the river becomes dark colored and more toxic. This fact emphasizes that the key to clean water lies in keeping the areas around the river unpolluted. The Moshassuck, which was named by the Narragansett Indians, means "river where moose watered." Historically, the river was basically a sewer for industrial and human wastes. In fact, during the 19th century, the cholera epidemics that occurred in the area are believed to have come from the deplorable conditions of the river. As old textile industries closed, the water quality of the Moshassuck improved. Further improvement came about with the Clean Water Act of 1972, but the river is still full of toxic chemicals and garbage. This river then empties into the Narragansett Bay, further compromising the condition of this very important coastal estuary. In essence, Lime Rock Preserve is the Moshassuck's greatest ally. The preserve is not only critical for its dolomitic marble and its splendid plant display but for being a source of pure water for a river that has suffered its fair share of pollution and toxic overload. A visit to the preserve is beautiful any time of the year as the flowers bloom and the deciduous trees change their color in the fall. On the western side of the preserve, an old electric rail bed offers a stopping point to observe a scenic view overlooking the Manton Reservoir.

Further Reading

Chapman, William K., Valerie Conley Chapman, Alan E. Bessette, and Arleen R. Bessette. *Wildflowers of Massachusetts, Connecticut, and Rhode Island in Color.* Syracuse, NY: Syracuse University Press, 2008.

Henshaw, Carol. *Natural Wonders of Connecticut & Rhode Island: Exploring Wild and Scenic Places.* New York: McGraw-Hill, 2000.

Nature Conservancy. "Lime Rock Preserve." http://www.nature.org/wherewework/northamerica/states/rhodeisland/preserves/art5572.html.

NARRAGANSETT BAY RESERVE

The Narragansett Bay Reserve is a rich repository of natural and cultural history for the state of Rhode Island. Located in the center of Narragansett Bay, the reserve occupies territory of the bay itself and land on four islands: Prudence, Patience, Hope, and Dyer Islands. The reserve manages and protects nearly 4,400 acres of land and water and is committed to conducting the most current research in the estuarine ecosystem and promoting long-term environmental education and stewardship.

Patience Island is 207 acres of this critical reserve. The island teems with black cherry, shadbush, blueberry, bayberry, red cedar, and a state rare plant species called the seablite. Wildlife that populate the island are white-tailed deer, red fox, and many waterfowl, including the common loon, horned grebes, great cormorants, and quahogs. Historically, all of the islands were utilized and traversed by the Wampanoag and Narragansett Indians prior to colonial settlement. Patience Island used to be a large farm in the 17th century, until the Revolutionary War provoked the burning of all the farm buildings by the British. Afterward, the farm was rebuilt and remained in existence until the mid-20th century, when the island was targeted as a resort haven. Construction for the resort was never completed. Patience Island only has about 200 full-time residents, but during the summer months, the population explodes.

Occupying a central location within Narragansett Bay, Prudence Island boasts a rich salt marsh community with spike grass, cord grass, salt meadow grass, marsh lavender, marsh elder, fiddler crabs, green crabs, and snails. The plant life on the island reflects its history of farming within the last century. It is a mix of deciduous forest and shrubland. Prudence Island is known for hosting a deer population that is unmatched in any other part of New England. This island is a site for the state's rare golden aster and the seaside sparrow, which is becoming increasingly rare in Rhode Island. In 1637, Prudence Island was purchased from the Narragansett Indians by Roger Williams and John Northrop. Although Williams and Northrop did not live on the island, they both visited the island frequently and promoted farming and settlement.

Hope Island is 91 acres of uninhabited land with rocky shoreline and bluffs. Unlike Patience Island, Hope Island is closed during the summer months due to its significance as a nesting place for colonial birds such as great egrets, snowy egrets, black-crowned night herons, Canada geese, herring gulls, and black-backed gulls. The island has an agricultural history and was once used as a storage location for ammunition during World War II.

Continual research and monitoring of the Narragansett Bay estuary is a high priority of the reserve in order to protect and manage the environmental quality of this important area. The biggest threats to the bay and the islands are development, pollution, and ecologically damaging forms of land use. To encourage understanding of the ecological sensitivity of the bay and its natural communities, many educational opportunities are provided by the reserve, including volunteer days for cleaning the beaches, open houses, statewide presentations and displays, and exhibits at the reserve's learning center. The reserve also offers a coastal training program for individuals who want to play a more active role in managing the estuary's natural resources. Some of the ongoing stewardship projects involve supporting the nesting areas for osprey, monitoring invasive species, protecting eelgrass beds, constructing shelters for barn swallows, and restoring meadow, salt marsh, and pine barren communities. A promising outlook for the Narragansett Bay and its watershed and islands is that there are numerous efforts at the federal, state, and local levels dedicated to working toward enhancing the ecological value of this beautiful natural area.

Further Reading
Henshaw, Carol. *Natural Wonders of Connecticut & Rhode Island: Exploring Wild and Scenic Places*. New York: McGraw-Hill, 2000.

Narragansett Bay Research Reserve. http://www.nbnerr.org.

National Estuarine Research Reserve System. http://www.nerrs.noaa.gov/Narragansett Bay/.

RODMAN'S HOLLOW

Situated 12 miles off the coast of Rhode Island, Block Island is home to numerous nature preserves, the Block Island National Wildlife Refuge, rocky bluffs, peaceful trails, clear ponds, golden beaches, and other scenic coastal areas. It provides habitat for the endangered American burying beetle and 40 other rare and protected species. This 6,200-acre island was formed by glaciers many thousands of years ago, and what exists today is a treasured island protected by state, local, and federal environmental management agencies as well as the stewardship of its residents. Block Island is an important stop for migratory birds along the Atlantic Flyway. It supports coastal shrubs, morainal grasslands (grasslands containing glacial deposits), and a rich cultural heritage.

In the southwest region of Block Island is a 230-acre glacial depression called Rodman's Hollow. The depression was formed from glacial melt water that eroded the south end of the island. Within the hollow are three large holes that were formed by the melting of three large ice chunks. The Rodman's Hollow preserve is a home for the bushy rockrose, which is endangered in the state of Rhode Island. Bayberry, arrowwood, and shadbush also adorn this coastal ecosystem.

Another important fact about Rodman's Hollow is that it is one of the last remaining habitats for the Block Island meadow vole. This is vole is a subspecies of the meadow vole that is commonly found on New England mainland. The Block Island vole was discovered by naturalist Outram Bangs in 1899 and has a few distinguishing characteristics: its body is more rounded, it is a lighter shade of brown than the mainland vole, it has a gray belly, and it is slightly larger. While the life span of a meadow vole is only about one and a half years, the females can produce up to 100 offspring in one year. The voles live above ground and tunnel their way through the grasses and leaves, creating chambers and travel networks. They eat seeds, flowers, and grasses and are a vital food source for preying birds, especially the marsh hawk and northern harrier.

Because of its unique geological features, Rodman's Hollow is the site that marks the origin of conservation efforts on Block Island. After being discovered by vacationers as a beautiful location, a development boom began in the early 1970s that was then curtailed by a man named John Robinson Lewis. Along with other residents on the island, Lewis began the Block Island Conservancy to preserve and protect the open space and undeveloped areas on the island. Rodman's Hollow became permanently protected when many residents donated their lands to the conservancy. But this was only the beginning of conservation on Block Island. Now, decades later, it has been estimated that 40 percent of the island's open space has been preserved by the Block Island Conservancy. Included in this effort was the establishment of the Block Island National Wildlife Refuge. Founded in 1973, it is 127 acres of natural habitat for wildlife. It is a stopover spot for the endangered piping plover and the largest colony of gulls in the state.

Other important areas include the Hodge Family Wildlife Preserve, which supports migratory birds, maritime shrubland, and other species significant for Block Island. Additionally, there is a preserve called the Nathan Mott Park and Turnip Farm that is protected, in part, by the Block Island Conservancy. A state endangered plant known as the northern blazing star thrives here more than in other part of the state, and, because of this preserve's higher elevation, it offers broad sweeping views of Block Island's open space. The conservation efforts have been incredibly successful on this teardrop-shaped island, helping to maintain both its natural wonders and its rural charm.

Further Reading

Ball, Martha. *Block Island: Rhode Island's Jewel.* Beverly, MA: Commonwealth Editions, 2007.

Sterling, Dorothy. *Outer Lands: A Natural History Guide to Cape Cod, Martha's Vineyard, Nantucket, Block Island, and Long Island.* New York: W. W. Norton, 1992.

WOOD RIVER

Rolling through Arcadia Wildlife Management Area is the sparkling Wood River. Considered a wild and scenic waterway, the Wood River is stocked with trout and home to beavers, warblers, hawks, dragonflies, wood turtles, and damselflies. Along the banks of the river are red maple trees, pitch pine, oak, and colorful wildflowers in the warmer months. The Wood River is critical in supporting the forest, stream, and wildlife habitats in the Arcadia Wildlife Management Area. Keeping residential development at a minimum has been key for keeping this river vibrant and clean.

The Headwaters of the Wood River is a 56-acre tract of land managed by the Nature Conservancy that connects already-protected blocks of land. The significance of this area is to add to the expanse of protected forest that runs from Boston to New York to form a vast area of preserved woodland and streams. The headwaters region is just north of Arcadia and contains rough trails for hiking. Arcadia has an extensive trail system. Some of the most scenic and inspiring trails are Arcadia Trail, John B. Hudson Trail, and Breakheart Trail.

The Wood River is one of the purest rivers in Rhode Island. It has this reputation because of the condition of the forest lands within the Wood-Pawcatuck watershed. The high soil quality in Arcadia strongly contributes to the health of both the Wood and the Pawcatuck rivers. The water from these rivers provides drinking water to most of southern Rhode Island. In recent years, these rivers have become a focus of priority concern because of the increased development that is threatening the quality of these clear waterways. Efforts to reduce the increasing amount of pollution entering the rivers involves educating homeowners who live in the watershed, specifically those who are close to the river banks. Planting trees and providing a shoreline buffer helps to filter out toxins before they drain into the river water. The Nature Conservancy and Wood-Pawcatuck Watershed Association are working to protect the integrity of these rivers that are not only essential to the people who live in these areas but for recreational purposes as well. These rivers provide some of the best canoeing and fishing opportunities in the state.

The Wood River also provides important educational environments for regional schools. It has been used by local schools as an outdoor laboratory for learning about the river's ecology. Students test the river's oxygen levels, pH, its chemical and biological properties, and they study its plant and animal species. Students learn that the presence of a variety of different species is a strong indicator of the health and condition of the river. A number of schools participate in this learning opportunity, which, ultimately, provides a more thorough study of the Wood River. Meanwhile, students become actively involved in a concern critical to their own communities, they learn about watersheds, ecology, biodiversity, and the impact of humans on one of our most precious natural resources—water.

Keeping the Wood River clean is dependent upon keeping the surrounding forests in western Rhode Island healthy and intact. Arcadia Wildlife Management Area not only supports the Wood River, but, of all the state-managed natural areas in Rhode Island, Arcadia is the largest. Nearly 14,000 acres, Arcadia is awash in the deep green of white pine trees and is teeming with wetlands, wild rivers, ponds, trails, and wildlife. Residents in the towns of West Greenwich, Hopkinton, Exeter, and Richmond in western Rhode Island call Arcadia home. Fox, raccoon, mink, white-tailed deer, cottontail rabbits, squirrels, ruffed grouse, and wild turkey are just a few of the regular inhabitants of this natural area that are nourished by the wild Wood River and its surrounding woodlands.

Further Reading

Henshaw, Carol. *Natural Wonders of Connecticut & Rhode Island: Exploring Wild and Scenic Places*. New York: McGraw-Hill, 2000.

Nature Conservancy. "Headwaters of the Wood River." http://www.nature.org/wherewework/northamerica/states/rhodeisland/preserves/art4093.html.

Wood-Pawcatuck Watershed Association. http://www.wpwa.org/.

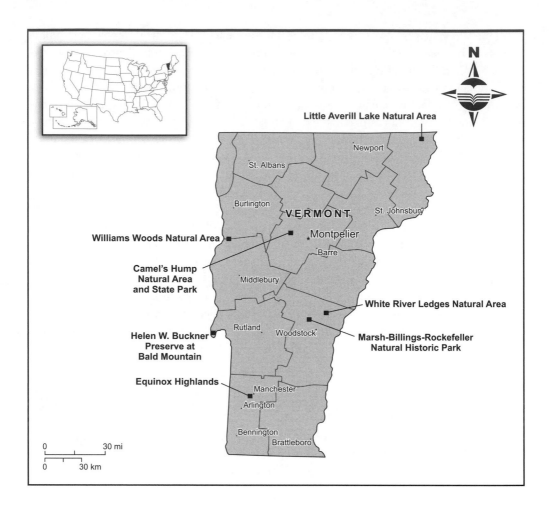

Little Averill Lake Natural Area

Newport

St. Albans

Burlington

VERMONT

St. Johnsbury

Williams Woods Natural Area

Montpelier

Barre

Camel's Hump
Natural Area
and State Park

Middlebury

White River Ledges Natural Area

Rutland

Woodstock

Marsh-Billings-Rockefeller
Natural Historic Park

Helen W. Buckner
Preserve at
Bald Mountain

Equinox Highlands

Manchester

Arlington

Bennington

Brattleboro

0   30 mi

0   30 km

Camel's Hump Natural Area and State Park, 144

Equinox Highlands, 146

Helen W. Buckner Preserve at Bald Mountain, 147

Little Averill Lake Natural Area, 149

Marsh-Billings-Rockefeller National Historic Park, 150

White River Ledges Natural Area, 152

Williams Woods Natural Area, 154

VERMONT

Vermont's story is one of ecological and social recovery. A state that was once indiscriminately ravaged by the timber industry, it is now known for its verdant northern hardwood forests, gently rolling rural hills spotted with farms, vibrant fall foliage, sparkling Lake Champlain, and its commitment to sustainability and stewardship at both the state and local levels. It is the state that, in the 19th century, inspired George Perkins Marsh at his home in Woodstock near Mount Tom to write *Man and Nature* in 1864 to challenge prevailing notions that human activities had little impact on the natural environment and its ecosystems. Often referred to as the father of the conservation movement, Marsh and his environmental ethic questioned the perception of America as the land of limitless resources. Marsh inspired fellow native Vermonter Frederick Billings, who implemented the most sustainable farming practices of his time in Vermont and led conservation movements in the American West.

Vermont is nicknamed the Green Mountain State to reflect its recognition of one of its most valued natural resources and to claim its green hilly terrain as a distinct feature of its state identity. The Green Mountain National Forest is perhaps the largest expression of this identity, spanning close to 400,000 acres across a vast portion of central Vermont. The forest is a rich tapestry of red, peach, russet, and gold in the fall, while in the summer, it is an outdoor recreation attraction and a place to take refuge in one of its lush, tranquil hollows.

A major factor that has helped to develop Vermont's strong land ethic and "green" reputation is the success of its leading organizations that have pioneered conservation efforts. One of the most vital stewardship organizations in the state is the Vermont Land Trust (VLT). A highly effective nonprofit organization, the VLT provides financial and stewardship assistance to communities, landowners, and other state agencies to conserve Vermont's natural resources and its rural economy. According to Nora Mitchell and Rolf Diamant, "the success of VLT has made it a model for many other smaller land trusts in the Northeast and across the country." In 2006, a survey conducted for the VLT by the University of Vermont Center for Rural Studies found that the participants of the survey place high value on the state's natural environment, working farms, locally grown food, and nonmotorized recreational areas. It is VLT's willingness to serve the needs of the people of Vermont while protecting the state's natural resources that contributes to its statewide and regional success.

Another state initiative that is working to conserve Vermont's natural resources is the Clean and Clear Program that began in 2003 and is dedicated to improving the state's water quality. One of the most serious water-quality threats for Vermont is phosphorous that gets into the water supply as runoff from developed areas and causes toxic algae blooms. With funds supplied by the Clean and Clear Program, ecosystem restoration projects are being formed to reduce the concentration of phosphorous that is polluting the water and threatening biological communities.

Vermont is also actively researching the impact of climate change on the state's natural environment. The Vermont Commission on Climate Change investigates the existing and potential negative impacts of climate change to Vermont's ecology, public health, and economy. It also seeks to discover new ways to reduce greenhouse gas emissions and provide education to citizens and business about energy conservation and reducing carbon emissions. This commission was formed by Governor Jim Douglas upon the recognition of the "profound implications that global warming and climate variation could have on the economy, environment, and quality of life in Vermont."

The state of Vermont has experienced a substantial recovery of its natural heritage since its logging legacy because of its belief in the importance of public engagement. Participatory democracy is highly valued by the people of Vermont. Communities across the state hold annual town meetings that are well attended to discuss conservation concerns as well as the state's budget and other important matters.

CAMEL'S HUMP NATURAL AREA AND STATE PARK

In central Vermont, in the Green Mountains, a mountain formed from advancing glaciers called Camel's Hump reaches higher than 4,000 feet high and is the focal point in Camel's Hump Natural Area and State Park. Totaling a little over 23,000 acres, the Camel's Hump region and summit is one of the most widely recognized landforms in Vermont because of the mountain's double-humped shape that resembles a camel's back. Cartographer Ira Allen in 1798 called the mountain Camel's Rump, which evolved into Camel's Hump a few decades later. But even before that, the mountain was named lion couchant or resting lion by early explorers, and a Waubanaukee word meaning "saddle mountain" was also used to describe this distinctive mountain. The park and forests of Camel's Hump are known for their lush, green vegetation, abundant wildlife, and breathtaking beauty.

This large, preserved parcel of land began with 1,000 acres that Colonel Joseph Battell owned to protect the mountain from logging and to preserve the aesthetic beauty of the mountain summit. The mountain, particularly the summit, had already undergone devastating logging practices in the mid-19th century that threatened the red spruce population on the mountain because of its wide use in home building materials and for the production of paper. In 1969, surrounding forest areas were designated a park, while the summit and its supporting acres remained a natural area. Farming, a massive fire on the mountain in the early 1900s, insects, and various diseases are also part of the mountain's ecological history. Because of the summit's environmental fragility, recreational activities are permitted but highly limited.

An attraction for many visitors to Camel's Hump is the summit's arctic-alpine vegetation. Alpine bilberry, mountain cranberry, mountain sandwort, Labrador tea, and Bigelow sedge are some of the plants that grow in the alpine zone. Because the high altitude climate is not conducive to a diversity of wildlife, a few birds such as ravens and sparrows can occasionally been seen hovering near the summit, while mice and voles tunnel through the vegetation below. In the park, however, there is quite an abundance of wildlife. Moose, bobcats, porcupines, and bears inhabit the park amid the birch, maple, beech, ash, spruce, and fir trees.

Camel's Hump is an attraction to hikers who can traverse the extensive trail system, and it is also a place of considerable interest to researchers who wish to study the arctic-alpine natural community and the devastating impacts of acid rain. Because of the high elevation of Camel's Hump, the summit region is occasionally surrounded in polluted cloud cover that deposits a fine mist on the trees. This cloud mist is often more concentrated with acids deadly to trees than when it falls in the form of rain, thus producing a significant threat to the vegetation near the summit. Trees, such as the red spruce, on other sections of the mountain seem to be in decline, with evidence suggesting acid rain is either killing the trees or weakening them so that they more easily succumb to diseases and fungal infections. Researchers continue to study the forest damage at Camel's Hump due to acid rain.

As a uniquely visual landmark and important symbol of Vermont's natural heritage, Camel's Hump Natural Area and State Park is a wilderness habitat, a home for rare species, and a protection site for the Gleason Brook drainage area. It is a central location for the study of air pollution and its effect on forests and a carefully managed recreation area that offers visitors hiking, skiing, hunting, camping, and snowmobiling in designated areas.

Further Reading

Gardner, A. Blake. *Untamed Vermont: Extraordinary Wilderness Areas of the Green Mountain State*. North Pomfret, VT: Thistle Hill, 2003.

Johnson, Charles W. *The Nature of Vermont: Introduction and Guide to a New England Environment*. Hanover, NH: University Press of New England, 1998.

Scofield, Bruce. *High Peaks of the Northeast: A Peakbagger's Directory and Resource Guide to the Highest Summits in the Northeastern United States*. Amherst, MA: New England Cartographics, 1994.

EQUINOX HIGHLANDS

In southwestern Vermont, there are forest regions so vibrant and abundant with life that ecologists refer to them as rich northern hardwood forests, or RNHFs. The Equinox Highlands, located in Manchester and Dorset, are the largest of these rich forest natural areas in New England. Covering Mount Equinox and, to a smaller extent, Mother Myrick Mountain, the 2,000 acres that make up the Equinox Highlands are treasured forests and critically important to the state of Vermont.

The Equinox Highlands are part of the Taconic Mountains, a slender range of marble, slate, shale, and limestone in southwestern Vermont that stretches down into Connecticut. Mount Equinox, at 3,852 feet, is the highest peak in the Taconic range. The rich northern hardwood forests that create the highlands are predominately sugar maple forests, making for a stunning foliage display in the fall. Other trees that are common to the forests are white ash and basswood and occasionally black cherry, sweet birch, and butternut.

But it is not just the trees that make the Equinox Highlands so rich and blooming with biodiversity. In the spring, the forest floor is dancing with wildflowers, some of which are quite rare. The moist, nutrient-rich soils of the highlands offer habitat to the uncommon Goldie's wood fern, puttyroot, Hooker's orchis, and wood millet. The herbs that grow in the highlands are particularly lush with wild ginger, blue cohosh, wood nettle, maidenhair fern, hepatica, and Dutchman's breeches, to name a few. The RNHFs are known for having one of the most concentrated medleys of herbaceous plants than any other natural area in New England. Two important aspects make these forests so rich: the combination of the marble and the limestone, which weathers quickly to deposit important nutrients into the soil, and the downslope topography that gathers these nutrients in the lower areas, creating a soil that is akin to compost.

Along with the presence of more than 40 species of birds, there are falcons, bears, bobcats, moose, flying squirrels, and many other animals common to the northern forests residing in the Equinox Highlands. This area is home to two rare species of bats: the Indiana bat, and the eastern small-footed bat. Wild brown and brook trout can be found in the Batten Kill River as the rainwater filters down through the mountains, becomes more purified, and provides fresh water for the fish and for the people of Manchester.

Unfortunately, like many of the natural areas in the United States, the Equinox Highlands are being threatened by invasive species, overdevelopment, logging, and an overwhelming deer population. Some of the steps being taken to manage the area's critical resources include protecting the natural forest composition, the native species, the downslope movement of nutrients, the high biodiversity, the herbaceous species, and the rapid decomposition of organic matter that creates the rich soil. Also of great importance is the implementation of responsible and strategic timber management practices so that the forests can support the region's economic needs while still maintaining its high ecological value. Work is being done to improve the network of hiking trails for nearby residents and visitors who are drawn to these unforgettable forests. On an international scale, protecting the Equinox Highlands is critical due to the alarming rate of deforestation around the world that is contributing to climate change and the destruction of migratory bird habitats. The Campaign for the Equinox Highlands, initiated in 2007 by the Vermont chapter of the Nature Conservancy, hopes to address all of these conservation issues in the highlands as well as finalize the purchase of thousands of surrounding acres to ensure that these rich forests will continue to thrive.

Further Reading

Gardner, A. Blake. *Untamed Vermont: Extraordinary Wilderness Areas of the Green Mountain State*. North Pomfret, VT: Thistle Hill, 2003.

Johnson, Charles W. *The Nature of Vermont: Introduction and Guide to a New England Environment*. Hanover, NH: University Press of New England, 1998.

Thompson, Elizabeth H., and Eric R. Sorenson. *Wetland, Woodland, Wildland: A Guide to the Natural Communities of Vermont*. Middlebury, VT: Department of Fish and Wildlife and the Nature Conservancy, 2000.

HELEN W. BUCKNER PRESERVE AT BALD MOUNTAIN

Part of the Southern Lake Champlain Valley, the Helen W. Buckner Preserve at Bald Mountain is a wellspring of biodiversity, beauty, and thriving natural communities. In the midst of gentle farmland and the southern portion of Lake Champlain, Bald Mountain is home to peregrine falcons that nest in the cliffs and float over the valley and wetlands below. The 3,776-acre preserve contains marsh habitat, upland forest, wetlands, 11 unusual animal species for Vermont, 18 rare plant species, and 10 plant communities. The biodiversity level at this preserve is the highest in Vermont, making it a likely candidate for priority ecological management.

The preserve is located in West Haven, Vermont, where it is bordered by the Poultney River and Lake Champlain. Because it is in a peninsula, the scenic views are of New York state as well as Vermont. Amphibians live at this preserve as well as wild turkeys, bobcats, black bears, bald eagles, and ospreys. The preserve is a colorful sweep of wildflowers in the spring and a bird-watcher's paradise year-round. The natural community that is most prominent at Helen W. Buckner is the forest of white and red oak, hophornbeam, shagbark, and bitternut hickory.

Hikers can enjoy two nature trails at the preserve: the Susan Bacher Memorial Trail and Tim's Trail. From Tim's Trail, hikers can observe talus slopes that are formed from rocks that fall from a cliff. The rock piles provide stable habitats, especially for reptiles. There are also magnificent overlooks from Tim's Trail. From the trail, hikers can enjoy views of Ward Marsh, an important wetland blanketed in cattails. The Poultney River and Birdseye Mountain can also be seen from the trail, and there are views of the town of

Whitehall, New York, and the Champlain Barge Canal. Along the trail, stone walls from the 19th century are likely indicators of early property boundaries. The trail is named after and dedicated to Timothy Cameron Kuehn, a young man who died in his early 20s. Tim grew up in West Haven and had a great passion for the beauty and peace of this natural area. There is also a trail of chestnut groves that connects Tim's Trail and the Susan Bacher Memorial Trail that offers views of Lake Champlain and Black Mountain.

There are many opportunities for local residents to volunteer to help with conservation efforts in the Southern Lake Champlain Valley. For the last two decades, volunteers have helped to control water chestnut populations in Southern Lake Champlain because of the damage this invasive species can do to ecologically sensitive wetlands. Thousands of pounds of water chestnut plants are pulled each year by dedicated volunteers. In fact, Tim's Trail was created by the hard work of volunteers who cleared and marked the trail and built the information kiosk.

The Buckner Preserve has remained relatively unpolluted and unexploited not only because of the careful stewardship of the Nature Conservancy, but also because of the diligent management of the larger landscape within which it resides. Several chapters of the Nature Conservancy from both Vermont and New York work to protect numerous nature preserves that help to maintain the area's mountains and wetlands. In addition to Buckner Preserve, the region is home to Shaw Mountain Natural Area, Hubbardton River Clayplain Preserve, Lower Poultney River Preserve, and Saddles Mountain Preserve. A walk through Buckner Preserve is a walk through hemlocks and mixed hardwoods, along old stone walls, and through woodland stocked with overlooks that inspire and evoke awe as the red-tailed hawks soar from behind the mountains and then disappear.

Further Reading
Champlain Valley Clayplain Forest Project. www.clayplain.org.

Gardner, A. Blake. *Untamed Vermont: Extraordinary Wilderness Areas of the Green Mountain State*. North Pomfret, VT: Thistle Hill, 2003.

Nature Conservancy. "The Helen W. Buckner Preserve at Bald Mountain." http://www.nature.org/wherewework/northamerica/states/vermont/preserves/art7277.html.

Thompson, Elizabeth H., and Eric R. Sorenson. *Wetland, Woodland, Wildland: A Guide to the Natural Communities of Vermont*. Middlebury, VT: Department of Fish and Wildlife and the Nature Conservancy, 2000.

LITTLE AVERILL LAKE NATURAL AREA

In the northeast corner of Vermont, close to the Canadian border, fishers who like to sit quietly in their boats on the glassy evening waters of Little Averill Lake may hear the call of a common loon in the distance as they are waiting for the fish to stir in the deep, cool water that spans 438 acres. Or they may not. The common loon has not been able to live up to its name, given that the water bird was once considered endangered in Vermont. The Little Averill Lake Natural Area, owned by the Nature Conservancy, is a location designated for the protection of nesting sites for the common loon, and the Vermont Institute of Natural Science carefully observes and studies the loon's breeding patterns in this important natural area in Averill, Vermont.

In the middle of the 20th century, common loon populations were in decline, mostly likely due to loss of habitat and contaminated waters. But, in the last several decades, there has been gradual increase of the common loon, possibly because of improved conservation efforts and greater advancements toward cleaning waterways of dangerous pollutants such as mercury and lead. However, recent studies by the Wildlife Conservation Society and the BioDiversity Research Institute indicate that mercury from coal-burning emissions is having a profound impact on the health, behavior, and breeding patterns of the water bird in the northern United States. Research to discover and implement alternative energy sources will need to continue to offset the devastating impact of dirty, dangerous, and unsustainable coal mining and burning that has been detrimental to the environmental health of the United States and is a leading contributor to global climate change.

The common loon is most abundant in Canada, Greenland, and the northern United States. They have red eyes and black-and-white plumage that is highly identifiable. They are superb swimmers but somewhat clumsy on land. Loons breed once a year during the warmer months and build their nests in grassy areas, often on peninsulas and islands. They prefer secluded lake areas and have a captivating, yodeling call that can be heard from a great distance. The common loon is perhaps most known for this haunting call, but perceptions of the bird vary widely. Fishers may see loons as competition for fish, and they carry a substantial number of body parasites. At one time, they were hunted for sport, but now they are probably most valued as symbolic of the northern lakes and wilderness. They are a food source for the Cree Indians in Canada, and, to some environmentalists, the well-being (or lack thereof) of the common loon is a powerful indicator of what is in store for humans if environmental standards are not improved.

While protection of the common loon's nesting site is one of the primary reasons why the secluded Little Averill Lake is a natural area of critical importance, there are other significant ecological features of this area. It is home to a northern white cedar swamp and a unique beach vegetation community. Round-leaved sundew, green wood orchis, bugleweed, and shrubs such as mountain holly, sourtop blueberry, and sweet gale grow on the sandy shores of the lake. Peregrine falcons can be seen flying overhead, and moose and other wildlife thrive in the area. Brousseau Mountain stretches above the lake, and the area is surrounded by northern hardwood forest and other forest communities. The Little Averill drains into the Great Averill Pond, which is a popular location for recreational activities. Although much of the surrounding area is used for timber production, Little Averill Lake Natural Area is remote and resplendent.

Further Reading

Johnson, Charles W. *The Nature of Vermont: Introduction and Guide to a New England Environment.* Hanover, NH: University Press of New England, 1998.

Tavener, Julien. *John J. Audubon's Guide: The Birds of the Northeast.* Boston: Audubon Masterpiece Collection, 2003.

Thompson, Elizabeth H., and Eric R. Sorenson. *Wetland, Woodland, Wildland: A Guide to the Natural Communities of Vermont.* Middlebury, VT: Department of Fish and Wildlife and the Nature Conservancy, 2000.

MARSH-BILLINGS-ROCKEFELLER NATIONAL HISTORIC PARK

In 1864, a book entitled *Man and Nature* was published that asked readers in the mid-19th century to rethink their perceptions of the American landscape as a place of limitless resources and to reconsider the logging, farming, and industrial practices at the time that were having a profound impact on forests, watersheds, and ecosystems. Often referred to as the father of the conservation movement, the author of that book is George Perkins Marsh, who grew up on the property that is now the Marsh-Billings-Rockefeller National Historic Park and whose childhood memories of living among the beautiful landscape of Woodstock, Vermont, would impact him for the rest of his life.

One individual who was deeply influenced by the writings of Marsh was Frederick Billings, who later bought the Marsh property near Mount Tom, bought additional nearby property, planted trees, created trails with spectacular views, and established a farm using the most progressive sustainable practices at the time in order to use the natural resources without depleting and damaging the landscape. After his death, his daughters took over the property, and, with careful stewardship and help, they maintained their father's commitment to sustainable forest management practices. In addition to being known for his farm in Vermont, Billings promoted the conservation of areas in the American West.

When the granddaughter of Frederick Billings, Mary French, married Laurance Rockefeller, a son of John D. Rockefeller, Jr., the union would see to it that the Marsh-Billings property would remain in the hands of owners who saw land stewardship as a central priority for the welfare of all. Coming from a family who made conservation efforts part of their national legacy, Laurance Rockefeller created Virgin Islands National

Marsh-Billings-Rockefeller National Historical Park. (Courtesy of Bryan Whalen)

Park and held the position of chairman of the Outdoor Recreations Resources Review Commission. In 1992, Mary and Laurance donated the property and surrounding forests to the National Park Service.

The Marsh-Billings-Rockefeller National Park was officially designated and opened in 1998. The park features many miles of scenic trails and roads skirted in hemlock, beech, and maple trees. Mount Tom consists of 550 acres of ecologically managed forest and has been certified by the Forest Stewardship Council as sustainable forest. Only about a mile from the park, hikers can embark on the famous Appalachian National Scenic Trail that extends from Georgia to Maine. A 14-acre pond called The Pogue is on the property as well as the mansion and gardens. In the mansion, visitors can see photographs and paintings of the American West by Frederick Billings that he sent back east while on his travels in order to provoke interest in conservation out west. Nearby is the Billings Farm and Museum, a dairy farm that connects visitors to the historic, rural life of Vermont. The National Park Service Conservation Study Institute is also located in the park, as well as the Carriage Barn Visitor Center that was refurbished by using white pine from the park and by utilizing local artisans to build the chairs, benches, and bookcases.

Dedicated to community outreach and stewardship education, the Marsh-Billings-Rockefeller National Park is also part of the Forest for Every Classroom program, which provides opportunities for educators to develop workshops and classes that foreground ecological sustainability, a sense of place, and stewardship practices. The program is deeply committed to enhancing the understanding of the interconnections between places and people and promoting active engagement in the care of public lands and places. In addition to its civic outreach goals, the park is a symbol of, and a testament to, its conservation history and the stewardship activities that make the park a model for a sustainable future.

Further Reading

Dorman, Robert. *A Word for Nature: Four Pioneering Environmental Advocates*. Chapel Hill: University of North Carolina Press, 1998.

Klyza, Christopher McGrory, and Stephen Trombulak. *The Story of Vermont: A Natural and Cultural History*. Hanover, NH: University Press of New England, 1999.

Marsh, George Perkins. *Man and Nature*. Cambridge, MA: Belknap Press, 1965. (Originally published in 1864.)

National Park Service. "Marsh-Billings-Rockefeller National Historic Park." http://www.nps.gov/mabi/.

WHITE RIVER LEDGES NATURAL AREA

Due to heavy agricultural use, floodplain forests have been greatly diminishing in Vermont, but on the shores of the White River in the White River Ledges Natural Area, such valuable floodplain natural communities are thriving with sturdy ash-leaved maple trees. As the yearly flooding overflows the banks of the White River, the slow receding river leaves behind clay and silt deposits that nourish the forest floor and support the growth of various herbs and voluminous ostrich ferns.

White River Ledges is also home to northern hardwood forest natural communities that are quite common for the state of Vermont. These forests teem with sugar maple, yellow birch, and American beech. Additionally, this preserve contains the rich northern hardwood forest natural communities that are formed from water filtering down hillsides through mineral bedrock, which creates fertile soil near the base of the hills and cultivates an abundance of spring flowers, herbs, and green vegetation. The diverse presence of herbs is a telltale characteristic that makes this natural community distinct from the northern hardwood forests.

There is yet another natural community that thrives in White River Ledges called the calcareous riverside seep. This natural community is formed when water that has a high calcium content trickles down through riverside rocks, supporting the growth of rich mosses and grasses, some of which are uncommon. Regular flooding and ice help to keep these rocks open for the seepage.

The 186-acre White River Ledges Natural Area is located in the towns of Pomfret and Sharon in the central Vermont Piedmont region, where the landscape has been shaped by the influx and retreat of glaciers that formed the hills, valleys, and waterways thousands of years ago. The White River is an old river. It has played a role in shaping the landscape as it furthers its course toward draining into the Connecticut River. The fact that it has remained unaltered by damming means that its natural flow and flooding patterns have been maintained. This seasonal flooding not only promotes the growth of floodplain forest communities, but many animal species rely on the regular flooding for their survival. The river is home to beavers, raccoon, bald eagles, blue herons, river otters, and bank swallows. Also, the Atlantic salmon swims upstream and is dependent upon the river's flow patterns.

One of the primary threats to the natural communities at White River Ledges Natural Area is the overgrowth of invasive species that threaten the local population of native plants. The Nature Conservancy has created a weed management plan to keep the exotic species at bay. Plants such as the common reed, honeysuckle, and Japanese knotweed add to the list of invasive plants that must be carefully managed.

Agricultural practices, such as sheep grazing, have greatly impacted some of the natural communities at White River Ledges, but the sheep have been moved to another location in order to protect this important natural area since the Nature Conservancy acquired the property in 1998.

This Vermont landscape has been highly populated by humans for thousands of years—from the Algonquin and Iroquois who burned the fields to fertilize the soil to the Europeans who, comparatively speaking, are newcomers to this region and promoted their agriculture. But the White River Ledges Natural Area still maintains much of its natural beauty. One only needs to walk the one-mile trail loop to see that this inspiring terrain with its unique and representative natural communities adjacent to the rolling White River is a vital natural habitat for plants and animals and an asset to the entire central Vermont Piedmont region.

Further Reading

Johnson, Charles W. *The Nature of Vermont: Introduction and Guide to a New England Environment.* Hanover, NH: University Press of New England, 1998.

Mitchell, Nora, and Rolf Diamant. "Stewardship and Sustainability: Lessons from the 'Middle Landscape' of Vermont." In *Wilderness Comes Home: Rewilding the Northeast,* edited by Christopher McGrory Klyza, 213–33. Hanover, NH: University Press of New England, 2001.

Thompson, Elizabeth H., and Eric R. Sorenson. *Wetland, Woodland, Wildland: A Guide to the Natural Communities of Vermont.* Middlebury, VT: Department of Fish and Wildlife and the Nature Conservancy, 2000.

WILLIAMS WOODS NATURAL AREA

A t one time, when European settlers first walked through woodlands near what is now northwestern Vermont, they most likely walked through a natural community called a valley clayplain forest. This forest type used to dominate the Champlain Valley, but it is now considered endangered and only occurs in small fragments. Valley clayplain forests contain a wide variety of trees, including white pine, white oak, red maple, red oak, shagbark hickory, white ash, bur oak, and others. This forest type contains a greater variety of tree species than any other forest community in the northern New England region. An abundance of plant and herbaceous communities are supported by the fertile clay soil of the clayplain forest. Some of these species are more common in southern regions, but they thrive in the warmer, Champlain Valley climate. Additionally, many animal species call the clayplain forest home because of the number of nut-producing trees that provide them with food. Williams Woods Natural Area is a 63-acre nature preserve that attempts to protect this threatened valley clayplain forest, which serves as a vital link to Vermont's ecological history. It also supports several other natural communities and is a laboratory for the study of storm damage in the Champlain Valley.

In addition to the valley clayplain forest, Williams Woods is home to mixed hardwoods, a regenerating field, a marsh area, and a white pine and hemlock community. The marsh area is near Thorp Brook, where tree frogs, salamanders, and other amphibians thrive. There are two very large swamp white oaks that are estimated to be more than 200 years old in Williams Woods and a trail loop that passes two bridges and circles within the center of the preserve, giving hikers and nature observers a view of the natural communities.

Numerous activities are taking place to protect Williams Woods and the valley clayplain forest ecosystem. The Nature Conservancy provides stewardship for Williams Woods by maintaining the hiking trail, monitoring and controlling invasive species, and engaging in research to study and support the effects of storm damage on the trees in Williams Woods. With the understanding that felled trees are a necessary aspect of forest health, trees that have fallen from high winds and storms are left to decompose on the forest floor for the study of how those rotting trees become habitats for species and help to regenerate the forest floor. In 2007, a weather event that brought down trees in the preserve prompted a reconstruction of the hiking trail in order to accommodate the fallen trees for the study of how natural disturbances assist in forest health and vitality.

Performing additional work to protect the clayplain forest region in northwestern Vermont is the Chaplain Valley Clayplain Forest Project. This program promotes the research, education, and stewardship of the valley clayplain forest ecosystem to foster understanding of the critical importance of this forest type and to encourage sustainable land use practices that help to preserve this important link to the Champlain Valley's ecological history. Activities include controlling invasive species (particularly honeysuckle), tree planting, and educational events that teach local residents about the unique and complex characteristics of the forest. Because of the warmer climate of the southern

Champlain Valley region, agriculture has been the dominating force that has disrupted the natural cycles and native species in this region of Vermont. Only roughly 10 percent of the original valley clayplain forest ecosystem still remains in fragments throughout the landscape. It is of critical importance that individuals and organizations continue their hard work at Williams Wood Natural Area and beyond to protect this rare but vital part of Vermont's natural heritage.

Further Reading

Brynn, David. "Vermont Family Forests: Building a Sustainable Relationship with Local Forests." In *Wilderness Comes Home: Rewilding the Northeast,* edited by Christopher McGrory Klyza, 234–55. Hanover, NH: University Press of New England, 2001.

Champlain Valley Clayplain Forest Project. http://www.clayplain.org.

Thompson, Elizabeth H., and Eric R. Sorenson. *Wetland, Woodland, Wildland: A Guide to the Natural Communities of Vermont.* Middlebury, VT: Department of Fish and Wildlife and the Nature Conservancy, 2000.

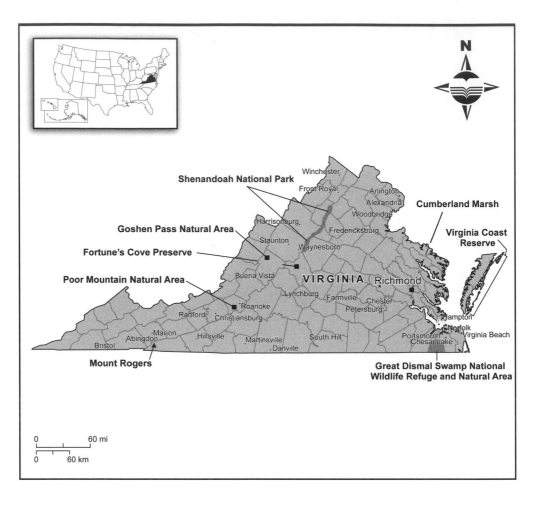

Cumberland Marsh, 158

Fortune's Cove Preserve, 160

Goshen Pass Natural Area, 161

Great Dismal Swamp National Wildlife Refuge and Natural Area, 162

Mount Rogers, 164

Poor Mountain Natural Area, 165

Shenandoah National Park, 167

Virginia Coast Reserve, 168

VIRGINIA

The territory of the eastern United States that is now called Virginia has a rich natural heritage and cultural history. Once home to a large population of indigenous tribes and thick with forests and wildlife, Virginia is a modern-day pastoral expression of its colonial landscape. Its history includes battles of the Revolutionary and Civil Wars and the foundation of the famous Jamestown Settlement in 1607 with its triumph, tragedy, and stories that have evolved into myth.

Virginia's great biodiversity is rooted in its geophysical landscape, which is comprised of five regions. The coastal plain or tidewater region to the east borders the Atlantic Ocean and the Chesapeake Bay. This region includes the barrier islands with their salt marshes and tidal mudflats that are feeding and nesting grounds for birds. Two prominent threats to this region are pollution and an invasive species called *Phragmites australis,* also known as the common reed. To the west of the coastal plain after the fall line is Virginia's Piedmont region, which has forests, parks, preserves, historic sites, and gentle hills that roll across the state. Crucial river systems and hardwood forests in the Piedmont still need to be protected before these areas are lost to development. Invasive plant species, incompatible forestry, and disruptions of natural water flow are the primary threats to this region. Farther west is the Blue Ridge Mountain range. This region is part of the Appalachian Mountain range. As the trees and plants of the Blue Ridge convert sunlight, rain, and nutrients into food, they give off a water vapor that blankets the region in a barely perceptible blue haze. This process of photosynthesis is what gives the Blue Ridge Mountains their descriptive name. To the west of the Blue Ridge is the valley and ridge region, the location of Virginia's Great Valley and other scenic valleys bordered by rugged hills. Finally, Virginia's fifth region is the Appalachian Plateau in the far west corner that is known for its coal.

Virginia has numerous conservation concerns. A priority for the state is to maintain its natural heritage as a home to rare and endangered species and natural communities that can be found nowhere else in the world. The state of Virginia also recognizes the importance of water quality and the risks of toxic mercury levels in waterways that advance the presence of mercury in the environment and make fish consumption a problem. Mercury is dangerous to the health of humans and wildlife and can cause cardiovascular diseases as well as reproductive and neurological disorders.

Virginia is also actively researching the impact of climate change on the state's natural environment. The Governor's Commission on Climate Change investigates the existing and potential negative impacts of climate change to the state's ecology, public health, and economy. It also seeks to discover new ways to reduce greenhouse gas emissions and educate citizens and business about energy conservation and reducing carbon emissions. The Virginia Energy Plan has set a goal to reduce the state's greenhouse gas emissions by 30 percent by 2025.

Other entities that support Virginia's environmental vitality are the Virginia Land Conservation Foundation (VLCF) and the Land Trust of Virginia. The VLCF provides state funding for the protection of lands that are special to Virginia, such as historical sites, natural areas, parks, and forests. The Virginia Department of Conservation and Recreation manages many of these natural areas in the state that contain rare species or natural communities critical to the state's natural heritage. The Land Trust of Virginia has statewide and local projects that protect Virginia's lands from development. The Land Trust works with landowners to secure conservation easements that encourage open spaces, forests, recreation areas, and sustainable farming. Recognizing that Virginia's undeveloped landscapes are slowly diminishing, these organizations are committed to preserving Virginia's verdant lands.

CUMBERLAND MARSH

Like many regions along the eastern seaboard, central eastern Virginia is an area experiencing environmental duress. The rivers and tributaries that flow into the Chesapeake Bay are suffering from ecological disturbances associated with overdevelopment. The wetlands and marshes are under threat as well, which is why places like Cumberland Marsh Preserve are so important for helping to maintain the ecological balance and natural integrity of Virginia's tidewater region.

Cumberland Marsh Preserve, in New Kent County, is a critical area for conservation not only because it is a 1,094-acre parcel of protected freshwater tidal marshland for migratory birds and other wetland species, but also because it is home to the sensitive joint vetch, a rare plant that is native to the eastern United States. The plant is sometimes called the Virginia joint vetch. It can be found in a few other mid-Atlantic states, but Cumberland Marsh has the largest population of the plant in the world. It used to be found in Pennsylvania and Delaware as well, but factors associated to habitat destruction such as road construction, residential and commercial development, and water pollution are the probable causes for the plant's disappearance in those states.

The sensitive joint vetch is in the bean family because it sprouts an irregular-shaped legume. It gets its name from being sensitive to the touch. When the leaves are touched, they close slightly. It grows along marsh edges and intertidal zones, where it is inundated with water twice a day. Not inclined to compete with other plants, the joint vetch often spreads where the vegetation has been thinned out by foraging wildlife. Its native home is freshwater tidal marshes of the mid-Atlantic states. While the sensitive joint vetch may be found in other locations, Cumberland Marsh is one place where it is protected, which might be why the plant occurs here more than in any other location worldwide.

Cumberland Marsh is a superior freshwater tidal marsh and an excellent location to see ducks, Canada geese, great blue herons, osprey, and egrets. A boardwalk and a wooded trail lead to the wooded upland area of the preserve. In addition to the sensitive joint vetch, the bald cypress tupelo grows in the area as well as scrub oak and Parker's pipewort. Threats to the marshland include invasive plants and fish, inappropriate development, and fluctuating water levels. One of the biggest threats to Cumberland Marsh Preserve—and throughout Virginia's Chesapeake Bay region—is an invasive species called *Phragmites australis*, also known as the common reed. This plant grows in wetland areas and is highly aggressive. It grows in acidic as well as alkaline environments and spreads easily. Reasons for its widespread distribution along the eastern seaboard may have something to do with the fact that the reed grows very well in disturbed wetland areas. Since few wetlands along the East Coast have escaped human activity and some level of habitat destruction, the common reed has been able to invade coastal areas, profoundly impacting the ecology and biodiversity of wetland regions.

The Nature Conservancy has owned Cumberland Marsh Preserve since 1993. The marsh is important because of its location within the Chesapeake River Landscape Program, which aims to conserve and protect the tributaries that drain into the Chesapeake Bay. Rivers such as the Rappahannock, Mattaponi, and Pamunkey are part of this conservation program. Cumberland Marsh is located along the Pamunkey River. In addition to providing habitat for the endangered sensitive joint vetch, the preserve is a scenic spot for bird-watchers, nature observers, and bicyclists. The preserve also serves as a place for healing. It is the site of outdoor rehabilitation programs for a nearby children's hospital.

Further Reading

Badger, Curtis J. *A Naturalist's Guide to the Virginia Coast.* Charlottesville: University of Virginia Press, 2004.

Lippson, Alice Jane, and Robert L. Lippson. *Life in the Chesapeake Bay.* Baltimore: John Hopkins University Press, 2006.

Nature Conservancy. "Cumberland Marsh Preserve." http://www.nature.org/wherewework/northamerica/states/virginia/preserves/art1232.html.

Tate, J. R., Karen Terwilliger, and Susan L. Woodward. *A Guide to Endangered and Threatened Species in Virginia.* Granville, OH: McDonald & Woodward, 1995.

FORTUNE'S COVE PRESERVE

While it may be true that Virginia's mountainous western region and coastal east are brimming with ecologically diverse and significant natural areas, it would be a mistake to overlook the state's scenic central Piedmont region. Spanning across Virginia's midsection from the coastal plain to the Blue Ridge Mountains, the Piedmont ecoregion has forests, parks, preserves, and historic sites that host many visitors each year. One such place is Fortune's Cove Preserve in Nelson County near Lovingston and Charlottesville. Fortune's Cove is unique in that it lies partly along the Blue Ridge and partly in the Piedmont, giving it a unique plant combination, and there is a section of rocky glades that houses very rare plant species.

Resting within 29,000 acres of stable forest habitat, Fortune's Cove Preserve has a remarkable array of wildlife and songbirds. It is a popular spot for hikers and bird-watchers. The 5.5-mile trail climbs to the crest of a mountain for gorgeous ridge top views and then loops back down to the lower-lying Piedmont so that nature observers get a full range of what the preserve has to offer. Birds such as the cerulean, blue-winged warbler, orchard oriole, scarlet tanager, ovenbird, and Carolina wren are a few of the bird species that can be found at the preserve. Other wildlife include black bear, box turtle, red fox, and bobcat.

The rocky glades of Fortune's Cove make this preserve an important natural area for conservation because the plants found on the glades are very rare. Globally, there are less than 20 known sites where these plants occur. The glades are blanketed in lichen and rock mosses, and a species of prairie grass called little bluestem grows in the grassy area of the glades. The sweet-smelling fringe tree grows in the wooded areas. The oak-hickory forests in the preserve remind visitors that they are in Appalachia, even though the Piedmont landscape is nearby.

Under the guidance of the Nature Conservancy, the hiking trail and a parking area were created in 2002. Signs were posted to assist visitors and to make the beauty of Fortune's Cove more accessible to the public. The area falls under the conservancy's Central Virginia Piedmont Program, which aims to protect natural areas between the coast and the mountains of Virginia as this area becomes a hot spot for development and growth. Crucial river systems and hardwood forests in the Piedmont still need to be protected before these areas are lost to development. Invasive plants species, incompatible forestry, and disruptions of natural water flow are the primary threats to this region as more and more subdivisions and shopping complexes are opening.

Fortunately, much is being done to protect the Piedmont region of Virginia. The 755-acre Fortune's Cove Preserve has been expanded to 1,026 acres through land acquisition pursuits. Other parks and preserves in the Piedmont have received expanded protection through the acquisition of lands that adjoin their borders, giving them added conservation benefits. A Rivanna River Basin Commission was created that involves four local governments to help protect the health and integrity of the Rivanna River watershed for the well-being of central Virginia's ecological landscape and those who live within the watershed. Near the urban area of Charlottesville, the Rivanna River remains one of the cleanest rivers in Virginia's Piedmont. Home to rare species and providing fresh drinking water to central Virginia's growing population, conservation efforts hope to keep the river in healthy condition. The campaign called Virginia*forever* has been launched to further promote conservation through state and local funding efforts. With these initiatives and numerous other programs in place to offer environmental support for central Virginia, natural areas like Fortune's Cove Preserve have a promising future.

Further Reading

Nature Conservancy. "Fortune's Cove Preserve." http://www.nature.org/wherewework/northamerica/states/virginia/preserves/art7461.html.

Tate, J. R., Karen Terwilliger, and Susan L. Woodward. *A Guide to Endangered and Threatened Species in Virginia.* Granville, OH: McDonald & Woodward, 1995.

Winegar, Deane, and Garvey Winegar. *Highroad Guide to the Virginia Mountains.* Atlanta, GA: Longstreet Press, 1998.

Wofford, B. Eugene. *Guide to Vascular Plants of the Blue Ridge.* Athens: University of Georgia Press, 1989.

GOSHEN PASS NATURAL AREA

Nestled in the Appalachian Mountains of Rockbridge County, Virginia, is Goshen Pass Natural Area, a 937-acre preserve that provides sanctuary for an exemplary chestnut oak forest community, several rare plants, and the rare Appalachian jewelwing damselfly. Even if Goshen Pass did not provide protection for these important natural resources, it would still be a special place because of its elegant beauty and fascinating natural history.

Goshen Pass and its deep, narrow gorge were created by the unstoppable Maury River that for millions of years carved through the ridges of the Appalachian Mountains to form this lovely landscape. It is a relatively young natural area in terms of its formal dedication. In 2002, Goshen Pass was dedicated as a state natural area after being owned by the Virginia Department of Conservation and Recreation since 1954. Remarkably, the area was once an inland sea until the Appalachians began to buckle, rise, and form valleys and ridges. The geological makeup of this area is siltstone, sandstone, and quartzite. These erosion-resistant rocks are a good indicator of how powerful and persistent the determined waters of the Maury had to be in order to form the passage.

In addition to the chestnut oak forest, additional forest areas of the preserve are comprised of Table Mountain pine, pitch pine, and other mixed oak and hickory trees. Heath plants such as huckleberry, blueberry, and mountain laurel are the dominant shrub species. Three rare native plants grow in the preserve: marsh vetchling, freshwater cordgrass, and sand grape. The marsh vetchling and sand grape occur along the Maury River in sandy areas. In the nearby states of Tennessee, Virginia, and Pennsylvania, the sand grape is also listed as threatened or endangered. Freshwater cordgrass has few populations in

Virginia but can be found in larger populations in other regions of the United States. All three of these plants are more abundant in the Midwest.

Goshen Pass is a place to go for hiking and viewing wildlife along one of its hiking trails. The view from the swinging bridge is unforgettable. The primary threat to Goshen Pass is nonnative invasive plants that may jeopardize the survival of the area's biodiversity. Ongoing study of the plant life at Goshen Pass will help researchers develop effective conservation plans to protect this Virginia treasure. Adjoining wildlife management areas also help to safeguard the preserve.

Near Goshen Pass to the west is Warm Springs Mountain Preserve in Bath County. Warm Springs Mountain Preserve is 9,296 acres of protected land that connects other conservation areas in western Virginia's Allegheny Highlands to provide a green corridor for plants and wildlife. This preserve is important to Goshen Pass and other preserves and natural areas in western Virginia because it protects a broad expanse of lands and waters in the region. The preserve harbors an unusual montane pine barren community and a variety of rare plants and invertebrates. The word *allegheny* is Algonquin for "endless," and Warm Springs Mountain Preserve helps to protect the endless natural beauty of western Virginia by being a vital link in this Allegheny Highlands greenway. Threats to this region are nonnative invasive species, residential development, incompatible forestry, and diseases or insects that threaten trees. Local, state, and federal agencies work together to maintain these natural areas by acquiring lands, applying sound ecological management, influencing public policy to promote conservation efforts, and through education and outreach programs that help to foster an appreciation for nature and assist local communities in the development of activities that work toward preserving the cultural and natural histories of the region.

Further Reading

Tate, J. R., Karen Terwilliger, and Susan L. Woodward. *A Guide to Endangered and Threatened Species in Virginia.* Granville, OH: McDonald & Woodward, 1995.

Virginia Department of Conservation and Recreation. "Goshen Pass Natural Area." http://www.dcr.virginia.gov/natural_heritage/natural_area_preserves/goshen.shtml.

Winegar, Deane, and Garvey Winegar. *Highroad Guide to the Virginia Mountains.* Atlanta, GA: Longstreet Press, 1998.

GREAT DISMAL SWAMP NATIONAL WILDLIFE REFUGE AND NATURAL AREA

Spanning across the Virginia border and into North Carolina is the Great Dismal Swamp National Wildlife Refuge and Natural Area. With 82,000 acres in Virginia and 38,000 acres in North Carolina, this is one of the largest swamps in the northeast United States. In the center of the swamp lies Lake Drummond, the largest natural lake in Virginia. Ecologically speaking, the swamp has seen better days, before logging operations dramatically changed the landscape by impacting the area's natural hydrologic processes and decimating the native cypress and Atlantic white cedar stands. But the Great Dismal Swamp is still considered a wilderness, and it is a natural area teeming with wildlife, plant communities, and historical value.

Despite its shortcomings, the Great Dismal Swamp has plenty to offer. It is an important resting location for hundreds of species of migratory birds, many of which have nesting areas in or near the refuge. Swainson's warbler and Wayne's warbler are two species that are common and noteworthy in the swamp. Three plants—dwarf trillium, silky camellia, and log fern—are important to the refuge. Although most of the tupelo bald cypress and Atlantic white cedar trees were logged, there are isolated locations where these trees still exist. Other trees in the swamp include red maple, oak, gum, and poplar. The swamp has a remnant marsh and a sphagnum bog. Because of its loblolly pine and pond pine trees, the Great Dismal Swamp has been targeted as a habitat for the red-cockaded woodpecker. This special bird was listed as a federally endangered species in 1970 due to its loss of habitat and because of its very particular preferences for nesting. It likes to live in pine trees that have been infected with red heart fungus. The diseased tree has softer wood than healthy pines, allowing the bird to dig a hole in the tree where it can roost. Interestingly, the sap that drains from the hole keeps snakes away from the nest.

Of great historical interest is the role of the Great Dismal Swamp in supporting the Underground Railroad. Early colonists deemed the swamp impenetrable and bleak. However, around 1747, the Dismal Swamp Land Company, of which George Washington was a founder, used slaves to dig ditches to drain water from the swamp, to acquire timber, and to build a 22-mile canal that connected the Chesapeake Bay in Virginia and Albemarle Sound in North Carolina. Because of its extremely dense vegetation, soft, soggy earth, mud, snakes, insects, and other wildlife, the swamp was not traveled by many whites, and the slaves knew this. It became well known that many African American slaves traveled through the swamp seeking freedom, and many who sought refuge in the swamp lived out their lives there in higher-level areas living on wildlife and what provisions they could steal.

There is good news for this fascinating, historical, natural area. In 2006, the U.S. Fish and Wildlife Service compiled a document called the Great Dismal Swamp National Wildlife Refuge Comprehensive Conservation Plan. According to this plan, impressive efforts are being made to restore the Great Dismal Swamp by prioritizing research that will provide answers to questions about habitat diversity and restoring remnant species. Roads that were built to support the logging operations inflicted unimaginable damage to the swamp by altering its natural water regime. The result is flooding and areas of stagnant water. Efforts to control water levels and movement are essential for the survival of the plant and animal communities. There are trails for hiking and biking, but recreation does not seem to be an urgent threat to the area. Unwanted wildfires occasionally adversely impact the swamp, but prescribed, carefully controlled fire is considered a valuable method of maintaining habitats. The considerable movement toward restoring this unique, protected natural area suggests that the Great Dismal Swamp is on the rebound. It will never return to its original condition prior to colonial exploitation, but it has the potential to become even more diverse and a magnificent laboratory for environmental research and study.

Further Reading

Fergus, Charles, and Amelia Hansen. *Wildlife of Virginia, and Maryland, and Washington D.C.* Mechanicsburg, PA: Stackpole Books, 2003.

Simpson, Bland. *The Great Dismal Swamp: A Carolinian's Swamp Memoir.* Chapel Hill: University of North Carolina Press, 1998.

Tate, J. R., Karen Terwilliger, and Susan L. Woodward. *A Guide to Endangered and Threatened Species in Virginia.* Granville, OH: McDonald & Woodward, 1995.

U.S. Fish and Wildlife Service. "Great Dismal Swamp National Wildlife Refuge." http://www.fws.gov/northeast/greatdismalswamp/pdf%20files/Highlights3–06.pdf.

Mount Rogers

Located in the George Washington and Jefferson National Forests, the Mount Rogers National Recreation Area (MRNRA) is home to the highest point in Virginia. Reaching 5,729 feet, the Mount Rogers summit is within the Lewis Fork Wilderness Area in western Virginia and can be reached from the Appalachian Trail. Blanketed in a red spruce/Fraser fir forest, Mount Rogers hosts the northernmost occurrence of Fraser fir and is decked with rhododendron, rocky outcroppings, grassy meadows, and mountain balds.

An abundance of plant an animal species can be viewed in the Mount Rogers National Recreation Area. Trout lily, bellwort, bluets, summer bee balm, mountain laurel, and flame azalea can be seen blooming during the warmer months. Many varieties of hawks and songbirds can be found at Mount Rogers, along with peregrine falcons and saw-whet owls. Other observable wildlife in the area includes bobcats, black bear, white-tailed deer, gray fox, and eastern cottontail. Although there is no view from the summit of Mount Rogers, other mountaintop balds and outcroppings provide incredible vistas of hardwood forests, subalpine beech, and spruce forests. The Crest Zone within the MRNRA hosts a wild pony herd that grazes in the fire-maintained open meadows.

The mountain balds are probably the most distinguishing features of this stunning Blue Ridge landscape. Mountain balds are high-elevation areas that are not forested but covered in grass or heath vegetation. It is not clear what created these high-elevation windswept meadows. Perhaps the mountains were overgrazed by cattle owned by early settlers, or perhaps lightning strikes that cause occasional fires have kept the slopes open. Regardless of their origin, they are popular attractions for photographers due to the far-reaching scenic vistas where layered mountain ranges with sunlit peaks and shadowed valleys can be seen for miles.

The MRNRA features several famous hiking trails: the Virginia Creeper Trail, Iron Mountain Trail, the Appalachian Trail, and the Daniel Boone Heritage Trail. But with more than 400 miles of trails in the area, there are also primitive trails, old logging roads, and converted railroads that serve as trails for horses and bicycles as well as foot traffic.

The picturesque region of southwest Virginia also includes the Mount Rogers Scenic Byway, from which many of the area's most beautiful landscapes can be admired. Near Mount Rogers National Recreation Area is Grayson Highlands State Park and White Top Mountain. At 5,520 feet, White Top Mountain is the second highest peak in Virginia behind Mount Rogers. Grayson Highlands State Park also contains a pony herd that runs wild in the park and is the location of a popular fall festival that celebrates the region's bluegrass music heritage and local culture.

To protect this diverse habitat and scenic area, the U.S. Forest Service implemented a program called the Limits of Acceptable Change (LAC) program to monitor and correct the impact of recreational activities in the Mount Rogers High Country, which covers roughly 20,000 acres within the national recreation area. If a hiking trail or campsite shows signs of damaging recreational impact according to acceptable use standards, then the trail or campsite will be closed until it is restored. Camping, hiking, horseback riding, and bike riding are very popular activities in this area and do pose a threat to the environmental integrity of the region. In fact, finding solitude in the high country of Mount Rogers in the summer might be difficult except on lesser-known trails in the wilderness area. One of the primary goals of the LAC program is to preserve the distinctive features and natural heritage of the Mount Rogers High Country. But even with its heavy visitor use, the Mount Rogers National Recreation Area is a unique place and an ecologically vital natural area.

Further Reading

Molloy, Johnny. *Mount Rogers National Recreation Area Guidebook*. 2nd ed. Knoxville: University of Tennessee Press, 2008.

U.S. Forest Service. "Mount Rogers National Recreation Area." http://www.fs.fed.us/r8/gwj/mr/.

Winegar, Deane, and Garvey Winegar. *Highroad Guide to the Virginia Mountains*. Atlanta, GA: Longstreet Press, 1998.

POOR MOUNTAIN NATURAL AREA

Along the Appalachian Mountain range, there are a few places where the climate is dry, strongly acidic, and not particularly hospitable to a wide variety of plants and animals, but it is sometimes surprising what can be growing on a harsh, rugged terrain. Poor Mountain Natural Area Preserve near Roanoke, Virginia, derives its name from the nutrient-poor soils from metamorphosed sandstone, and yet it is home to the globally rare and state endangered piratebush, making it quite rich in terms of its conservation status.

Totaling 925 acres just off the Blue Ridge Parkway, Poor Mountain is a pine-oak woodland where chestnut oak, scarlet oak, bear oak, Table Mountain pine, and pitch pine grow, while shrubs such as mountain laurel, huckleberry, and fetterbush dominate the understory. Table Mountain pine is an Appalachian mountain tree with long, spreading branches that grows on dry ridges and slopes. It was first found on Tablerock Mountain in North Carolina, thus giving the tree its name. Not only is Poor Mountain a curious location for the rare piratebush, but it hosts the world's largest population of this parasitic shrub. Piratebush can be found in eastern Tennessee and in western North Carolina, but Poor Mountain's selection is mysteriously abundant. Other than these three states, piratebush is found nowhere else in the United States.

Like pirates that steal what they need to survive at sea, the piratebush steals from nearby root systems what it needs to survive. Because it doesn't need as much chlorophyll as other plants, it has a light green color. It is believed that this shrub's original host plant may have been the Carolina hemlock tree, but studies indicate that the piratebush may be able to survive with numerous different kinds of trees and plants as hosts. It seems to grow best in areas that are fire maintained. Indeed, one of the threats to this species includes lack of periodic fire that would cause habitat succession. Other threats include overcollection of specimens and branches falling from trees growing over the piratebush. The piratebush is sometimes 10 feet high. It can grow up to 15 feet, but is generally only 3 or 4 feet high. It turns yellow in the fall and grows small flowers in the spring.

Near Poor Mountain, which is the tallest mountain in Roanoke County, is Bottom Creek Gorge Preserve, which is home to Virginia's largest population of Carolina hemlock. There is a beautiful old-growth hemlock forest in the preserve, and the area serves as the headwaters of the Roanoke River. Bottom Creek provides critical habitat to native fish species, and the preserve houses the globally rare chestnut lipfern.

Poor Mountain continues to be a location of ongoing scientific research of this unique shrub, while recreational activities are limited to hiking, photography, and bird-watching. The rugged terrain prevents many other kinds of outdoor activities. While the view from Poor Mountain is characteristic of the Blue Ridge Mountains, the mountaintop itself is not what one would expect, with its gnarly trees and bushes, but with its significant piratebush population turning the mountaintop bright yellow in October, it can be said that there is no other place like Poor Mountain on earth. Managed by Virginia's Department of Conservation and Recreation Natural Heritage Program, Poor Mountain is a significant site of conservation and stewardship for the state of Virginia and an attraction for botanists from all over the world.

Further Reading

Tate, J. R., Karen Terwilliger, and Susan L. Woodward. *A Guide to Endangered and Threatened Species in Virginia*. Granville, OH: McDonald & Woodward, 1995.

Virginia Department of Conservation and Recreation. "Poor Mountain Natural Area Preserve." http://www.dcr.virginia.gov/natural_heritage/natural_area_preserves/poormt.shtml.

Winegar, Deane, and Garvey Winegar. *Highroad Guide to the Virginia Mountains*. Atlanta, GA: Longstreet Press, 1998.

Wofford, B. Eugene. *Guide to Vascular Plants of the Blue Ridge*. Athens: University of Georgia Press, 1989.

SHENANDOAH NATIONAL PARK

Where the northern trek of the Blue Ridge Parkway comes to an end near Waynes-boro, Virginia, another scenic highway called Skyline Drive begins. Following the gorgeous Blue Ridge Mountains, Skyline Drive meanders through one of the most famous national parks in the eastern United States. Shenandoah National Park is 300 square miles of Appalachian beauty, with roughly 40 percent of the park designated as wilderness. There are more than 500 miles of hiking trails in the park, including 101 miles of the Appalachian Trail. Shenandoah is a diverse mix of natural habitats as well as a site where the cultural struggles of America found expression.

With the Virginia Piedmont on the east and the Shenandoah Valley on the west, Shenandoah National Park rests in a location that supports a lush botanical landscape. Herbs, ferns, shrubs, flowers, and forests characterize a picturesque walk along one of the trails at Shenandoah. Oak-hickory forests dominate the canopy of the park, and inter-rupted fern, blueberries, trillium, jack-in-the-pulpit, azaleas, and lady's slipper orchids dress the forest understory. Yellow poplar and cove hardwoods also appear in the park.

The mountains of Shenandoah tell a fascinating geologic history that dates back to ancient times when lava flows, erosion, and remnants of mountains that existed before the Appalachians all came together to form the distinct topography of Shenandoah. Stacked cliffs from ancient lava flows created dramatic cliffs and waterfalls from streams that carved through the lava. Stony Man Mountain and Hawksbill Mountain are the two highest peaks in the park, each reaching over 4,000 feet and providing breathtaking vistas across the hill and valley terrain. The view over the landscape is well known for its blue hue typical of the Blue Ridge Mountain range. As the trees and plants of the Blue Ridge convert sunlight, rain, and nutrients into food, they give off a water vapor that blankets the region in a barely perceptible blue haze. This process of photosynthesis is what gives the Blue Ridge their descriptive name.

The Blue Ridge Mountain/Shenandoah Valley region before European settlement was populated by American bison, elk, otter, beaver, black bear, and the eastern cougar, to name a few. Some of these species disappeared entirely, but white-tailed deer, coyotes, bobcats, fox, turkeys, and many other species live in Shenandoah today. There are more than 200 bird species and 30 fish species that swim in the park's rivers and streams.

In addition to the park's natural history, Shenandoah was the stage for cultural con-flicts and struggles for equal rights in the 20th century. The park was officially established in 1935 and, during its earliest years, followed the separate-but-equal form of segregating visitors. Provisions at the park were provided for African Americans at a special area so that they did not interact with the white visitors. The sign at this designated area read: "Lewis Mt. Picnic Grounds for Negroes." This practice of segregating guests based on race continued until 1950, when the park accepted full integration.

The equal rights struggle for women was also an issue that evolved at Shenandoah. At one time, only men were permitted to hold positions as forest rangers. Eventually, women were granted jobs that allowed them to partially be rangers in addition to other responsibilities. In 1969, new standards were issued that approved women to be hired as full rangers, and, in 1978, women were permitted to wear the official ranger uniform and badge. It took many years of hard work and protest by women to change perceptions of the National Park Service that women were fully capable of holding positions that worked with nature and law enforcement.

Extensive research projects and stewardship programs are in place at Shenandoah. Ongoing activities include monitoring air and water quality, restoring processes that have been influenced by human activity, removing aggressive nonnative species, and controlling visitor interaction with wildlife. Unfortunately, the blue hue of the Blue Ridge Mountains in Shenandoah is slowly becoming a pollution haze. Reducing air pollution emissions is a goal of the National Park Service due to the high volume of tourism by car along Skyline Drive. Careful and diligent management will ensure that Shenandoah remains one of Virginia's most prized natural areas.

Further Reading

Gildart, Bert, and Jane Gildart. *Shenandoah National Park Pocket Guide*. Guilford, CT: Falcon, 2008.

Lambert, Darwin. *The Undying Past of Shenandoah National Park*. Lanham, MD: Roberts Rinehart, 2001.

National Park Service. "Shenandoah National Park." www.nps.gov/SHEN/.

VIRGINIA COAST RESERVE

Considering how much coastal land along the eastern seaboard of the United States has been developed into seaside resorts and vacation homes, areas that have been able to escape this fate are special places indeed. The Virginia Coast Reserve, owned by the Nature Conservancy, consists of 14 undeveloped islands along a strip of coastal land that lies between the Chesapeake Bay and the Atlantic Ocean. Spanning 38,000 acres along the Virginia coastline, the reserve is rich in biodiversity and is one of the most important migratory bird stopover points in the world. Also, the islands form a critical buffer area that protects developed areas of the Virginia coast from storm surge.

The islands of the Virginia Coast Reserve are pristine coastal wilderness areas frocked in windswept marsh grasses with no recreational trails. The beaches have been preserved in their natural state. There are 18 barrier islands, and the reserve protects 14 with the intention of keeping the islands free of development while also conducting research for projects that aim to restore the eelgrass and oyster populations on the islands. The islands are open to the public, but contacting the Virginia Coast Reserve office is recommended prior to visitation.

The islands, with their salt marshes and tidal mudflats, are a haven for birds. Songbirds, shorebirds, raptors, and waterfowl flock to the islands in droves, feeding and nesting in the marshes. Black ducks, snow geese, common terns, piping plovers, pelicans, royal terns, black skimmers, gulls, and sandpipers are just a few of the birds that can be seen on the islands during various times of the year. Birds known as red knots and American oystercatchers fly to the islands in vast numbers and are mesmerizing to any bird-watcher.

Encroaching development is the biggest threat to the islands of the Virginia Coast Reserve. In the 1960s, when developers acquired one of the islands to build a resort area, the Nature Conservancy and other organizations responded by forming a coalition that worked to purchase as many islands as possible within Virginia's Eastern Shore to preserve the beauty and spectacular ecological qualities of the islands. Other threats include invasive species, overfishing, incompatible forestry, recreation, and agricultural practices. Efforts to address these threats involve purchasing more lands for preservation as well as habitat restoration and enhancement by controlling invasive species and securing healthy nesting and feeding areas.

Other islands and coastal areas within the Virginia Barrier Islands region are owned by other agencies. The U.S. Fish and Wildlife Service owns several refuges, including Assateague Island, Fisherman Island, and Wallops Island. These areas are for the protection of wildlife and are not open to public access. The Virginia Department of Game and Inland Fisheries owns Mockhorn Island, which is open to the public. Wreck Island is owned by the Department of Conservation and Recreation and is closed during the nesting season for bird protection.

For boaters, a way to experience the coastal wildlife habitats is along the Seaside Water Trail. The trail meanders along the barrier islands, where oyster sanctuary reefs are located and mudflats with feeding birds can be seen. Turtles and marine mammals such as dolphins, manatees, whales, seals, and porpoises can sometimes be spotted along the trail. There are numerous launch sites in various locations along the Eastern Shore. While these islands are receiving high-priority protection from organizations that are committed to their ongoing preservation, the Virginia Coast Reserve and other islands along Virginia's Barrier Island corridor are very fragile natural areas. They are subjected to polluted waters from the Atlantic Ocean, and the Chesapeake Bay is considered extremely toxic. Additionally, natural weather-related erosion and movement is taking place along the islands, keeping the environment constantly in flux. With so few undeveloped coastal areas remaining on the East Coast, these lovely islands are critical conservation areas for Virginia.

Further Reading

Badger, Curtis J. *A Naturalist's Guide to the Virginia Coast*. Charlottesville: University of Virginia Press, 2004.

Minichiello, J. Kent., and Anthony W. White. *From Blue Ridge to Barrier Islands: An Audubon Naturalist Reader*. Baltimore: John Hopkins University Press, 2000.

Nature Conservancy. "Virginia Coast Reserve." http://www.nature.org/wherewework/northamerica/states/virginia/preserves/art1244.html.

Virginia Coast Reserve Long-Term Ecological Research. http://atlantic.evsc.virginia.edu/.

0   50 mi
0   50 km

Bear Rocks Preserve, 172

Cranberry Glades and Wilderness, 174

Cranesville Swamp Preserve, 175

Greenbrier Valley, 176

New River Gorge, 178

North Fork Mountain, 180

WEST VIRGINIA

K nown as the Mountain State, West Virginia lives up to its nickname, at
least by eastern U.S. standards. Its scenic, forested, jagged terrain invites
many outdoor enthusiasts and nature observers each year. Its Appalachian cultural heritage and history of labor conflicts stemming from undercompensated
and dangerous working conditions in its coal mines have shaped the state's history, defined its natural heritage, and have formed the unique rural character of
the state.

According to the Environmental Protection Agency, West Virginia has
three ecoregions that characterize its landscape. In eastern West Virginia is the
rugged and diverse ridge and valley region that the state shares with its eastern neighbor, Virginia. To the west is the central Appalachian region, which
is mostly forest covered and mountainous. This region of West Virginia holds
the majority of the state's coal mines that have created polluted waterways and
scarred mountains. Western West Virginia is known as the Western Allegheny
Plateau ecoregion. This region is hilly with deep forested valleys but is less rugged than eastern West Virginia. There are farmlands and coal mines in this
region. In eastern West Virginia, the Allegheny Plateau (also called the Appalachian Plateau) has an eastern edge known as the Allegheny Front. Serving
as the eastern continental divide, the Allegheny Front has a dramatic impact
on weather and drainage patterns. On the west side, precipitation drains into
the Ohio and the Mississippi rivers. Precipitation on the east side of the divide
drains into the Potomac River.

West Virginia is abundant in natural resources, which is perhaps the state's
greatest strength and its greatest downfall, ecologically speaking. Although
farming is not the backbone of its economic stability, peaches, corn, apples, and
tobacco are important products for the state as well as natural gas, salt, stone,
and oil. West Virginia's most-coveted natural resource is its coal, and the production of this nonrenewable form of energy has devastated the state's mountain
landscape and waterways. The drilling for natural gas and oil has also left behind
an environmentally toxic legacy.

There are several environmental threats facing West Virginia. Certainly, its lands and waters have suffered from the coal-based economic system. Acid mine drainage is a serious problem in the state and arguably its biggest source of water pollution. Mountaintop removal for the purpose of accessing coal seams has created enormous ecological disturbance in the state, destroying wildlife habitats and polluting valleys and streams with disposal sites in its hollows. Abandoned oil and gas wells by the thousands also pose a major threat for the state as these wells leak contaminants into the state's water sources. West Virginia also has a problem with combined sewer overflows (CSOs), which are older sewer systems that combine both storm water and waste water to be redirected to nearby waterways; therefore, raw sewage is flowing into some of the state's rivers, lakes, and streams. These CSOs could potentially cause outbreaks of serious communicable diseases. Illegal dumping and urban runoff are also concerns for the state.

Several entities are working to improve West Virginia's environmental condition. The West Virginia Environmental Protection Agency has many offices and programs working to improve the state's environmental health and is deeply involved in monitoring water quality in the state along with other local, state, and federal agencies. The Stream Partners Program is a community-based collaborative effort that identifies impaired watersheds and works to restore and protect water quality in rivers, streams, and watersheds. The West Virginia Conservation Agency also is a leader in the state's conservation efforts. Its mission is "to conserve natural resources, control floods, prevent impairment of dams and reservoirs, assist in maintaining the navigability of rivers and harbors, conserve wildlife, protect the tax base, protect public lands and protect and promote the health, safety and general welfare of the people."

BEAR ROCKS PRESERVE

In eastern West Virginia, the Allegheny Plateau (also called the Appalachian Plateau) has an eastern edge known as the Allegheny Front. Serving as the eastern continental divide, the Allegheny Front has a dramatic impact on weather and drainage patterns. On the west side, precipitation drains into the Ohio and the Mississippi rivers. Precipitation on the east side of the divide drains into the Potomac River. The scenic Bear Rocks Preserve is on top of the Allegheny Front in the Dolly Sods Wilderness Area, which is located in the Monongahela National Forest.

Created in 2000, the windswept Bear Rocks Preserve is 477 acres in Grant and Tucker Counties in the Central Appalachian Forest ecoregion. Dwarf dogwood, dwarf cranberry, three-toothed cinquefoil, mountain laurel, lowbush blueberry, black huckleberry, and rhododendron are common plants and heath vegetation that can be seen at Bear Rock. Spectacular views of layers of eastern mountain ranges are visible on clear days. Because of the air currents that flow over the mountains, Bear Rocks Preserve offers great opportunities to view southbound migratory birds, including hawks and eagles, making their way toward warmer climates in early fall. Near Bear Rocks is the Allegheny Front Migration Observatory for watching the annual hawk migration. The birds rest on the high sandstone outcropping of rocks that extend into the blue skies above West Virginia.

Bear Rocks Preserve is within the reasonably remote Dolly Sods Wilderness Area. Created in the 1970s, Dolly Sods has elevations from 2,000 to more than 4,000 feet and an extensive trail system. The area is roughly 15,000 acres. An additional 6,000 acres that were acquired in the 1990s created Dolly Sods North. Cranberry bogs and one-sided red spruce can be found at Dolly Sods, along with the Cheat Mountain salamander and West Virginia flying squirrel, both of which are federally endangered species. The spruce trees are one-sided because of the constant prevailing winds that prevent branches from growing on one side of the tree. Other wildlife that can be seen in the area include bobcat, black bear, white-tailed deer, wild turkey, and snowshoe hare. Red Creek, which has its origins on Allegheny Mountain, runs down through Dolly Sods Wilderness Area and contains trout. Because portions of the Red Creek have poor drainage, the ecology of Dolly Sods can be boggy. There is one note of caution about this area. During World War II, the areas that are now Bear Rocks Preserve and Dolly Sods were used as artillery training areas, creating a potentially dangerous situation if unexploded shells are found. Hikers and hunters are advised to stay on designated trails and to not touch shells if they are found.

Early settlers once felt that this general area was impossible to penetrate, but as the logging and coal industries acquired the means to clear the region in the late 19th century, the area was extensively logged. By the early 20th century, very little original forest was left standing. The hills were burned into grazing pastures. Acquired by the U.S. government in 1916, Dolly Sods was added to the growing Monongahela National Forest and then, in the 1970s, guarded under the National Wilderness Protection System. Dolly Sods Wilderness Area is protected as a high-priority area to allow natural processes of the area to emerge without human influence. Its importance for Bear Rocks Preserve is that it provides an essential buffer zone for the preserve. Without the protection of Dolly Sods as a Wilderness Area, the unique character and ecology of Bear Rocks would be much more vulnerable. Tourism and recreation are currently the biggest threats that compromise the integrity of Bear Rocks preserve and its surrounding wilderness.

For Further Reading

Clark, Jim. *West Virginia: The Allegheny Highlands*. Boulder, CO: Westcliffe, 1998.

Clarkson, Roy B. *Tumult on the Mountains: Lumbering in West Virginia 1770–1920*. Parsons, WV: McClain, 1997.

Nature Conservancy. "Bear Rocks Preserve." http://www.nature.org/wherewework/northamerica/states/westvirginia/.

CRANBERRY GLADES AND WILDERNESS

Bogs are quite common in the northeast United States, but a little less usual in places as far south as West Virginia, which is why the 750-acre Cranberry Glades Botanical Area is a special place for preservation. Within the glades are four bogs that are home to peatland vegetation not typical for West Virginia, making this their southernmost range of occurrence. A half-mile boardwalk crosses through the Cranberry Glades, passing along areas of open grassland as well as carnivorous plants. Wild orchid, sundew, pitcher plant, wild raisin, Indian pipe, bishop's cap, jewelweed, turtlehead, and false hellebore can be found here. It is often said that the bogs here blanketed in sphagnum moss are akin to the peatlands one might see in Canada.

Next door to the Cranberry Glades is another special place. Located within the Monongahela National Forest, Cranberry Wilderness is one of the most impressive wilderness areas in the eastern and mid-Atlantic United States. Managed by the U.S. Forest Service, there are over 50 miles of scenic hiking trails within the area that covers more than 35,000 acres. Designated a wilderness area in 1983, Cranberry Wilderness's beauty comes from its mix of Appalachian hardwoods and red spruce and its broad, sweeping mountains and sun-drenched valleys. Portions of the Williams River and Cranberry River drain into the wilderness area. Cranberry Wilderness is within the Black Bear Sanctuary, which protects bears in the area from hunting. Other wildlife in the area include wild turkey, white-tailed deer, mink, bobcat, and fox.

A major threat not only to the Cranberry Wilderness but also a concern for the entire Monongahela National Forest is the presence and spread of nonnative invasive species. Garlic mustard, Japanese stiltgrass, and honeysuckle are carefully managed and monitored because of their threat to sensitive species such as running buffalo clover, long-stalked holly, and nodding pogonia. The hemlock woolly adelgid and the emerald ash borer that feed on the trees in the forest are also of great concern. The Forest Service also monitors air quality, water quality in the region, timber production, soil quality, wildlife and vegetation diversity, as well as heritage resources and the impact of recreation on the area. Recent records indicate that more than 28,000 visitors make their way to the Cranberry Mountain each year. The Forest Service creates new trails, maintains existing trails, conducts leave-no-trace workshops to foster awareness about visitor impact, and builds boardwalks over fragile ecosystem areas.

The Cranberry Mountain Nature Center is committed to educating visitors to the Cranberry Mountain region and celebrating Appalachian culture. Various short films and interpretive programs are available. In September, the center hosts an annual Cranberry Mountain Shindig that draws a large gathering. The center is located along the Highland Scenic Highway, which runs along West Virginia Routes 39/55 and 150 through gorgeous West Virginia countryside with scenic overlooks of wildflower displays in the spring and summer months and picturesque fall foliage in October. Due to the high traffic that meanders along this scenic byway, air quality reduction from motorized vehicles is a consideration for the Forest Service.

Near Cranberry Wilderness, along the Highland Scenic Highway, is the Falls of Hills Creek Scenic Area. The falls are nestled in a deep gorge that is blooming with wildflowers and studded with cool rocks. The three falls at the site are 25, 45, and 63 feet (the second highest in the state). The diversity of this entire region that is home to mountains, valleys, rivers, bogs, waterfalls, a scenic highway, a rich Appalachian heritage, and remote wilderness is indeed a treasure for the state of West Virginia.

For Further Reading

Adams, Kevin. *Waterfalls of Virginia and West Virginia*. Birmingham, AL: Menasha Ridge Press, 2002.

Howell, Benita J. *Culture, Environment, and Conservation in the Appalachian South*. Champaign: University of Illinois Press, 2002.

Kavanaugh, James. *West Virginia Trees & Wildflowers*. Phoenix, AZ: Waterford, 2008.

CRANESVILLE SWAMP PRESERVE

Cranesville Swamp Preserve is a unique place located in a frost pocket, where the topography of the area and the surrounding hilly landscape hold moisture and cold air in a low area, forming a frosty terrain. The preserve is decked with an acidic conifer swamp forest of red spruce, eastern hemlock, and the southernmost population of larch trees, in addition to the larch population found at Finzel Swamp in Maryland. The forest helps to insulate the valley, keeping the cool air in and preventing sunlight from warming or drying the landscape. This huge wetland of 1,600 acres receives top-notch protection because of its size and its biodiversity; the area provides habitat to at least 50 rare species.

Cranesville Swamp is home to black bear, wood ducks, ravens, and the northern water shrew. The saw-whet owl, alder flycatcher, Nashville warbler, and golden-crowned kinglet are state endangered birds that can be found at the preserve.

This chilly yet soggy landscape features peat that measures more than three feet deep. Peat is partially decayed plant and animal matter. The preserve lies on the border between West Virginia and Maryland and contains sedges, speckled alder, roughish arrowwood, and sphagnum (or peat) moss. Sphagnum moss is a lime-green spongy moss that grows in the water of the bog. The round-leaved sundew—a carnivorous plant that traps insects in its sticky leaf blades—cranberry, and narrowleaf gentian are bog plants that can be seen at Cranesville Swamp Preserve. The sundews with their tiny glistening droplets of digestive enzymes ensnare a moving insect, render it debilitated with its mucilage, and then digest the insect into a protein that is absorbed into the leaves. The sundew is a smart plant. If a grain of sand or a dead insect falls onto the leaves, it barely moves, but if a live meal crosses its leaves, the tentacles move very quickly to encase the captured creature in its trap. The cool temperature of Cranesville Swamp supports the growth of several types of ferns including cinnamon fern and bog fern. Mountain laurel and rhododendron are two dominant shrub types that comprise the undergrowth. Also of interest at Cranesville Swamp is the presence of running pine, a vine that runs along the forest floor that is technically classified as a club moss.

The human activity that has historically impacted the area is timber harvesting. Much of the conifer forest was once logged, and those trees have been replaced in part by hardwoods and pine trees. The dense pine forest supports few species, but the hardwoods have encouraged beavers to live at Cranesville Swamp. The beavers have influenced the wetland through dam building and tree clearing that create small ponds.

The preserve is open for public access and has five designated trails and a board-walk for visitors who want to view the bog's exceptional grasses and birds. The Nature Conservancy has owned the preserve since 1960 and conducts research on rare species and maintains the walking trails. The unusual ecological conditions at Cranesville—including temperature, altitude, and precipitation—create a landscape that is biologically diverse and an attraction for bird-watchers and photographers. The Nature Conservancy regulates the occurrence of invasive species while promoting the growth of swamp plants, the spruce forest, and the northern larch or tamarack, which is uncommon as far south as West Virginia. In 1965, the National Park Service designated Cranesville Swamp Preserve a National Natural Landmark. Because of its exceptional biodiversity and its unusual ecological conditions as a frost pocket, it was one of the first natural areas in the United States to be designated this important status.

For Further Reading

Kavanaugh, James. *West Virginia Trees & Wildflowers*. Phoenix, AZ: Waterford, 2008.

Nature Conservancy. "Cranesville Swamp." http://www.nature.org/wherewework/north america/states/maryland/preserves/art135.html.

Tekiela, Stan. *Birds of West Virginia Field Guide*. Cambridge, MN: Adventure Publications, 2008.

GREENBRIER VALLEY

Few people would deny that West Virginia's nickname the Mountain State accurately describes the scenic topography of this mid-Atlantic, central Appalachian region of the eastern United States, but amid the rolling green hills and smoky morning valleys, there are other ecosystems that may not come to mind when one thinks of West Virginia. The Greenbrier Valley in the southeastern portion of the state is home to shale barrens and a vast underground cave system with passages that have never been explored.

The shale barrens in the Greenbrier Valley are dry ecosystems unique to central Appalachia, where slopes of exposed shale receive little rain and support sparse vegetation. The federally endangered shale barren rock cress can be found in this area along with yellow buckwheat, Kate's mountain clover, and shale barren evening primrose. Some of these plants can only be found in shale barren ecosystems. Near Lewisburg, West Virginia, is the Nature Conservancy's Slaty Mountain Preserve that protects and provides an excellent example of this important ecosystem. Allegheny plum can be seen at this preserve along with 12 other shale barren species. Birds, such as the blue-headed vireo, scarlet tanager, chestnut-sided warbler, and indigo buntings, are at Slaty Mountain along with a marvelous variety of butterflies. A dirt road crossing the shale barren can be used by hikers who want to observe the shale barren plants in bloom. Late summer is the best time to visit.

One of the biggest threats to the shale barren communities in the Greenbrier Valley is perception. Deemed useless and unattractive, shale barrens are frequently not appreciated for their ecological values and are therefore targets for dumping, construction, and utility projects. Efforts to clean polluted areas of trash, stave off nonnative invasive species that threaten the shale barren species, and create awareness of the environmental significance of the shale barrens are ongoing projects for the Nature Conservancy to ensure protection of this unique ecosystem.

One of the more famous cave systems in the Greenbrier Valley is the Organ Cave System near Lewisburg, close to the Greenbrier River and Greenbrier State Forest. Organ Cave is a national natural landmark and a national historic landmark. Archeological evidence suggests that Native Americans used the flint found in the caves for tools and arrowheads, and that Europeans came across the cave system in 1704. During the Civil War, saltpeter found on the walls and floor of the cave was used to make black powder, and the cave was used for processing the mineral into a more refined form. Organ Cave has large limestone, water-carved passageways and a calcite structure that looks like a large pipe organ, which explains the cave's name. Cave Organ is a commercial cave so the area experiences its share of foot traffic and tourism; however, 200 passages have never been explored, and exact lengths of some of the caves are still unknown. The Indiana bat and Virginia big-eared bat are endangered species that roost in Organ Cave as well as the eastern pipistrelle, the gray bat, Townsend's big-eared bat, and the rare silver-haired bat and small-footed bat. Many other common species of bats live at Organ Cave.

Similar to the shale barrens, caves have been polluted by illegal dumping and construction. The dumping primarily occurs at cave entrances. Quarries have already destroyed many caves in West Virginia. All of these activities have a negative impact on groundwater quality in the Greenbrier Valley. Protecting the shale barren and cave communities is essential not just for the preservation of rare species but also to maintain the historical and ecological integrity of the ecosystems. Some of the caves in the Greenbrier Valley were formed from water that took thousands of years to sculpt its way through rock that is millions of years old, and the process is still going on today.

For Further Reading
Howell, Benita J. *Culture, Environment, and Conservation in the Appalachian South*. Champaign: University of Illinois Press, 2002.

Rice, Otis K., and Stephen W. Brown. *West Virginia: A History*. Lexington: University Press of Kentucky, 1994.
Vanderhorst, Jim. "The Hot Zone: The Shale Barrens of Eastern West Virginia." *West Virginia Wildlife* (Fall 2005): 4–6.

NEW RIVER GORGE

I t is ironic that such an old river with a history that traces back to ancient times is called New River. With headwaters that are as far away as Blowing Rock, North Carolina, New River is close to 320 miles long and slices through the Appalachian Mountains, forming a corridor where eastern Piedmont species and northern mountain species come together. The New River is traced back to an ancient river called the Teays that was formed from the draining of the young Appalachians. The powerful Teays cut through the mountain range and formed a deep canyon that is now the New River Gorge. In some locations, the gorge is 1,500 feet deep. In 1998, the New River was named an American Heritage River, one of only 14 in the United States.

There is an extraordinary natural history that can be observed by viewing the V-shaped New River Gorge. It is not clear how many years it has taken this river system to carve the gorge and expose its shale, sandstone, and coal seams, but it likely took many millions of years. An unusual type of sandstone called Nuttall sandstone is predominantly quartz and is found in the lower part of the gorge, where other very old rocks can be seen. The fact that this river system was fierce enough to cut across the Appalachian Mountains gives testament to the powerful sculpting force of water. The corridor that it created between the eastern and central United States prompted the construction of a railroad, which is one of the many indicators of the presence of humanity in the gorge. But the age of the New River, its stunning gorge, its old rocks, geologic formations, and direct path through mountain range make this a natural area for high-priority preservation.

The gorge has seen its share of challenges. Two invasive species are being carefully watched in the New River Gorge: the emerald ash borer and the hemlock woolly adelgid. The emerald ash borer is an Asian beetle that feeds on and destroys ash trees. It has killed millions of ash trees in the Midwest and has been spotted in West Virginia near the New River Gorge. The hemlock woolly adelgid, native to Japan, is a small insect that infests hemlock trees for food, eventually killing them. Long-term solutions are still being researched, but there is fear that the eastern hemlock tree may become an endangered species if the woolly adelgid is not kept under control.

Water quality is an issue of great concern for the New River, and many contributing factors impact the river's health. The New River is subjected to runoff from winter road salt, industrial toxins, metal pollutants from mining, pesticides and even raw sewage due

The New River in West Virginia. (Courtesy of Malik Ismail Ahamed)

to the absence of well-performing sewage treatment plants. Air quality is also a concern as traffic, industry, construction, residential wood burning, and forest fires all impact the area. Unfortunately, illegal dumping is also a major problem. Trash and debris accumulate along the banks of the river, creating unsightly and dangerous problems for the gorge. Cleanup programs have been initiated, but solid waste pollution will likely remain a problem until more educational programs are created to inform visitors and residents of the health and safety issues related to illegal dumping. Visitors also negatively impact the area by trampling on fragile vegetation.

One promising program taking place in the New River Gorge is the Peregrine Falcon Program. The National Park Service and the West Virginia Department of Natural Resources are working together to reintroduce the peregrine falcon into the New River Gorge area. Due to pesticide use, the falcons had difficulty reproducing, and their numbers sharply declined in the 1950s. The goal of the program is to encourage the falcons to nest in the New River Gorge and become a permanent part of their historic range.

For Further Reading
Burns, Shirley Stewart. *Bringing Down the Mountains: The Impact of Mountaintop Removal on Southern West Virginia Communities*. Morgantown: West Virginia University Press, 2007.
National Park Service. "New River Gorge." http://www.nps.gov/neri.

NORTH FORK MOUNTAIN

E cologically speaking, West Virginia is a state full of surprises. North Fork Mountain in Pendleton County is a location that encompasses such biodiversity and amazing vistas that the area has received nods from magazines such as *Backpacker*, *Southern Living*, *Washingtonian*, and *Wonderful West Virginia*. The North Fork Mountain landscape is a fascinating mosaic of coastal pine barrens, cedar glades, a gorge, prairies, caves, red pine forests, mountain meadows, rocky slopes and cliffs, and a remarkable number of plant and animal species, some of which are rare, boreal (northern), and some that are native to Appalachia.

North Fork Mountain is arid and high, with a 4,300-foot summit where Pike Knob Preserve is located. Pike Knob was created in 1995 by the Nature Conservancy. The Allegheny Front nearby to the west influences weather patterns so that precipitation that falls to the west of the Front leaves North Fork drought prone but incredibly unique. A remote two-mile hiking trail leads to the summit and to a mountaintop meadow called Nelson Sods. Periodic burning has strongly determined the vegetation, which includes red oak, red pine, paper birch, Appalachian oak fern, and the Allegheny onion. Pike Knob is the southernmost native occurrence of red pine and a curious place for a coastal pine barren that has been maintained with fire.

Close to Pike Knob is a mountain peak called Panther Knob Preserve. Consisting of rugged wilderness and an elevation of higher than 4,500 feet, Panther Knob has no public access except for scheduled trips conducted by the Nature Conservancy. Beach heather, a shrub that grows on coastal sand dunes, grows on some sandy spots at Panther Knob, and variable sedge can be found in the areas that undergo fire maintenance. This area hosts the world's largest population of variable sedge. Species native to Appalachia thrive here as well as a boreal species of butterfly called the pink-edged sulfur butterfly, which is more commonly found in the north.

As if these two mountain peak preserves aren't enough to establish North Fork Mountain as a natural area worthy of ecological significance, the area also contains an 11-mile gorge called Smoke Hole Gorge, locally named Smoke Holes, and a vast system of underground limestone caves that harbor the endangered Virginia big-eared bat and the endangered Indiana bat. Smoke Hole Gorge was formed by the Potomac River, which cut a beautiful canyon through North Mountain and Cave Mountain and carved deep vertical walls that expose limestone, sandstone, and shale. The prairies and cedar glades near Smoke Hole host important plant species such as prairie flax and a mint called Smoke Hole bergamot. The North Fork Mountain Trail travels along the western rim of this canyon, offering extraordinary views of the misty gorge and its surrounding remote wilderness. The nearby Smoke Hole Caverns showcase some of the best caves in West Virginia. Some of the caves are closed to public access to protect the endangered bats. The caves provide habitats for large numbers of bats at a time when bats are increasingly losing their roosting areas.

Development is the biggest threat to the North Fork Mountain region. The Nature Conservancy's conservation plan involves furthering its land acquisition projects, controlling nonnative invasive species, researching the benefits of fire maintenance, and educating visitors and landowners about the conservation needs of North Fork Mountain.

Limestone quarrying is also a threat to the area and particularly a problem for the caves. With careful management from both the Nature Conservancy and the U.S. Forest Service, this outstanding natural area will continue to be one of West Virginia's most prized landscapes.

Further Reading
Clark, Jim. *West Virginia: The Allegheny Highlands*. Boulder, CO: Westcliffe, 1998.
Kavanaugh, James. *West Virginia Trees & Wildflowers*. Phoenix, AZ: Waterford, 2008.
Nature Conservancy. "North Fork Mountain." http://www.nature.org/wherewework/northamerica/states/westvirginia/preserves/art1213.html.

GLOSSARY

ATLANTIC FLYWAY   One of four North American waterfowl flyways. The Atlantic Flyway migration route follows the Atlantic coast stretching from Canada to locations off the coast of Florida and into the Caribbean Sea. The other North American flyways are the Mississippi, Central, and Pacific Flyways.

BOGS   Acid wetlands where the soil is comprised of partly decomposed plant matter and the land is often moist and spongy. The water supply of a bog is replenished by precipitation.

BOREAL   Having to do with northern regions, particularly areas dominated by coniferous trees.

BRACKISH   Water that has a high salt content, but not as high as seawater.

BROWNFIELDS   Sites that may be dangerous to restore or reuse due to the possible contamination of hazardous pollutants.

CRETACEOUS AGE   A geologic period approximately 145 to 165 million years ago that is most commonly known for its mass extinctions, such as the dinosaurs.

DOLOMITE   A sedimentary rock comprised of calcium magnesium carbonate that can be found all over the world. It is common to find the mineral in quarries of the Midwestern United States. Dolomite typically forms rhombohedrons, although different-shaped crystals have been found. It is frequently clear, pearly white, or pink.

DOMED BOG   A raised-level bog that receives most of its nutrients from precipitation.

EMERGENT MARSH   A diverse, shallow-water wetland type that is characterized by emergent and floating-leaved plants. Emergent marshes often occur along the shores of streams and lakes and are prone to flooding.

FEN Wetland area that has as its water source a stream or a spring. The water chemistry for a fen is either neutral or alkaline.

GEOGENOUS BOG A peatland that receives most of its nutrients from underground water and surface water. Geogenous bogs are the least acidic, allowing more alkaline-preferring wetland plants to thrive.

HABITAT ISLANDS Also called habitat corridors, these islandlike areas are green zones that provide safe pathways for animals through regions of agriculture and development. Animals often use these corridors to move from one larger natural area, such as a forest, to another.

HIBERNACULUM A location or protected area chosen by an insect or animal for hibernation.

KARST TOPOGRAPHY An unusual landscape characterized by caves, underground streams, springs, vertical shafts, and sinkholes caused by groundwater dissolving bedrock, particularly limestone.

LACUSTRINE SHALLOW-BOTTOM COMMUNITY A wetland where the shallow depth of the water allows for sunlight to hit the muddy and sandy bottom, supporting the growth of rare plants.

MACROINVERTEBRATE Often called benthic macroinvertebrates, these aquatic animals have no backbone but are large enough to be seen with the naked eye. A few examples include crayfish, clams, and snails. They live on rocks, logs, and aquatic plants. When they die and decay, they leave behind valuable nutrients for other life forms in the ecosystem.

MILLINERY TRADE The business of making and selling hats.

MIXED MESOPHYTIC FOREST A biologically rich and diverse temperate forest that is comprised of mixed species that have adapted to a moderately moist water supply. There are few undisturbed mixed mesophytic forests remaining in the world. The Appalachian Mountain region of the United States contains extraordinary examples of this forest type.

MONADNOCK A geologic term used to describe an isolated area that is much higher than its surrounding landscape due to erosion.

MORAINAL GRASSLANDS Grasslands containing glacial deposits.

MOUNTAIN BALD High-elevation area that is not forested but covered in grass or heath vegetation.

MOUNTAIN PEATLAND Also called mountain bogs, these peatlands have highly acidic, low-nutrient, water-saturated soils that foster the growth of only certain kinds of plants that have adapted to these conditions. These bogs and the plants that grow in them are becoming increasingly endangered.

PALUSTRINE WETLAND One of five types of wetland classifications. Palustrine wetlands are nontidal wetlands that contain trees, emergent plants, and shrubs. The other wetland types are lacustrine, riverine, marine, and estuarine. Palustrine wetlands border lakes, ponds, rivers, and streams and are freshwater areas. They are also swampy areas where water fills in low-level areas or ground depressions.

Pesticide Treadmill An ecologically destructive and toxic spiral caused by the over-use of pesticides, particularly in agriculture. Through evolutionary processes, life forms such as mosquitoes often develop resistances to the pesticides, prompting the use of stronger pesticides. This poisonous cycle frequently does more harm to predators of the insects, such as birds, bats, and fish, than it does to the insects.

Phragmites Australis Also known as the common reed, phragmites is a tall, hardy wetland grass that can be found in every state in the United States. It is particularly prevalent along the Atlantic coast in wetland areas, where it is considered a highly inva-sive plant responsible for the dramatic reduction of native wetland vegetation.

Ramsar Convention Formed in the 1970s, the Ramsar Convention promotes the sustainable use and conservation of wetlands from around the world. This international treaty was created in Ramsar, Iran, with the official title The Convention on Wetlands of International Importance, Especially as Waterfowl Habitat. The convention developed as a response to rapidly declining wetlands and to support the ecological and cultural importance of wetlands.

Relict Forest Forest ecosystem that at one time covered a large amount of territory, but is now confined to an isolated space.

Riparian Community Natural community that exists along river banks.

Sandplain Grassland An ecosystem comprised of native grasses and shrubs that is maintained by periodic burning. These grasslands were formed from melting glaciers many thousands of years ago when the glaciers dropped their sand and the streams from the melting water formed sandy plains. The deep sand deposits beneath the grassland allow water to percolate down quickly. Due to the high sand content of the soil, water and nutrients drain away easily, creating a climate that is perhaps prone to drought but also creating a very rare natural community

Serotinous A type of plant that protects its seeds in a cone or seed case until the seeds are released through fire. Pine cones, for example, may hold viable seeds for several years until they are exposed to fire and disseminated.

Serpentine Grasslands Rare grasslands that contain species that grow in soil that has a greenish color due to a high amount of magnesium and other metals. The soils are toxic to many species of plants, so those that grow in a serpentine community have adapted to the harsh soils.

Serpentine Outcrop An unusual geologic bedrock formation that is comprised of magnesium-rich rock that is greenish-gray in color and is accompanied by a natural com-munity that is globally rare.

Speleology The study of caves and other karst formations.

Stalactites Cave formations that hang from the walls or ceilings of limestone caves. Stalactites are comprised of calcium carbonate and other minerals.

STALAGMITES   Cave formations that rise up from the floor of limestone caves caused by calcium carbonate and other minerals that drip from the ceiling of the cave.

SUBALPINE   The zone on mountain slopes just below the tree line. Trees in this region are often stunted due to high winds.

TALUS SLOPE   An unstable buildup of rock debris at the base of a steep mountain or cliff.

TERRACE COMMUNITY   A natural community that exists at high levels along a river, often on outcrops and cliffs.

UPLAND FOREST BLOCK   The rolling hills and wooded areas that occur in valley slopes and highlands, often near a gorge.

VERNAL POND   A temporary pool of water most frequently appearing in the spring from melting snow and rain. Although some vernal ponds are dry during the summer months, they are vital habitats for various wetland species.

WATERSHED   A land area where all of its water sources drain to the same place. All life forms in a watershed depend on the same water flow pattern.

BIBLIOGRAPHY

Anderson, Roger, C., James S. Fralish, and Jerry M. Baskin, eds. *Savannas, Barrens, and Rock Outcrop Plant Communities of North America*. New York: Cambridge University Press, 1999.

This book provides detailed information about some of the most imperiled ecosystems in North America. Serpentine barrens, savannas, and rock outcrop natural communities are covered in relation to their historic and current occurrences. The vegetation, soil, and geologic formations of these communities are described.

Badger, Curtis J. *A Natural History of Quiet Waters: Swamps and Wetlands of the Mid-Atlantic Coast*. Charlottesville: University of Virginia Press, 2007.

At the intersection of cultural and natural history, this book sets out to confront the negative perceptions and neglect of swamps and wetlands of the mid-Atlantic coast. Badger presents a convincing argument for the protection of wetlands as valuable natural communities that need to be preserved rather than paved. The Great Dismal Swamp and other important wetlands of the mid-Atlantic are discussed.

Berry, Wendell. "An Entrance to the Woods." In *The Norton Book of Nature Writing*, Edited by Robert Finch and John Elder, 764–74. New York: Norton, 1990.

In this essay, Berry describes a September camping trip where he spent two nights in the dark hollows of the Red River Gorge in Kentucky. He describes the trees, flowers, and gurgling stream around his campsite. His philosophical approach to the experience reminds readers that we have become desensitized to the frenzied, mechanized world and that it takes time to adjust to the sights and sounds of the wilderness.

Cronon, William. *Changes in the Land: Indians, Colonists, and the Ecology of New England*. New York: Hill and Wang, 2003.

This book presents an interdisciplinary approach to the environmental history of New England. Cronon's analysis explores the impact of Native American cultures and colonists on the ecology of New England by showing the transformation of the Northeast's landscape and plant and animal species after the shift from Native American to European influence.

Forman, Richard T. T. *Pine Barrens: Ecosystem and Landscape*. New Brunswick, NJ: Rutgers University Press, 1998.

This book is a thorough exploration into the history and ecology of the vast New Jersey Pine Barrens. This detailed study discusses the original inhabitants of the Pine Barrens, the exploitation of the natural resources of this extraordinary ecosystem as well as its climate, soils, plant and animal species, and hydrology.

Hammerson, Geoffrey A. *Connecticut Wildlife: Biodiversity, Natural History, and Conservation*. Hanover, NH: University Press of New England, 2004.

This book provides a lengthy, comprehensive look into the ecosystems of Connecticut. Well illustrated and detailed, Hammerson's book covers wildlife in the state from the smallest of life forms to its largest mammals, and likewise explores specific and wide-ranging ecosystems. It is an authoritative source for the study of Connecticut's natural world and biodiversity.

Jewett, Sarah Orne. *The Country of Pointed Firs*. New York: Anchor, 1989. (Originally published in 1886.)

This American literary classic beautifully captures the local color of New England through the author's brilliant use of language, character, and setting. Jewett's novel describes seaside villages, farms, old houses throughout the countryside, and people who share an interdependent relationship with their environment and are defined by it.

Johnson, Charles W. *Bogs of the Northeast*. Hanover, NH: University Press of New England, 1985.

Johnson's thorough and detailed presentation of the ecology of the Northeast's peatlands dispels misconceptions about these often misunderstood environments as it describes the plants, animals, and geography of swamps, fens, and bogs. Scientific yet gracefully written, this book's final message is a call for preservation of these peatlands, which harbor rare species and are essential for the protection of the Northeast's natural heritage.

Judd, Richard W. *Common Lands, Common People: The Origins of Conservation in Northern New England*. Cambridge, MA: Harvard University Press, 1997.

As the title suggests, this book rewrites the history of conservation by arguing that ordinary citizens of New England rather than intellectual elites were central in creating movements toward the protection of natural resources in the 19th century. Judd's book is an important study of land use, the struggles of common people who were deeply committed to environmental conservation, and 19th-century attitudes toward nature.

Klotter, James C., and Freda C. Klotter. *A Concise History of Kentucky*. Lexington: University Press of Kentucky, 2008.

This historical overview of the bluegrass state covers Kentucky's Native American history, its frontier period, its diverse regions as well as many other aspects of the state, including its conflicts, government, education, arts, and 26 goals for the future of the state.

Klyza, Christopher McGrory. *Wilderness Comes Home: Rewilding the Northeast*. Hanover, NH: University Press of New England, 2001.

Making a compelling argument for restoring and protecting wilderness areas in the Northeast, this collection of essays examines wild lands that currently exist, lands that have the potential to be designated as wilderness areas, and ways to promote biodiversity through forest stewardship and species recovery.

Maine Natural Areas Program. http://www.mainenaturalareas.org.

This Web site offers an extensive list and overview of natural areas in Maine that contain rare species, natural communities, and lands that are significant to Maine's natural heritage. For each identified area, the program provides a description, information regarding the area's protection status, and conservation considerations. As part of the Maine Department of Conservation, this program presents important information to policymakers so that they can make informed decisions related to Maine's natural resources.

Marchand, Peter J. *North Woods: An Inside Look at the Nature of Forests of the Northeast*. Boston: Appalachian Mountain Books, 1987.

This book is a study of the landscape development and ecology of the Northeast's forests. Marchand describes boreal natural communities, including spruce-fir woodlands, heath bogs, and northern hardwood forests and concludes his book by identifying acid deposition as one of the primary threats to the forests of New England.

Mohlenbrock, Robert H. *This Land: A Guide to Eastern National Forests*. Berkeley: University of California Press, 2006.

This book is an informative and straightforward guide describing the important ecological features of the national forests in the eastern United States. Partially derived from Mohlenbrock's "This Land" column from *Natural History* magazine, this book discusses wilderness areas and tourist attractions to appeal to both naturalists and a general audience.

Moser, Susanne C., and Lisa Dilling, eds. *Creating a Climate for Change: Communicating Climate Change and Facilitating Social Change*. New York: Cambridge University Press, 2007.

This collection of essays is aimed at bridging the gaps between environmental science, public policy, and social change. The ideas presented acknowledge the importance of education and public outreach to create awareness about climate change and facilitate citizen response through practical suggestions.

National Audubon Society. http://www.audubon.org.

Focusing on birds and wildlife, this Web site is an educational resource that provides information about conservation and ecosystem restoration as habitats are continuously vanishing. State chapters and Audubon centers and sanctuaries can be accessed through this site. Readers can also learn about current conservation issues, such as climate change and energy, and how the society is addressing those concerns.

Nature Conservancy. http://www.nature.org.

This Web site provides a wealth of information about natural areas, nature preserves, and extraordinary landscapes around the world. The Nature Conservancy is a major conservation organization that purchases and manages areas of critical priority, particularly areas that harbor rare, threatened, and endangered species. The organization uses a science-based approach to address threats to conservation and presents information about the most current environmental concerns facing the world today.

New Jersey Department of Environmental Protection: Environmental Justice Program. http://www.state.nj.us/dep/ej/.

This Web site provides a useful definition of environmental justice, an overview of the history of the environmental justice movement, and why environmental justice is an important issue in New Jersey. The site presents information about policies and committees committed to addressing environmental inequities and offers specific examples of how the state is taking action to promote fair treatment for all people in the implementation of environmental laws.

New York State Department of Environmental Conservation. http://www.dec.ny.gov/.

A valuable research tool, this Web site has a wide variety of topics related to the state of New York's natural resources. Information pertaining to the state's flora and fauna, lands and waters, pollution, and outdoor recreation is available. The Web site has important information regarding how the state is addressing the issue of climate change. Educational resources for teachers and students are also offered.

Rappole, John. H. *Wildlife of the Mid-Atlantic: A Complete Reference Manual*. Philadelphia: University of Pennsylvania Press, 2007.

Taking into account the diverse geography, climate, and biology of the mid-Atlantic region, Rappole presents a comprehensive guide to the habitats and conservation status of the wildlife of New Jersey, Pennsylvania, Maryland, Delaware, Virginia, and

West Virginia. With more than 500 species described in detail, this book is a valuable resource for environmental professionals and students alike.

Raymo, Chet, and Maureen E. Raymo. *Written in Stone: A Geological History of the Northeastern United States*. Hensonville, NY: Black Dome Press, 2001.

This book follows the history of the northeast United States by presenting its geologic evolution since the era of the dinosaurs. The landscape of the Northeast is explained by the authors, who describe forces such as volcanoes, earthquakes, and mountain-building processes, which are written in the rocks and stones and tell the story of this diverse terrain.

Terrie, Philip G. *Contested Terrain: A New History of Nature and People in the Adirondacks*. Syracuse, NY: Syracuse University Press, 1997.

As an investigation into the relationship between the Adirondacks its landholders, *Contested Terrain* outlines the ongoing conflicts over land use in Adirondack Park. Disagreements between those who believe the land should be preserved and those who want to promote development or exploit the natural resources of the Adirondacks are discussed by Terrie. The book is a valuable history of the Adirondacks as a place of unparalleled beauty and conflict.

Thompson, Elizabeth H., and Eric R. Sorenson. *Wetland, Woodland, Wildland: A Guide to the Natural Communities of Vermont*. Middlebury, VT: Department of Fish and Wildlife and the Nature Conservancy, 2000.

More than simply a guide book, *Wetland, Woodland, Wildland* is an exhaustive study of 80 distinct Vermont natural communities, including rich northern hardwood forests and boreal bogs. This book provides detailed ecological information related to the vegetation, wildlife, soil, and geology of Vermont's ecosystems.

Thoreau, Henry David. *Walden, Civil Disobedience, and Other Writings*. New York: Norton Critical Editions, 2007. (Originally published in 1854.)

Thoreau's classic literary work, *Walden*, is a masterpiece of American nature writing that presents an environmental ethic for living with simplicity and peacefully coexisting with the natural world that is as relevant today as it was in the 19th century, if not more so.

Thoreau, Henry David. *The Maine Woods. Henry David Thoreau: A Week on the Concord and Merrimack Rivers, Walden; Or, Life in the Woods, The Maine Woods, Cape Cod*. New York: Library of America, 1985. (Originally published in 1864.)

Written as three essays, *The Maine Woods* is a chronicle of Thoreau's expeditions into the Maine wilderness. The book details his observations of "Ktaadn," "Chesuncook," and "The Allegash and East Branch" and his reactions to the indigenous tribes of the region. Published posthumously, *The Maine Woods* is a historical record of the Maine landscape in the 19th century and a Transcendentalist text that illuminates human interactions with the natural world.

United States Environmental Protection Agency. http://www.epa.gov.

> The EPA Web site has a wide variety of resources available that support the agency's mission to protect the environment and human health. The Web site includes current scientific research related to air quality, water quality, climate change, pollution, and an extensive list of specific topics related to environmental issues in the United States. The site offers practical suggestions for developing a green lifestyle, and it provides educational resources for teachers and students.

Vermont Land Trust. http://www.vlt.org/index.html.

> The Vermont Land Trust (VLT) is one of the leading nonprofit land trust organizations in the Northeast. This Web site provides information pertaining to the VLT's latest projects aimed at conserving land in Vermont, and it provides stewardship information, current conservation reports, the *VLT Newsletter,* and other publications.

Weidensaul, Scott. *Mountains of the Heart: A Natural History of the Appalachians.* Golden, CO: Fulcrum, 1994.

> Weidensaul's book travels back millions of years to outline the formation and evolution of the spectacular Appalachian Mountain range that spans from Alabama to Canada. The author describes the more current degradation of the mountains as pollution and industrial exploitation of Appalachia's natural resources have devastated ecosystems. The book also explains conservation efforts to restore the Appalachians.

Wessels, Tom. *Reading the Forested Landscape: A Natural History of New England.* Woodstock, VT: Countryman, 2005.

> A portrayal of the forests of New England, this book examines the woodlands of this region and how they have changed over the centuries. By describing the clues that indicate natural and human-induced forest disturbances, the author demonstrates how we can better understand New England history by reading its landscape.

INDEX

Acid rain, 70, 74, 104, 120, 145

Allegheny Front, 171, 172, 173, 180

Allegheny National Forest, 117, 128, 129

Allegheny Plateau, 120, 128, 130, 171, 172

Appalachian Mountains, 23, 34, 62, 97, 104, 122, 157, 161, 168, 178

Appalachian Trail, 10, 37, 42, 43, 70, 77, 85, 97, 99, 123, 164, 167

Arctic tern, 66

Atlantic Flyway, 19, 91, 92, 108, 139

Atlantic salmon, 71, 153

Atlantic white cedar, 1, 8, 17, 47, 81, 82, 94, 134, 135, 163

Audubon Society, 38, 104, 120, 134, 135

Bald cypress, 54, 55, 58, 159, 163

Bald eagle, 3, 39–44, 80, 88, 94, 111,147, 153

Balsam fir, 70, 79, 88, 89, 105

Bangs, Outram, 139

Barrens: alvar, 109–10; blueberry, 37; pine, 46, 86, 91, 95, 99, 100, 103, 106, 113, 114, 180; serpentine, 124–25; shale, 53, 176–77

Belgrade Lakes, 44

Berkshire Mountains, 69

Berkshire Taconic Landscape, 10, 11, 70

Berry, Wendell, 24

Billings, Frederick, 143, 150, 151

Black bear, 7, 43, 70, 82, 83, 85, 88, 97, 111, 113, 115, 122, 123, 127, 128, 130, 147, 160, 164, 167, 173, 175

Block Island, 133, 139, 140

Bluegrass, 23, 26, 30, 31, 165

Blue heron, 61, 66, 107, 153, 159

Blue Ridge Mountains, 157, 160, 166–68

Blue Ridge Parkway, 165, 167

Bobcat, 2, 4, 7, 43, 44, 57, 70, 88, 110, 113, 115, 128, 134, 145, 146, 147, 160, 164, 167, 173, 174

Boghaunter dragonfly, 7, 8, 47, 135

Bogs: boreal, 127; cranberry, 67, 88, 127–28 geogenous, 40; heath, 37; mountain, 24, 57; raised 48

Buffalo, 23, 26

Cadillac Mountain, 38, 39
C&O Canal, 61, 62
Caribou Pond, 40
Carson, Rachel, 117
Catskill Mountains, 103, 113, 114
Caves, 30, 53, 56, 57, 113, 114, 118, 119, 121, 177, 180, 181
Champlain Valley Clayplain Forest Project, 114–15
Chesapeake Bay, 14, 15, 17, 53, 54, 59, 118, 157, 158, 159, 163, 168, 169
Chesapeake Bay Program, 159
Clean Water Act, 2, 78, 137
Climate change, 2, 43, 54, 66, 67, 70, 74, 77, 78, 84, 85, 89, 91, 92, 144, 147, 149, 158
Coal mining, 23, 117, 118, 149
Coastal sandplain, 45, 63, 65
Coverdale Farm, 16
Cree Indians, 149
Cumberland Gap, 24

Daniel Boone National Forest, 32, 34
Davis, Rebecca Harding, 117
Delmarva Peninsula, 13, 14, 53
Dinsmore, James, 26
Dinsmore, Martha, 26

Eight Mile River, 2, 26
Emerald ash borer, 174, 178
Emerson, Ralph Waldo, 65, 83, 103
Environmental justice, 92
Environmental Protection Agency, 2, 103, 171, 172

Fallingwater, 120, 121
Fen(s), 44, 49, 127
Follensby Pond, 103
Frost, Robert, 77
Furnace Town, 60

Godfrey Pond, 5
Grasslands, 23, 28, 45, 46, 53, 63, 65, 66, 68, 69, 73, 94, 106, 107, 110, 125, 133, 139

Green Mountains, 69, 114, 144
Griffith, William, 30

Hardwood forest, 1, 8, 9, 10, 18, 20, 37, 47, 70, 77, 85, 88, 95, 97, 98, 103, 104, 120, 121, 122, 123, 127, 128, 135, 143, 146, 150, 152, 153, 157, 160, 164
Hawthorne, Nathaniel, 70
Heathland, 65, 66, 68
Hemlock woolly adelgid, 25
Hessel's hairstreak butterfly, 8, 17, 48, 82, 135
Hickory, 7, 8, 18, 20, 30, 37, 47, 73, 77, 80, 111, 114, 135, 136, 154, 161
Hope Island, 138
Housatonic River, 1, 70
Hundred Acre Pond, 30

Indigo bunting, 59, 177
International Alvar Conservation Initiative, 110

Karner blue butterfly, 107, 108
Karst topography, 30
Kentucky Natural Lands Trust, 24

Lake Champlain, 114, 115, 143, 147, 148
Least tern, 3, 40, 66, 92, 108
Lenni Lenape Indians, 95, 99
Lewis, John Robinson 139
Logging, 10, 30, 35, 37, 43, 88, 129, 130, 144, 146, 150, 162, 163, 173
Long Island Sound, 1, 2, 3, 7, 77–78
Loverens, Joseph, 82
Lowell, Amy, 83

Mahican Indians, 70, 107
Maine Natural Areas Program, 38
Maine Woods, The, 37
Maliseet Indians, 37, 38
Mammoth Cave, 23, 29, 30

Man and Nature, 143, 150
Marsh, George Perkins, 143, 150
Martha's Vineyard, 65, 68, 69
Melville, Herman, 70
Mercury, 2, 104, 133, 149, 158
Micmac Indians, 37, 38
Mixed mesophytic forest, 24
Moby Dick, 70
Mohawk Trail, 63, 70
Monongahela National Forest, 172–74
Moody, James, 98, 99
Moose, 37, 43, 48, 70, 79, 82, 83, 85, 88,
    103, 137, 145, 146, 150
Mount Katahdin, 37, 42, 43

Nanticoke River, 13, 17, 18
Narragansett Indians, 138
National Park Service, 34, 62, 66, 67,
    151, 152, 168, 176, 179
Nature, 65
Northern blazing star, 45, 46, 140

On Golden Pond, 44
Ordway, Katherine, 5
Overdevelopment, 99, 146, 158

Parker, Desire, 8
Pasamaquoddy Indians, 37, 38
Patience Island, 137
Peatlands, 40, 48, 49, 57, 127, 174
Penobscot Indians, 37, 38
Peregrine falcon, 39, 44, 92, 94, 109, 115,
    147, 149, 164, 179
Pesticide treadmill, 56, 119
Piping plover, 3, 66, 92, 93, 94, 108, 125,
    126, 139, 168
Piratebush, 165, 166
Pitch pine/scrub oak forest, 46, 49, 65, 66,
    69, 86, 106
Pocono Mountains, 117, 121, 127
Prudence Island, 138
Pushaw Lake, 40
Prine, John, 29
Proctor, Edna Dean, 83

Ramsar Convention, 93
Red River, 32, 33
Red-tailed hawk, 66, 73, 148
Rhododendron, 1, 8, 24, 97,
    120, 122, 123, 127, 134, 135,
    164, 172, 176
Running buffalo clover, 26, 31, 174

Salt Marsh, 20, 66, 67, 80, 94, 95, 133,
    138, 157, 168
Sensitive joint vetch, 158, 159
Shawangunk Mountains, 103,
    113–14
Shawnee Indians, 33, 34
Silent Spring, 117
Smith, John, 17

Thoreau, Henry David, 37, 65, 70,
    73–75, 83
Tranquility Project, 39

Underground Railroad, 163

Vermont Land Trust, 143
Virginia big-eared bat, 32, 177, 180

Wabanaki Indians, 38
Walden, 65, 74
Wampanoag Indians, 137
Waterfalls, 30, 97, 113, 120, 121, 122,
    123, 130, 167, 175
Watts Creek, 26
*Week on the Concord and Merrimack Rivers,
    A*, 65
White pine, 8, 11, 39, 43, 48,
    73, 80, 86, 105, 110,
    114, 127, 130, 135, 141,
    152, 154
White Mountain National Forest, 77, 84,
    85, 88
White River, 152, 153
Whittier, John Greenleaf, 83
Wood turtle, 46, 83, 140
Wright, Frank Lloyd, 120

About the Author

Donelle Nicole Dreese is a nature writer and an assistant professor at Northern Kentucky University, where she teaches multicultural literatures and environmental literatures. Her interests include the relationship between people and the places they inhabit, environmental racism, and other social justice movements. Dreese has published a wide variety of creative writing and scholarship in her fields of study.